WHAT WAS ONCE EAST PAKISTAN

WHAT WAS ONCE EAST PAKISTAN

SYED SHAHID HUSAIN

Second Edition with a new Preface

OXFORD
UNIVERSITY PRESS

OXFORD
UNIVERSITY PRESS

Oxford University Press is a department of the University of Oxford.
It furthers the University's objective of excellence in research, scholarship,
and education by publishing worldwide. Oxford is a registered trade mark of
Oxford University Press in the UK and in certain other countries

Published in Pakistan by
Oxford University Press
No. 38, Sector 15, Korangi Industrial Area,
PO Box 8214, Karachi-74900, Pakistan

ISBN 978-0-19-070729-3

Typeset in Adobe Garamond Pro
Printed on 68gsm Offset Paper

Printed by Delta Dot Technologies (Pvt.) Ltd., Karachi

Dedication

I dedicate this book to my entire family—my mother, brothers, sisters, and in particular my late father, Dr Syed Hamid Husain.

My father arrived in Karachi by sea from Kanpur (India) in early February 1948 along with my mother and his two older sons (I being the eldest), and settled in Sindh. The values he instilled in me have endured the challenges of living in a world with declining standards of morality. He declined to visit me in East Pakistan when I was posted there because he did not want to die away from home. He passed away soon thereafter.

My family suffered a great tragedy when my youngest brother, Dr Khurshid Hamid, died quite suddenly and mysteriously in the US within 29 days of his marriage to an Indian lady no one had ever known. It was a shattering experience for all of us. In a tragic irony of fate, I went to the US to attend his wedding but was required to attend his funeral before returning home. Khurshid worked as a specialist in internal medicine in Cooper Hospital, NJ.

I also dedicate this to my mother, Azra Hamid, who lived with Khurshid for ten years till she moved in with my brother Sajid whose account the reader would find in this book. She now lives with him in Chicago.

Contents

Preface to the 2021 Edition

More than ten years have gone by since the publication of this book. I received mixed reactions (hostile, encouraging, and polite) from friends and acquaintances. Did the book change the minds of people? Hardly. People have their views and they hold fast to them. Their comfort zones and the fear of being proved wrong, do not allow them to let go of their dearly held views.

I have received some sharp and polite reactions from those who disagreed with my conclusions. The critics have difficulty blaming General Yahya Khan for not transferring power after he organized reasonably fair elections because they think that since he was a drunkard he could be easily 'misguided' by his advisers—a case of tail wagging the dog.

Surprisingly, a substantial majority of people in Pakistan love to pile up major blame, if not in its entirety, on Zulfikar Ali Bhutto. He evokes strong reactions as much in favour as against. His detractors refer to his threats to break the legs of the elected representatives who would dare to attend the National Assembly session in Dhaka or for 'allegedly' proclaiming that 'Udhar tum idhar hum' (you there and we here),[1] easily forgetting that there was no session to attend as General Yahya had postponed *sine die* the first session of the National Assembly he had belatedly called. Even in Bangladesh people prefer Bhutto to Yahya for the blame.

My account, however, lays the blame for the calamity, squarely and unequivocally, at the doorstep of Yahya because he was the president, prime minister, the army chief and all else rolled into one. His drinking and philandering were his personal failures. However, he and his Generals cannot absolve themselves of all responsibility for their decisions which led to the breakup of Pakistan. At no stage did his military colleagues appear to have dissuaded him from the disastrous undertaking. They were his unflinching supporters to the end and way beyond.

The deadliest culmination of events was on 25 March 1971 when Yahya decided to punish the entire population of East Pakistan for voting the way they did or for demanding that he follow up on the results by suddenly and surprisingly postponing National Assembly session *sine die*. Most of his Generals crowed that they would shoot their way through.

Stiff resistance from the people of East Pakistan paid put to their dreams. Also, intervention by India had not formed part of their equation. The Generals mused that they were dealing with a 'domestic' problem and as a sovereign nation they were within their rights to deny the 'elected' sovereigns a share in power.

When I hear people in truncated Pakistan grieve for the loss of East Pakistan, less and less with the passage of time, it is never for losing the people but the land they occupied. That speaks volumes about our mindset. We value real estate more than anything else. Balochistan has lots of real estate and we made full use of its vastness and barren beauty— shaking it up a little by testing our much-touted nuclear weapons in 1998. That is our gift to the poor people of Balochistan.

Over the years there have been arguments to justify not so much the invasion of East Pakistan as if it was populated by the enemy; but its eventual loss at the hands of the joint India-Bangladesh (Mukti Bahini) Forces. The Generals were confident they would cow the Bengalis down and assumed that India would be a silent spectator. Besides, even if India tried, the US (ever the military's supporter) will prevent them because President Richard Nixon was beholden to General Yahya for arranging Henry Kissinger's secret trip to China in July 1971. But once the outcome became clear on 16 December 1971, they rushed to characterise the debacle not as a military defeat but as a political one—implying that the politicians were to blame. The Generals were not prepared to share an iota of responsibility for the outcome.

However, no politician had any power at the time. When military takes over the running of a country they become the politicians. It is therefore their failure at both the political and military level.

With the passage of time and some more reflection, I have come to the conclusion that one cannot blame the army entirely for the East Pakistan fiasco. The West Pakistanis are also responsible as they did not protest either Yahya Khan's illegal grab of power or his patently illegal act of refusing to transfer it to the elected representatives after he had organized elections, which he himself claimed to be fair and free. We did not empathize or speak up for our compatriots in East Pakistan who suffered untold miseries at the hands of the army between March and December 1971. We should have, at least made our repugnance known at the horrid treatment of the people of East Pakistan. And all, for what? What was their crime? Winning elections? We were so brainless that we refused to consider the facts and chose to be spoon-fed by Yahya's self-serving lies.

Responsibility has layers. Ordinary people have the lowest responsibility but higher the position in the societal pyramid, more is the responsibility. On that scale, the highest responsibility lies at the doorstep of the top Generals who formed the core of Yahya's support system and benefited from his illegal grab of power from yet another military dictator, General Ayub Khan. Next layer was the politicians and intellectuals. And so on! If only half a dozen generals had protested not so much to defend the Constitution but to save themselves from the inevitable disaster and forced Yahya's hand to transfer power to the elected representatives of the people even if temporarily, the action of 25 March may have been avoided.

Admiral S.M. Ahsan who was the Governor of East Pakistan was the only honourable exception who apparently refused to be a part of the senseless course of action Yahya was determined to pursue. But then he was from a junior service and the army could ignore him and the service he represented. General Sahibzada Yaqub Khan is also rumoured to have opposed the action, but one never heard him speak publicly during his exceptionally long public career, as if he had taken a vow of silence. No civil servant showed any distaste or disapproval for the action and not one of them went on long leave in protest. They continued to deploy their expertise in the service of a dictator and his mad pursuit of power.

We collectively owe an apology to the people of Bangladesh for the treatment we meted out to them. Former prime minister, Nawaz Sharif, and former dictator, General Pervez Musharraf, came close to accepting responsibility, when they 'regretted' the 1971 role of the Pakistani troops in East Pakistan.[2] But our relations have since then gone downhill. Bangladesh is closer to India than to its religious compatriots in the west.

The agony of the people of East Pakistan, the breakup of the country, and the humiliating mass surrender of our troops before India could have been avoided only if Yahya had not refused to talk to and negotiate with Mujib. He is reported to have offered to Bhutto—before reluctantly transferring power—to execute Mujib. The India-Pakistan war that Yahya triggered could have brought the world to the brink of a nuclear holocaust as documented by Daniel Ellsberg (Pentagon Papers fame). According to him, East Pakistan is one of the twenty-five actual nuclear crises that can be documented for the last half of the twentieth century, as a flashpoint. To quote:

> Threats and nuclear-capable naval deployment in 1971 to deter (according to Nixon) a Soviet response to possible Chinese intervention against India in the Indo-Pakistan war, but possible also, or mainly, to deter India from further military pressure on Pakistan.[3]

Sadder part is that two big Muslim countries in the subcontinent are barely on speaking terms. Visas are routinely denied although the travel should have been easy and visa free. We cannot blame India for its intransigence when two Muslim countries in the subcontinent cannot do business. With better relations between Pakistan and Bangladesh, India would perhaps have been more accommodating to our point of view.

To this day, the understanding of the 1971 infamy and its causes eludes our intellectuals. Only if we were united, that is the refrain one hears from drawing room intellectuals, such things won't happen! A strong country in their imagination is one that is completely under the control of one Salahuddin Ayubi symbolized by who else but the chief of armed forces. In fact, the country is as strong as its people and 1971 is proof. United States is strong because of distribution of power to States, counties, and cities. Soviet Union was weak despite concentration of all power in the Central Communist Party. People were poor, disenfranchised, and angry. The system was unsustainable and simply imploded. Even the atomic weapons or the huge army they possessed could not save it from collapse. Its collapse could provide a face saving to Pakistan if it ever came to the brink under similar circumstances.

Break up of Pakistan has done quite lot of good to the former East Pakistan mainly because of devolution of power which resulted from the break up. Otherwise all decisions were made in Islamabad. Social and economic indices present stark differences.

Pakistan is poorer today than it was in 1971. Its population estimated at 221m (58m in 1971), is a fourfold increase. Pakistan is the fifth most populous country in the world and grows annually at 2 per cent. This rate is exceeded only by Nigeria, Congo, and Tanzania. Even Iran, with its theocratic government, has 1.3 per cent annual increase. Bangladesh has 161m population and the growth rate is 1 per cent. In 1971, East Pakistan had 64m people and was growing by 3.01 per annum.

We cannot even organize a decennial census because of opposition from communities and provinces who fear being undercounted. However, if a census is planned then the military must be mobilized for security but then the results are not acceptable and not allowed to be officially announced. Census due in 2010 took place in 2018 under Nawaz Sharif, and to date, the government cannot make the count official, which determine among other things the seats in the national and provincial assemblies.

UNDP indices present stark contrast between two former parts of one country. According to UNDP Human Development Index (HDI) ranking, Bangladesh is at 133 and Pakistan at 154.[4] Life expectancy at birth in Pakistan is 67.3 years; expected years of schooling 8.3 years and GNI per capita $5005 (PPP—Price Purchase Parity). Comparable Bangladesh figures are 72.6, 11.6 and $4976, respectively. Higher per capita income for Pakistan conceals greater disparity of incomes. The direction is obvious. We are going downhill.

The future is uncertain; the only certainty is that it will be quite different from the status quo. Covid-19 is a life changing event. Economic life as we know is going to be difficult and much worse. There will be change in manufacturing, services, and economic relations. Globalization has been halted principally by the US and its Western allies all to check an emerging Asian power—China. West does not want a competitor. They are comfortable with the monopoly of power in their hands. A deeper nexus between the US and India is evolving as a counterweight to China. Nothing will please the West more than a military conflict between India and China. They will sell arms to India and assure an outcome where both countries are weaker and dependent.

China has avoided armed conflict so far, but can it do so in the future despite grave provocations by the US? The economic war is ongoing. All technological cooperation is being denied to China which will be forced to evolve its own answers. Trade relations will undergo a sea change as a result of the pursuit of economic war to hurt China by all means. Two obvious economic blocs are emerging.

The US is undermining the international trade regimes and coercing Europe to follow. Barack Obama administration's pivot to Asia,[5] intensified by Donald Trump, will be pursued by Joe Biden. Pakistan and Bangladesh may be asked to choose.

In terms of democracy that was the raison d'être for its creation, Bangladesh has not done well. It did not have a smooth sailing. Soon after 'liberation', the 'founding father' was murdered along with his family except for the few who escaped or were abroad. Military organized coups and counter coups and all met a sad end. General Ziaur Rahman was killed and General Hussein Mohammad Ershad was jailed for several years unlike in Pakistan, where we failed to jail General Pervez Musharraf even for a day and the PM Nawaz Sharif who tried it, was shown the door. Musharraf's conviction by a tribunal was promptly undone by higher courts and he was allowed to leave the country. Bangladesh, on the contrary, appears to have established the writ of the state, barring accidents. There have been no more coups since General Ershad. It has gone on an executing spree. 'Collaborators' mostly belonging to the

Jamaat-e-Islami Bangladesh (now banned as a political party) have suffered the most.

Democracy has survived if only in form. It is a shell. Sheikh Hasina's government may look legal but lacks legitimacy in the eyes of most objective observers. Continuity of Sheikh Hasina in power for twelve years and counting raises suspicion regarding the system or its legitimacy. Trappings of democracy do not equal freedoms that ordinary people enjoy in a democratic society. Press is careful and cautious. Courts are far more careful and follow the lead. Civil service has been completely cowed down. Orders are obsequiously carried out without question.

The elephant in the room is the Bangladesh Army. Surprisingly, it has not responded to its inherent itch to take over. Reason is tighter control by the Sheikh Hasina government of the levers of power or sheer luck. A friend from Bangladesh assures me that India has to be thanked because it acts as a proxy for the civilian oversight of army leadership.

Opposition has been neutralized; Khaleda Zia, the leader of the main opposition party, was jailed on 'corruption' charges. Sheikh Hasina 'won' the 2018 boycotted elections.

Corruption is a charge which is always used to neutralize the opposition. The last elected government of Nawaz Sharif was shown the door by the Establishment, a euphemism for the army, with overt and covert help from the Supreme Court. It does not matter if the people framing charges are themselves corrupt. The entire opposition comprising two major political parties in Pakistan is being hounded by the current hybrid dispensation with corruption cases being framed on an industrial scale. In Bangladesh, Sheikh Hasina's government is following a similar script and is succeeding. The normal reaction of people such as *gherao-jalao* has long since disappeared, perhaps on account of improvement in their economic lot. They now have a stake in the system which they formerly lacked.

The world will be poorer as a result of Covid-19 and Pakistan will not be able to get external help that it has in the past to close the gap between its expenditure and resources. We have already reached a point where pay and pensions are not being paid to nurses, teachers, sanitary workers, bus drivers etc. The crisis will reach higher echelons. Pakistan is in dire straits. Its undoing may be its defence expenditure which the resources simply do not justify and never did. It has survived on borrowing. Its so-called circular debt is Rs 2.1 trillion and increasing and there is no way to pay that amount. There are no domestic or international resources in sight. Covid-19 has decimated economies the world over and no one has the spare cash. Our Middle Eastern co-religionists are going through financial crises of their own. They are heavily indebted. Oil is no more the currency of the times. If anything, the world is moving to renewable energy and oil may soon be a thing of the past.

Remittances we relied upon to fill the hole may decline sometime in the future because our workers in the Middle East are coming back in hordes in spite of rosy projection by the World Bank that the two South Asian countries will see increase in remittance flow despite the pandemic. The World Bank predicted in its report[6] that Pakistan would witness increased remittance flow as a consequence of depreciation and greater resort to formal channels rather than 'hawala' and will secure eighth position in the world in terms of inward remittance flow in 2020. Analysts and experts said remittances to Pakistan may rise 5 per cent to hit another all-time high mark of $23 billion during the ongoing fiscal year despite a slight decline in inflows during the July-September 2019 quarter.

World Bank has also projected that Bangladesh will also witness increased remittance inflow and will secure eighth position in the world in terms of inward remittance flow in 2020. Bangladesh will gain 8 per cent more remittance this year, according to the report. The total remittance flow will be $20 billion, the World Bank projected.

Tectonic shift in economic relations the world over as a consequence of Covid-19 may present unpleasant surprises. All forecasts and fancy model may fall by the way side. Only the societies that seize opportunity at the right moment will go forward.

To conclude, the Establishment's involvement (overt and covert) in politics continues in Pakistan; it wields absolute power and there are dire consequences for those who are a threat: Ayub Khan destroyed all politicians Pakistan had at the time of independence; first elections under the 1956 constitution were thwarted by Ayub; the first genuine elections in 1970 on the basis of one man one vote resulted in the breakup of Pakistan; Zulfikar Ali Bhutto was hanged; Benazir Bhutto was assassinated; Nawaz Sharif was thrown out because he had some funny ideas like striking peace with India.

Ayub, Ziaul Haq, and Musharraf ruled for thirty years between them. If the streets heat up they replace one protégé with another. The vicious cycle continues, and Pakistan pays the price.

NOTES

1. According to Dr Muhammad Reza Kazimi, Bhutto never said 'Udhar tum, idhar hum'. This was a headline concocted by Abbas Athar of the *Azad*, Lahore, 15 February 1971. The second and third headlines said that Bhutto wanted one Pakistan. See: 'Musharraf's Interview,' *DAWN*, August 13, 2017. Also, 'Idhar hum, udhar tum: Abbas Athar remembered,' *The Express Tribune*, May 8, 2013.

2. See: David Blair, 'Musharraf Apology to Bangladesh,' *The Telegraph*, July 31, 2002. Also, 'Bangladesh Expects Pakistan Apology on 1971 War,' *Zee News*, October 31, 2010.

3. Daniel Ellsberg, *The Doomsday Machine: Confessions of a Nuclear War Planner* (Bloomsbury, 2017), para 17, p. 321.

4. Pakistan's HDI value for 2019 is 0.557—which put the country in the medium human development category—positioning it at 154 out of 189 countries and territories. Human Development Indicators, United Nations Development Programme: http://hdr.undp.org/en/countries/profiles/PAK. Also, 'Human Development Report', United Nations Development Programme, (2020) http://hdr.undp.org/en/content/latest-human-development-index-ranking.

5. Kenneth G. Lieberthal, 'The American Pivot to Asia,' *Brookings*, Wednesday, 21 December 2011; https://www.brookings.edu/articles/the-american-pivot-to-asia/.

6. World Bank, 'COVID-19 Crisis Through a Migration Lens,' Migration and Development Brief, no. 32, World Bank, Washington, DC, 2020.

Preface

It is always helpful to study history. Our nation does not believe in history unless of course it is the doctored version which students are taught at schools and colleges. If history repeats itself, proverbially, we will be caught napping. 1971 was the year of national infamy. A watered down version of events in the Hamood-ur-Rahman Commission report became known to the people of Pakistan three decades later, courtesy the Indian press.

History is no more than an opinion and no less than a dynamic point of view which varies with the background and learning of the author. It is written and rewritten. A hero may become a rogue and vice versa. This version of events may present a slightly different perspective because I lived for about two years with the people of East Pakistan and developed a deep empathy for them. When Yahya Khan and his crew were dilly-dallying in summoning the assembly session, an East Pakistani friend, an engineer posted in Khulna, asked pathetically: 'Don't we deserve to get the government having won so convincingly?' I had no answer.

I first visited the province in 1966 as a civil service probationer. I went back three years later on regular posting under the inter-wing transfer scheme as the sub-divisional officer (SDO) of Serajganj (now a district) and then served as the additional deputy commissioner of Rajshahi and finally Khulna. The man-made disaster that East Pakistan eventually became is seen differently in the two former wings of the country. People of what was then West Pakistan view the use of force and a strong central government as the best guarantee for national integrity. People of the former East Pakistan, who are more democratic in nature, see the entire year-long saga as a military adventurer's attempt to deny power to the people, using military force as a means of achieving that end. That the military lost in the end was an unforeseen outcome. Otherwise the military personnel were heard saying: 'Give us two good riflemen and we will set the...right.' When in Dhaka, on my way back to West Pakistan, I heard the firing of bazookas for the first time, that too against the civilian population, I asked a *jawan* what did the fire denote and when was it used? The naïve answer was that 'it is fired when an officer orders us to do so.'

What follows in these pages may arouse some strong sentiments, particularly in present-day Pakistan, because the country's intelligentsia does not espouse democratic values, but one wonders if this would be accepted as a true version of events even in the former East Pakistan. The people there view the tragedy as having been engineered by Zulfikar Ali Bhutto and till today most of them apportion blame on him rather than on Yahya Khan.

The reader would find a very strong bias for democracy in this narrative, perhaps accentuated on account of the most brutal assault by the military on the unsuspecting civilian population of East Pakistan on 25 March 1971.

Introduction

One may wonder why I took so long to write this book. East Pakistan happened many years ago and as they say, it is now history. There is little interest in the subject—least of all in Pakistan where people prefer not to talk about this most tragic event in the nation's history. At the National Defence College where I spent a year this subject was taboo. Although the syllabus was comprehensive, based on elements of national power with subjects like politics, economics (even Islamic economics), sociology and the relationship of the country's resources with its military strength, East Pakistan was not mentioned even in passing. The usual explanation was that the event occurred too far back in history, even though at that point only seventeen years had elapsed since the country had split into two separate entities; the rationale for the creation of Pakistan and the Two-Nation Theory had been irrevocably undermined. If Muslims constituted a separate nation in the subcontinent then the creation of Bangladesh was an enigma for the purists. The subject is never too old for future generations as they would continue to reflect on the most devastating national tragedy that befell the largest Muslim country in modern times.

The other reason for writing this book is to provide an alternative perspective to students of history. History is never outdated. One would like to understand the current situation in the context of one's past. People usually offer superficial reasons for the separation of East Pakistan. Even the language used in the discourse reflects the biases of the interlocutors. The 'fall of Dhaka' is a phrase most commonly used in Pakistan to describe the break-up of the country. 'Separation' is another word often employed as if it were the Bengalis who chose to separate and not us who pushed them out. The year-long crisis of 1971 is often described as a 'civil war' implying that the Bengalis were fighting the Sindhis or the Biharis or some other group. Yes, there was animosity between the Bengalis and the Biharis but that was no 'civil war'. If there indeed was a 'civil war' then one must view the Pakistani military as one of the two parties to the conflict. But since the military is not a component of what is 'civil society', this characterization of the conflict cannot be justified as that would, in fact, be a wanton assault on the liberties and aspirations of a country's population.

Then there are people who describe the events of 1971 as a rebellion of the East Pakistanis against the government. They forget that Yahya's rule was illegal, more so after the people of East Pakistan had won the elections and were entitled to form the government. Besides, it was not the people of East Pakistan who attacked Yahya or his men. It was Yahya and his military that attacked the unsuspecting people of that province. Four months after the vote was counted and people saw no progress towards transfer of power, they protested peacefully. This civil resistance cannot be equated with rebellion.

Some people say that Pakistan split because of elections. Among the luminaries was one late Z.A. Suleri, previously editor of the defunct *Pakistan Times*, whom I heard making this claim during a lecture at the National Defence College in 1988. What a travesty of facts! Pakistan was split not because of the elections but because the election results were not acceptable to the rulers.

The ruling elites are reluctant to let people know the facts. The Hamood-ur-Rahman Commission Report (HCR)—a watered down and only partially true record of events—was withheld till such time some enterprising people unearthed the Report, thereby forcing the military regime of General Pervez Musharraf to allow a sanitized version to be made public.

When I landed in Karachi from Dhaka on 2 April 1971, I had a silly notion that the people of West Pakistan would be furious at the military junta for the atrocities heaped on the hapless Bengalis. The first man I encountered in Karachi was a taxi driver who was enthusiastically supportive of the military action and wished more Bengalis were killed to rid Pakistan of its enemies. An impression was deliberately created that the military intervened to save the Biharis who were being killed by the hundreds. The Hamood-ur-Rahman Commission appears to have swallowed this untruth. Although the Biharis were indeed apprehensive at the prospect of transfer of power to the Bengalis and looked to the West Pakistani elites as their ultimate support, yet there were no killings. The controlled press in those days gave only a sanitized version of events but to the best of my knowledge and contrary to what Yahya wished the West Pakistanis to believe there was no killing except may be one or two here and there. One was in touch with colleagues who were serving in almost all parts of the province. As a matter of fact, Sheikh Mujibur Rahman told his people that any one who lived in East Bengal was a Bengali. This was not only meant to reassure the Biharis but also to deny Yahya any pretext for refusing to transfer power to the people. Mujib's statement had a calming effect on the Biharis as there couldn't have been any greater acceptance of the Biharis by the Bengalis. However, it was the Biharis who opted to stay apart as was evident during the 1970 elections when they opposed *en bloc* all Bengali candidates.

Holding Bhutto responsible for the break-up of Pakistan and claiming that the calamity did not represent a military defeat but a political failure was another canard deliberately spread by the West Pakistani establishment, the military being its most powerful component. Ironically, this was a phrase Bhutto used soon after taking over power in the winter of 1971. In keeping with the traditions established by his predecessors, General Pervez Musharraf too blames Bhutto for the break-up of Pakistan in his book *In the Line of Fire: A Memoir*.[1] In doing so, Musharraf ignores the fact that the country was then under military rule and Bhutto, the elected leader of West Pakistan, was not in any position of power until after the Pakistan army had surrendered to Indian and Bangladesh forces on 16 December 1971.

This convenient explanation of pinning the responsibility on Bhutto exculpates the role of the military in dismembering the country. It should be remembered that Yahya had scrapped the 1962 Constitution and under a Legal Framework Order (LFO) arrogated for himself dictatorial authority to rule the country. The argument that Bhutto cannot be held responsible because he was neither the prime minister nor the president nor the chief of army staff—all three hats worn so enthusiastically by Yahya Khan—is countered by the claim that Yahya was a drunkard, a womanizer and a debauch, and therefore, by implication not culpable for his actions. It is also argued that Yahya was handicapped because he was not literate and erudite like Bhutto was, as if to say that his guilt rested solely on his education or the lack of it. Bhutto's infamous statement '*udhar tum aur idhar hum*', or his threat to break the legs of any West Pakistani member of the National Assembly who dared attend the session in Dhaka, are said to have contributed to the eventual break-up of the country. But Yahya was the all-powerful chief martial law administrator and could have assured members of the national assembly protection and taken Bhutto to task if he attempted to deliver on his threat. People conveniently find facts to fit preconceived notions. Very few remember that Yahya visited Larkana soon after the election results hit him as an unforeseen calamity, and was Bhutto's personal guest for three days. He did not go there to discuss trivialities. Contrary to an unfounded belief deliberately nurtured by the West Pakistani establishment, Yahya was an ambitious man and had engineered the ouster of his benefactor, Ayub Khan. All his subsequent actions were geared to remaining in power even if the price was national ignominy and the largest military surrender in recent times. He entered into an alliance with Bhutto against Mujib and democracy even though Bhutto was hardly in a position to influence events. Perhaps Bhutto saw in Yahya's adventure an opportunity to get rid of the military dictatorship.

By supporting a military usurper (so declared by the Supreme Court only after Yahya had ceased to hold power and perhaps to pre-empt future criticism against a pusillanimous judiciary) rather than Mujib who was leader of the majority, Bhutto clearly violated all principles of democracy. He was not prepared to accept the position of leader of the opposition even though that was the only honourable course of action for a statesman and leader of his stature. During the brief but phoney parleys that Yahya had with the two leaders, Mujib pleaded with Bhutto to support him or else, he cautioned, after sorting him (Mujib) out Yahya would sort out Bhutto.

The National Defence College, now a full university with a charter to award degrees, prepares senior military (and a few civilian) officers for assuming higher responsibilities some of which are not necessarily related to their profession; the content of the course strongly suggests this bias. The course I attended had subjects that dealt with the state's national power as reflected in the nation's economy and governance; this required us to visit all chambers of commerce and industry in the country. Yet the course content made no mention of the constitution or its significance in national life. A lack of knowledge of the constitution was evident on one occasion when a brigadier attending the course insisted that the constitution provided a 10 per cent job quota in the civil services for retired army officers and refused to accept the correct position. At least up to a few years back, the huge ornate library of the newly-built National Defence College in Islamabad did not have a single copy of the constitution even though one could find some less known commentaries.

NOTE

1. Pervez Musharraf, *In the Line of Fire: A Memoir*, Simon & Schuster, Adult Publishing Group, 2006.

Part I

Part 1

1

My First Visit to the Former East Pakistan (1966)

I saw East Pakistan for the first time in 1966. I had joined the civil service and together with a group of 39 other officers went on a three-month long familiarization tour of that province. I spent a month at the Comilla Rural Development Academy, one month on attachment to a district—Mymensingh—and the rest in travelling. Dr Akhtar Hameed Khan was the director of the academy and informed us in his very first address that we had to share spartan accommodation, polish our own shoes and stand in queue to get food. This appeared quite simple, but some of my colleagues felt offended at what they felt was demeaning treatment meted out to elite officers of the civil service; besides they were dissatisfied with the quality of food served in the canteen. There were moments of minor rebellion. We later learnt that Dr Khan had reported all of us to the federal government asking that disciplinary action be taken against us. Somehow the issue was resolved in our favour but I never found out how.

One night at the academy I was standing in the veranda of the first floor of our dormitory quietly gazing into the darkness. Abdul Qayyum, an East Pakistani friend and a foreign service officer, was alongside me. He remarked, perhaps half in jest, that the place would be 'their' civil service academy in the future. He did not use the name Bangladesh, and even I thought it was unlikely that East Pakistan would become independent. But one didn't realize the depth of resentment our military leaders had created in the hearts and minds of the Bengalis and the fatal effects the denial of their democratic rights had have on the body politic of the country.

My batch at the Civil Service Academy had thirty civil and ten foreign service officers. For visits to various parts of East Pakistan the batch was divided into four groups so as to lighten the burden on our hosts. My group of ten comprised only two West Pakistanis. When we went on a

3

visit to a district or divisional headquarters we were stuck with one another for almost the entire day. There were disputes, debates and discussions which occasionally degenerated into ugly acrimony. The pressures were such that our East Pakistani colleagues eventually stopped talking to us. Thus, when travelling by road in a coach if the two of us from West Pakistan happened to be seated apart, one in the front and the other at the back, we would go the entire way without being able to speak to anyone. Although my recollection may not be accurate, the arguments were mostly on how East Pakistan and its people were mistreated by the federal government. We became very familiar with their grievances as these were articulated regularly and supported with facts. We somehow felt that we had to be the devil's advocate and defended the indefensible.

We visited different places but the most memorable experience was the drive from Chittagong to Rangamati. The whole valley was breathtakingly beautiful. Rangamati itself was a very scenic place. I had not seen such breathtaking greenery before having lived my entire life in arid parts of Sindh where it wouldn't rain for years. A visit to Geneva a few years later did not erase the lingering impressions of East Pakistan.

As had become our wont, on arrival at a new place we would make a run to grab the best accommodation and this race I almost always lost. We did the same when we arrived at the Police Academy at Sardah but to my pleasant surprise there was no need for such antics because our accommodation had already been earmarked in order of seniority. Two groups of ten including that of the foreign service officers had arrived simultaneously. The police officers believed in seniority and being number one in my group I was accorded the status of the senior-most officer. In fact, I was even given priority over officers from the foreign service because that was considered a junior service. I ended up getting the best accommodation and was also assigned some ceremonial duties. It was fun playing the role of a senior for a few days.

A scene I witnessed when travelling by train in an air-conditioned compartment haunts me to this day. While eating lunch served to us from the train's dining car at the Ishurdi railway station, I noticed a score of hungry, half-naked boys and girls throng in front of our compartment. When the waiter stepped onto the platform with our retrieved trays, the children rushed towards him. Initially somewhat perplexed, I soon understood the cause of this commotion. The hungry, emaciated lot were waiting for leftovers but the bearer threw the leftovers to the children on the dirty and dusty platform and said, 'It would have been better to give it to the dogs.' I cannot forget the sight of hungry children running to pick whatever they could before the dogs got there. This was a sad reflection on the relationship between the Biharis and the Bengalis—the waiter was a Bihari and expected us to empathise with him. Another illustration of this relationship was provided by a Bihari servant, dark as anyone else there, of a Punjabi colleague who, on learning that his master was about to marry a Bengali girl, said, 'How can that be? Bengalis are all dark coloured and therefore no good for the fair skinned sahib.'

As part of this tour we were attached for a month with the deputy commissioner of Mymensingh. There were two of us, the other being Anwar Mahmood. He was an introvert and kept mostly to himself, and in spite of living together in one place and sharing meals three times a day we failed to develop any bonds of friendship. He was otherwise an extremely likeable person. Regrettably, he was caught in the wake of the military action in East Pakistan in the Tangail area, formerly part of the Mymensingh district and suffered agonizing moments and in the process came very close to death. He was living there with his wife and at one point was made to dig his own grave. His captors' womenfolk intervened to save him and his family. He came back to West Pakistan soon thereafter but didn't live long and died within a few years.

2

Three Years Later (1969–1971)

I next went to East Pakistan on a two-year posting as part of the inter-wing exchange programme. A decision had been taken to post West Pakistani civil service officers to East Pakistan and vice versa. The scheme had earlier worked well but was later abandoned under pressure from powerful West Pakistani bureaucrats who did not wish to have their sons posted to that distant province. While officers from East Pakistan welcomed this inter-wing posting, the same was not true for the West Pakistanis. An officer of my batch who was posted to the Bandarban sub-division in East Pakistan deserted his post because the district's name reminded him of 'our' ancestors. He was so prejudiced that he refused to advance his watch by one hour to read local time.

The inter-wing exchange scheme was revived at the fag end of President Ayub Khan's rule. Each batch of civil service comprised about thirty officers with equal numbers from the two provinces. Since fifteen officers were thought to be too many to exchange in one go, they were sent in two groups, six months apart. I was part of the second group of my batch. I landed in Dhaka in July 1969 and in spite of the fact it was raining that day, Ishrat Hussain was at the airport to give me a warm welcome. Ishrat was a year senior in service and subsequently went on to serve the World Bank. He rounded off his career by serving as governor of the State Bank of Pakistan during General Pervez Musharraf's rule. He was always kind to his colleagues and friends.

General Yahya Khan had taken over a few months earlier after months of turbulence following countrywide protests against Ayub Khan. East Pakistan had had more than its share of violence. '*Gherao, Jalao*' was the order of the day. A few of my senior colleagues experienced violence but were fortunate to have escaped death. Surprisingly, the whole movement died down the moment Yahya took over as if its leaders were waiting for this to happen. The Round Table Conference (RTC) called by Ayub Khan in the dying days of his regime was attended by almost all important leaders including Sheikh Mujibur Rahman who was arguably the most important of the lot. Mujib was undergoing trial in the infamous Agartala conspiracy case and Ayub was forced under public pressure not only to release him but also withdraw the case. Bhutto boycotted the conference on the pretext that he would put pressure from the outside. Too many coincidences pointed to an orchestrated preparation by Yahya to launch a *coup*. The RTC was a landmark political development as Ayub conceded to the demand to have a parliamentary form of government as opposed to the presidential form so dear to military usurpers.

After a few days in Dhaka, we proceeded to our respective places of posting which had been decided on the basis of merit. I landed in Serajganj, a large sub-division which had nine *thanas* (police and revenue jurisdictions being co-terminus) and a population of 1.2 million. Travelling by train from Dhaka, I crossed the River Jamuna in a steamer and re-boarded a train on the other side. It was an interesting experience. The river was in high flood and the situation worrying. My official residence in Serajganj was on the river bank with the bedroom opening towards the river.

Journalists in Dhaka were keen to get a daily update of the rising river, particularly the erosion it was causing. My lack of knowledge of the Bengali language was a serious handicap but I managed reasonably well because of the goodwill on both sides. The flooded river was causing serious erosion which was a cause for anxiety; a year or two later the sub-divisional officer's residence as well as the nearby rest house were washed away. The rest house enjoyed a place of honour because the Quaid-i-Azam had briefly rested there during his visit to the area; the people were proud of this fact and mentioned it very fondly.

14 August arrived suddenly. I had no idea that Independence Day was a big occasion for the East Pakistanis. It turned out that every small place had some celebration or the other to commemorate this day. As sub-divisional officer (SDO), I was chairman of a committee that had to chalk out a programme for Independence Day celebrations. My schedule was usually very crowded and I had to work hard to attend to official business so this meeting seemed an unnecessary distraction. I asked Akhtar, my personal assistant (PA), whom I met again when I visited Bangladesh in 1998, what momentous decisions was this meeting likely to take? Hadn't they celebrated Independence Day last year? He replied in the affirmative, so I inquired if things had gone well to which he again replied in the affirmative.

So, I went to the meeting armed with this intelligence. About fifty prominent citizens were present, all eagerly looking forward to the opportunity of having a discussion and in the process getting to know the new SDO. At the outset I asked how had the celebrations fared the previous year and was told that they had gone very well indeed. In that case, I announced, the same programme would be adopted this time around and before they could recover I took leave and left. This was the briefest meeting of my career. In hindsight I feel it must have been a public relations disaster. After all, everyone has an urge to speak and that urge had been denied. 14 August turned out to be a big day full of festivities.

The main function started with a congregation of all students at the college ground of the largest college in town where I was to give a speech. This was another test for me. I could not speak Bangla, Urdu would have been a disaster, and English, although not disliked as much, would not be understood. So I agonized over the matter and after some debate with myself decided to make a speech in Bangla. Obviously, it had to be brief to avoid making too many mistakes of syntax and pronunciation. So, I had it written in Roman and practiced it several times with my PA as the audience. Hesitantly, I went to the podium, and unsure of the response, started reading it. Judging from the response of a few thousand people, mostly students and the gentry of the town, I felt people were pleased, not so much at the quality or content of my speech but for the effort of delivering it in their language they held so dear. Their devotion to their language was beyond belief. The day ended with a cultural programme that went on till past midnight; other events including boat racing etc. had taken place earlier during the day. The enthusiasm and fervour with which the Independence Day was celebrated clearly showed their love for Pakistan and yet they were accused of secessionism, sedition and rebellion.

I was transferred to East Pakistan from Tank, a town situated in the semi-tribal part of the NWFP. A task that kept me quite occupied in Tank was renewing licenses for guns, pistols and revolvers. They were almost 10,000 such licenses and it was difficult for me to properly scrutinize the papers before signing them. I had imagined I would encounter a similar situation in Serajganj but to my surprise they were such a peace loving people that the entire sub-division did not have more than a dozen weapons. When the crunch came they had to struggle hard to acquire weapons in a hurry in response to the military assault of 25 March 1971; all hopes of transfer of power had by then been extinguished and they found themselves pushed against the wall. By July 1971, they had enough arms to be able to disrupt military movements.

The Bengalis chewed *paan* by the mouthful. They did not cut a leaf into several portions in the manner done elsewhere; instead they would put the entire leaf in their mouth, making speech difficult. As chairman of the local municipal committee, I thought of raising the octroi tax on *paan* to increase revenue. The opposition from the house—a hybrid of elected and non-elected officials known as 'basic democrats', a gift of Ayub Khan—was so intense that I had to withdraw the proposition.

On being promoted to the senior cadre, I was transferred to Rajshahi as additional deputy commissioner and given the simultaneous charge of chairman of the municipal committee. I decided to put up signboards for street names. The problem was that if street names were written in Bengali, people like me would not understand and if they were in any other language they would be useless for the Bengalis. English was useless anyway, so I decided to have bilingual signs, in Bengali and Arabic. The Bengali deputy commissioner (DC), who was my boss, resented this innovation and remarked that I had, in fact, put up Urdu signs. He was an extremely suspicious man when it came to the Urdu/Bengali issue. Besides, language could stir emotions of the Bengalis like nothing else. There was no other reaction besides this.

One day some teachers of municipal schools came to see me but I noticed they were so old they could barely walk. I asked my staff how it was that such elderly and infirm teachers were still in service. Had they not turned sixty? It turned out that they were Hindus and on nearing retirement had presented religious evidence from their priests to establish that they were younger than their ages on record. I called for the files of all teachers and found that there were eight of them. I cancelled the birth certificates given to them by the astrologers, ordered their immediate retirement and quickly arranged for replacements for fear that the process might be interfered with by my superiors. I gave the candidates a written test and without going through interviews, prepared a merit list and ordered the top eight to be appointed. On learning this, the DC asked me to take the old teachers back because he said no less a person than the secretary-general of the Awami League (who was from Rajshahi) wanted this done. I ignored his request and went ahead with the fresh appointments. When I met the DC next time, he showed his displeasure at my disregard of his orders and added that I had probably appointed Biharis to all the eight places. Every non-Bengali including a Punjabi or a Sindhi was referred to as Bihari. The DC's accusation had me worried for a while because in truth I had not determined the ethnicity of the fresh appointees. Fortunately, not one of them turned out to be a Bihari.

Then there was the case of Khan Abdul Qayyum Khan, head of his own faction of the Muslim League, who was to come to Rajshahi to address a public meeting. He was campaigning for the forthcoming elections. The DC, who was also the acting commissioner, was away to Dhaka so the entire burden of administration fell on me. The local hosts of Qayyum Khan wanted permission for their leader to stay in the Circuit House quoting the rule that former federal ministers and chief ministers were entitled to this facility. Since many rooms in the Circuit House were vacant there was no reason for me to decline this request and I allowed the permit to be issued. On learning this, the DC was furious and reportedly said I had permitted Qayyum Khan to stay in the Circuit House because he was a West Pakistani. In any case, Qayyum Khan's public meeting was a disaster with very sparse attendance even though his party enjoyed the patronage of Yahya and his coterie.

Rajshahi was a big town but lacked facilities for disposal of night soil. There were a score of small animal carts which would haul this cargo every morning to a disposal point and an equal number of buffaloes for pulling them. This process was nauseating and the entire city had to suffer the stench and the unseemly sight every day. I visited the animal shed and was disgusted with their state of health. The buffaloes were weak, haggard and underfed. An allowance of Rs 5 per month was paid to the sweepers for procuring feed for the animals but like the rest of us the sweepers looked after themselves instead of the animals. I decided to mechanize the system and arranged for the auction of the animals and bought a couple of tractors that could haul several carts in each trip. Now the problem was of adjusting the carts to hook up with the tractors but eventually these too were fixed. I was happy at this transformation. Hopefully they may have by now put a modern sewerage disposal system in place after over three decades of independence.

During the period I held charge, municipal sweepers struck work. I decided to take a hard line and refused to talk to them. Obviously, the sanitation situation during those three days deteriorated but I held my ground The DC didn't like this and asked me to talk to them. I raised all sorts of objections including my trump card, that I did not know enough Bangla. To my utter bewilderment and some embarrassment the DC roared with laughter and told me that the sweepers in East Pakistan spoke Urdu. I hadn't known this.

I willy-nilly called the sweepers to my office for talks in an attempt to resolve their grievances. They all stood there arguing with the sanitary inspector in attendance. After about an hour of this back and forth, the inspector realized that I wasn't getting anywhere. He finally lost patience and decided to intervene. He addressed me thus: 'Sir that is not the way to talk to sweepers, addressing them with *aap* and *janab*.' 'So, how does one talk to them then?' I asked. He didn't say a word but demonstrated how. He took off his shoe and menacingly held it towards the crowd following this up with an equally threatening speech. They all disappeared in less than a minute. 'That is how,' he said with satisfaction at achieving results by using methods he knew worked best. That taught me a lesson though, that you don't deal with everyone the same way. Methods have to vary.

I was soon transferred to Khulna where I stayed till after the military operation. Many people ask me if I was taken as a prisoner of war (POW). I tell them that not for a second did I think that military action against the Bengalis would succeed mainly because it was not justified and secondly because the odds were stacked against an occupying force. Also, I had made up my mind to leave at the first opportunity. It is a long story how I left. The entire province had ceased to function. Nothing moved— trains, carts or aircraft. One couldn't even walk without incurring serious risks. I left Khulna for Jessore with a military convoy along with my batch mate Roshan Zamir and Nawazish Ali Zaidi, a banker and a friend; all three of us travelled in Zaidi's car. From there we flew off to Dhaka in a PIA Fokker that the army had commandeered to ferry arms and ammunition,

Since I had no official authorization to leave Khulna except verbal acquiescence of the local military brass, someone remarked that I might be dismissed from service unless I had obtained permission from Islamabad. I told these 'well-wishers' that it was better to be dismissed and stay alive rather than die in service. The only CSP officer who had the misfortune to be taken as a POW was Khalid Mahmood of the 1966 batch; as a matter of fact his fate was much worse because he remained a POW longer than all the rest. He died in Canada in 2007 after migrating there on retirement from service. Khalid had many grievances against Bhutto and held him responsible for every problem the country encountered. He was prepared to forgive Mujib, but not Bhutto.

Most officers of the civil service managed to return safely by following one ruse or another because travelling after 25 March 1971 had become a suicidal undertaking. Three unfortunate people failed to make it and died brutal deaths. Muhammad Iqbal of Hyderabad was reportedly killed together with his pregnant wife inside the local jail where Bengali militants had incarcerated them. Vaqar, an additional deputy commissioner in Kushtia, was the third victim. He was killed and his body dragged tied to the back of a jeep. I was in Jessore with the brigade commander when pleas for help from the small military posse stationed in Kushtia were answered by false promises of reinforcement. The army tried to link up with the Kushtia contingent but could not go beyond the outskirts of the town and returned to the cantonment. The fourth victim was the SDO Naogaon, Nisarul Hameed, but the circumstances of his death are not known. They all died because of Yahya's resolve to hang on to power for as long as he could, elections being only a ruse to distract an enraged population.

Perhaps Yahya may have actually wished for a few high profile deaths of civil servants so that he would not have to belabour himself in finding a rationale for launching his military operation. Mujib was wise enough not to provide him the excuse and kept his people in check. But that was before Yahya went on a rampage on 25 March. In the aftermath of the military operation to combat Mujib's so-called obduracy, obstinacy, and refusal to talk sense, the Bengalis were left with no leader because Mujib was arrested and the others either fled to India or went into hiding. As soon as the Bengalis organized themselves they committed some despicable crimes of their own.

After arriving safely in Jessore we thought we owed it to Khalid Mahmood to alert him to the dangers of the situation; he was SDO Satkhira, a sub-division of Khulna district. We finally got through to him with some difficulty on a military telephone and asked him to come to Jessore. He did not give a clear answer but from what he said we realized he was not prepared to come. When we met a few years later he told me that he did not want to leave his station because he felt responsible for the treasury. It so happened that on the very same evening or perhaps the next day, the Bengalis took him prisoner and wanted to parade him before killing him with a fanfare deserving of such a high value target. Satkhira was a border sub-division and fortunately for him some Indian troops were already in the area. Luckily for Khalid, a Sikh officer rescued him and saved him from certain death.

Subsequent events narrated by Khalid suggest that the Indians initially treated him well till they realized that he did not have a clue of Yahya's plans. The Indians thought that our civil servants were part of the policy-making process. They then dumped him in an ordinary jail in Alipur in

West Bengal. It was only the intervention of our batch mate in the foreign service, Khalid Saleem, who was part of the delegation negotiating repatriation of the POWs that this category of officers, who were not given the status of POWs, was repatriated.

3

Killer Cyclone (1970)

In November 1970, I was posted at Khulna as additional deputy commissioner for development. Most of the districts had three additional deputy commissioners—general, revenue, and development. My two-year tenure in East Pakistan was due to end in June the following year; I was keen to visit the famous Sunderbans which fell within the jurisdiction of Khulna district before leaving for West Pakistan.

The post of a DC was a privileged position which carried with it a number of luxuries—launches with exotic names for visiting parts of the district not otherwise accessible by road and a Mercedes car for official duties. Enam Chaudhry, the incumbent DC, had been injured in a road accident and I was acting in his place. This meant I had the use of his official launch. On the morning of 6 November, the day I was to leave for the Sunderbans, the crew of the DC's launch arrived and refused even on pain of punishment to embark on the journey because of bad weather.

Natural disasters afflicted that part of the country quite often and insensitive people of the Western wing would describe these as their much-deserved punishment. However the local administration was always prepared to deal with such calamities. The signal for the impending cyclone on the morning of 6 November was four or five (on a scale of one to ten), and to my mind this did not portend disaster. I tried to persuade the crew that the danger was not too great and therefore we should stick to our plans. But they would not budge. The local population seemed to have a better instinct about an approaching cyclone, although on that day they too did not appear overly concerned. In the tsunami of 2004 it was the animals that had a forewarning of the disaster and some people saved their lives by following them to higher ground. Anyway, I had no choice but to postpone the visit to the next day.

There were some gusty winds on 6 November but the weather did not appear very threatening. I took all this in stride and didn't think the situation was very alarming. So did perhaps everybody else.

The next day I was woken up very early in the morning by a telephone call from the relief commissioner's office in Dhaka who wanted to know the extent of the damage caused by the storm. But at that point there had been no official reports of any damage. Embarrassed at having to admit my ignorance, I asked for time and promised to call back. I opened my window to look outside and saw a few fallen branches but the trees were all standing. I called back to report that the extent of damage in Khulna district had not been extensive because the storm had not been very severe and that only 20 per cent of the trees had been damaged. Perhaps this became the source of information for subsequent press announcements by the relief commissioner. I did not know what had happened in other districts, but it seemed that nobody else knew either.

As planned, I proceeded on my trip to the Sunderbans the next day. I met the local magistrate at Chalna port, which is almost midway to the Sunderbans, chatted with him for a few minutes and then continued on my journey. I later realized that he too had been completely oblivious of the calamity that had struck the previous day. On the way I saw a tiger royally resting after a meal with his eyes half open and fully satisfied with the state of affairs. He completely ignored me. I reached the Sunderbans after a 12-hour river journey and saw a few deer carcasses, perhaps victims of the storm, but no other visible signs of the catastrophe that had struck the previous day. I did not think much of it. The official rest house was perched on bamboo poles about 10 feet high. I spent about ten to fifteen minutes surveying the scene and returned satisfied that I had accomplished my mission. I could now count myself amongst those few West Pakistanis who had been to the Sunderbans.

On the way back I again stopped midway at Chalna port and met the same magistrate. This time it was different because he was extremely worried and had some ominous news. He startled me with the information that a huge disaster had struck the coastal areas. He asked if I had known about this disaster on my way out but obviously I knew nothing at the time. He said that the cyclone which had been dismissed as inconsequential devastated wide swathes of the coastal areas of East Pakistan and about 500,000 people were estimated to have died.

It was several days later before the enormity of the catastrophe was fully comprehended. The international response to this huge human tragedy was overwhelming. The US sent men and material and there were volunteers from the Salvation Army. People did not have much use for the tinned food and a number of other food items sent by the US because they suspected these were not *halal*. India understood the needs better and sent items like kerosene lamps, pots and pans, etc. which were of immediate use to the marooned people. Some international aid was shipped to Karachi but I believe most of it never reached East Pakistan. A large number of officers from other districts were deputed for special duty to the affected areas; I was sent to Bhola Island in district Barisal in December and stayed there for a month.

The government was slow to react and made some token effort at providing relief to the victims. Ironically, Yahya was in Dhaka on that fateful day but went back to West Pakistan without knowing what had really happened. He returned soon thereafter when he learnt about the enormity of the calamity and carried out an aerial survey of the cyclone hit areas. He perhaps felt that the situation was not sufficiently serious for it to warrant his presence so after issuing some half-hearted orders to the military to get involved in the relief, went back to Islamabad.

The first relief effort was seen in the affected areas some ten days after the tragedy. The army showed up eventually but there were reports that soldiers were stealing relief goods. Blankets were the most valuable item because many of the poor Bengalis did not know what they were and thought they were something very precious. The Hamood-ur-Rahman Commission was told that Pakistani soldiers refused to handle Bengali dead bodies. I am witness to a large number of dead bodies lying unburied. A cynical comment one heard was that the Bengalis did not want the dead buried so as to attract greater sympathy. The fact is that the survivors were too few and even they were not equal to the task because they had gone hungry for days and lost many members of their families. There was a glaring contrast in the manner in which the world rushed to provide succour to the Bengalis as against the passivity of the Islamabad government. Several years later, in the mid-1990s, as in-charge of the emergency relief cell controlled by the cabinet division, I discovered that relief goods meant for the 1970 cyclone were still lying in our warehouses.

Because there were not many structures left in Bhola after the cyclone—in fact very few existed even before—I was given a bunk in the deputy commissioner's boat anchored in the *khal* (a water inlet). The first thing I saw on arrival was a dead baby floating face down next to the boat. I had never seen a dead body before. But I was soon to see scores of them all along the two banks of the sea inlet—bloated and exuding an unbearable stench. It was impossible to breathe. I wondered how I would survive in such an inhospitable environment but within hours I ceased to smell the stench or feel perturbed by the ugly sight. I was tasked to ferry food and other relief material on a barge to areas where no one had gone since after the cyclone. The sight of dead bodies lying on either side of the narrow inlet was ghastly and the strong stench permeating the air simply overpowering. The people we met on the way had not eaten anything for close to a week, surviving on leaves or whatever else they could get.

I had brought my cook along but felt I would not be able to eat in the midst of such ghastly sights and unbearably disgusting odour. But within a few hours I ceased to notice any of this and ate as normally as I would otherwise. So, acclimatization to the most extreme conditions takes place sooner rather than later. God has given enormous adaptability to a human being.

We stopped *en route* at places where we saw some survivors, and handed over food and clothes to the one from amongst them who looked sensible. A Red Cross team had also accompanied me and we had agreed that distribution of the relief material would be a coordinated affair with mutual consultation. One arrangement was that only one blanket would be given to each individual. So when I saw a young man carrying two or three blankets I thought the arrangement had been breached, and asked the man how come he had more than one blanket. The poor recipient of the valuable item broke down and said he was only organizing his people to off load the relief material from the barge although he had lost all thirteen members of his family. I was embarrassed. We came across one group of hungry people who nearly raided the boat. We gave them some flour bags but they started fighting amongst themselves and in the melee one bag fell overboard. The man who last had the bag kept hanging on to it for dear life even though there was danger he might drown. The fight for this valuable cargo continued but we moved on even though I kept wondering for how long did the bag hold.

I stayed on the barge for the next three to four days. The last point of our journey presented a desolate and forlorn look. People were marooned and had not eaten anything for days. The storm had been so strong that a sea-going ship had been blown two miles inland and had come to rest not far from where we were. Palm trees that were nearly 30 feet high had water marks near their top. I asked a man with lacerations on his chest what had caused the injury. His reply was revealing. He had climbed a tree to escape the killer waves but they kept pounding against him like gigantic blows from a hammer. Yet the man was determined to survive and fought against the fury of the cyclone for hours, clinging to the tree for dear life and bravely enduring the rough tree trunk on his chest.

The commissioner of Chittagong was the overall in-charge of relief for the calamity stricken areas in Barisal and started to take measure of the damage the day he arrived. He asked how many livestock were lost in the cyclone and the concerned official gave a constant figure of 60,000 cattle or part thereof for each *thana*. He obviously had no clue about the losses and was quoting random numbers in an attempt to hide his ignorance. He adopted a simple formula—if there was a feeling that in a given *thana* there had been a total loss, he would quote a figure of 60,000 and if there was an opinion that the losses might not have been so grave, he would quote a number of 30,000. After he left someone pointed out that the losses of one *thana* had not been accounted for; the livestock man was recalled and asked to give an estimate and he promptly quoted yet another figure of 60,000. The commissioner was not amused because this rendered the whole estimate suspect, prompting him to remark that the livestock man was like cattle and should be counted as such.

Then there was Waheed, who was the local additional deputy commissioner, an officer of EP Civil Service. He and I shared bunks on the boat which belonged to the district. He would wake up early, smoke a cigarette and then start shaving using a small mirror hanging on the wall. One day as he was about to leave I noticed some soap on his face and pointed this out to him. He looked into the mirror, wiped the soap off his face and said that it did not really matter as he was only going to meet the superintendent of police (SP). I mention this to highlight the relationship between the police and the civil service; the police in the former East Pakistan, unlike their counterparts in the Punjab, respected the administrative hierarchy and accepted its subordination to the law/magistracy.

Early one afternoon there was great commotion on the boat with everybody running to and fro. The entire furore was about heating water for Waheed *bhai's* bath. This upset my calculations as Waheed was about to demolish my theory that he was essentially an animal of dry land and averse to water. I called my friend Tasneem Siddiqi (a civil servant colleague who retired from Katchi Abadi development of Sindh), who was also in the area on relief duty, on a rickety and ancient phone to share this news with him. We had been sharing the idiosyncrasies of Waheed *bhai* on a regular basis. Tasneem had a great sense of humour and was quick to join the fun, urging me to dissuade Waheed from this venture. So I reasoned with Waheed *bhai*, telling him that it was not the best of times to undertake such a risky enterprise. But he seemed determined to proceed and I finally gave up.

When Waheed *bhai* surprisingly reappeared very quickly after entering the bathroom, I remarked that he had been very fast indeed. He replied solemnly that he changed his mind about having a bath because with the sight of water came the realization that discretion was the better part of valour. For the month that we stayed together, Waheed *bhai* did not venture to have a bath. Mind you, although this was the month of November/December, winter in Bengal is very mild.

An interesting episode relates to the distribution of relief goods and cash amongst the victims of the cyclone. I decided not to issue relief material on a daily basis but hand over everything pro rata in a single day. I felt there was no point in requiring the same set of surviving population to queue up everyday as all relief goods were meant for them and it didn't matter if they received it piecemeal or in one go. However, I insisted on a queue and although people had a problem comprehending this concept I stood my ground till they finally conceded. Not surprisingly, women, children and the weak were at the tail end of the queue. Tasneem was present and had a brilliant idea. He advised me to start the distribution from the rear—which left the enterprising people in front feeling obviously cheated. Tasneem later made a name for himself both here and abroad for his pioneering work in *kutchi abadis* (resettlement in urban slums).

The events that followed, in particular the electoral sweep of the Awami League, had as much to do with other factors as with the cyclone because the calamity had been tardily and ineptly handled by the central government.

4

Six-point Programme

The six-point programme of the Awami League was made out by West Pakistani rulers to be at the heart of the problem, but it was there for everyone to see before the electoral process had started. It represented the political platform of the Awami League and called for maximum autonomy for East Pakistan. If the smaller provinces of West Pakistan chose to have lesser autonomy, the leader of the Awami League said he would have no problem in accepting their position. But the mere mention of the six points had become a mantra to charge the Bengali crowds although one can safely say that many of them didn't really know what they implied. I was surprised to note on one occasion that the secretary-general of the Awami League who belonged to Rajshahi did not go beyond the first or second point in a discussion he was having with the DC. Most Bengalis believed these six points were the means of gaining control of their own resources, but it is possible that they may have represented a maximalist bargaining position which politicians usually adopt.

When Mujib met the US Ambassador at Dhaka in February 1971, he told him that he 'wanted a just and rightful share of foreign aid, and not a mere "20 per cent as heretofore. With 60 per cent foreign exchange coming from my country, how can Islamabad justify the crumbs which they have thrown us?"[1]

Sirajul Huda, a friend and an engineer by profession who served in the National Highway Authority before retiring, once travelled with Mujib in a train from Chittagong to Dhaka. He confirmed to the author that during the journey Mujib said that the six points were negotiable as they were not the words of God. This narration has to be accurate because the views that Huda holds are such that he would love to believe anything to the contrary.

A careful reading of these points does not suggest anything more sinister than a demand for greater provincial autonomy. Even if the objective was to create a confederation, which these points did not seek, it was still a preferable option in comparison to the bloody mess the military imposed. In a desperate bid to retain power and to justify his unprovoked attack on the East Pakistanis, Yahya made his infamous speech on 26 March, but all he could accuse Mujib of was 'obstinacy, obduracy and refusal to talk sense.'

The West Pakistanis were not as politically conscious as the Bengalis and were led to believe that Mujib's six-point programme was actually an agenda for secession. This argument, on the one hand, deflects the blame from the real culprits, and on the other, finds a convenient and acceptable scapegoat. In the context of this narrative it is important to recall the six points (reproduced below):

1. The Government shall be federal and parliamentary in which elections to the Federal Legislature and to the Legislature of the Federating Units shall be direct and on the basis of universal adult franchise. The representation in the Federal Legislature shall be on the basis of population.

2. The Federal Government shall be responsible only for Defence and Foreign Affairs and, subject to conditions provided in (3) below, currency.

3. There shall be two separate currencies mutually or freely convertible in each Wing for each region, or in the alternative a single currency, subject to the establishment of a Federal Reserve System in which there will be regional Federal Reserve Banks which shall devise measures to prevent transfer of resources and flight of capital from one region to the other.

4. Fiscal policy shall be the responsibility of the Federating Units. The Federal Government shall be provided with requisite revenue resources, which would be automatically appropriable by the Federal Government in the manner provided and on the basis of the ratio to be determined by the procedure laid down in the Constitution. Such Constitutional provisions would ensure that the Federal Government's revenue requirements are met consistently with the object of ensuring control over the fiscal policy of the Governments of the federating units.

5. Constitutional provisions shall be made to enable separate accounts to be maintained of the foreign exchange earnings of each of the Federating Units, under the control of the respective Government of the Federating Units. The foreign exchange requirements of the Federal Government shall be met by Governments of the Federating Units on the basis of a ratio to be determined in accordance with the procedure laid down in the Constitution to negotiate foreign trade and aid within the framework of the foreign policy of the country, which shall be the responsibility of the Federal Government.

6. The Governments of each of the Federating Units shall be empowered to maintain a militia or para-military force in order to contribute effectively towards national security.[2]

A reading of these six points with an open mind and some under-standing of constitutional matters does not lead one to conclude that East Pakistan wanted to secede. A point wise examination is in order.

The first point required a federal and parliamentary form of government with elections to the legislature held on the basis of universal adult franchise. There was nothing sinister about this. All it asked for was a more democratic polity that was participatory in nature and would allow each adult voter one vote. The one-man-one-vote principle had been denied for twenty-five years on the basis of a contrived formula of parity. This in itself was a negation of the principle of democracy because it gave the 44 per cent people of West Pakistan an equal mandate to the 56 per cent people of East Pakistan. Both Ayub Khan and Yahya Khan had conceded this Bengali demand. The 1970 elections were held on this basis.

The second point limited the functions of the federal government to defence and foreign affairs and by implication allowed the remaining subjects to the provinces. Unified foreign and defence policies with a common flag provided the best guarantee against the break-up of a country which eventually the ambitious forces of West Pakistan so blatantly engineered. This point had no treasonous overtones, more so because provincial autonomy constitutes the most enduring guarantee for a strong federation. It was this withholding of autonomy that created the crisis in 1971 and continues to plague provincial relationships in Pakistan even today. The strength of the United States lies largely in the autonomy all its fifty states enjoy under its Constitution; this is also true for India as indeed for all other federations. Maximum autonomy is also a guarantee against an incipient Bonaparte lurking in the wings.

Unfortunately, it seems to be an article of faith with many people, particularly those of the subcontinent, that a strong centre guarantees progress and power. This represents a fascistic streak in their thinking. It should be obvious that a federating province that is unwilling to remain part of the federation cannot and should not be coerced into doing so for long. Every citizen should have a sense of participation in the affairs of a country because that guarantees a strong federation. In the context of the six points, the extent of provincial autonomy was neither debated nor determined by the National Assembly; in fact the assembly was not even allowed to convene after the 1970 elections.

These six points were integral to the Awami League's political manifesto on the basis of which it contested the elections. If the military rulers believed that these six points were detrimental to the interest of the federation they could and should have disallowed electioneering on any or all points; after all, the regime had empowered itself by promulgating the Legal Framework Order (LFO) to replace the 1962 Constitution and imposed a large number of restrictions on what the political parties could or could not do. For instance, the prescribed punishment under the LFO for criticising even a foot soldier of the Pakistan Army was seven years imprisonment while politicians were free to sling mud at each other so long as they left Yahya and his regime alone.

That they permitted the six points to be freely discussed and debated implied that either the rulers found nothing wrong with them or else they had sinister designs and anticipated events to unfold the way they did. They perhaps felt that by permitting uninhibited propagation of the six points they would prepare grounds to eventually charge the Bengalis for attempting to secede.

Justice A.R. Cornelius, a retired Chief Justice of Pakistan who served as a constitutional expert in Yahya's military regime, had this to say to the Hamood-ur-Rahman Commission:

> He (Yahya) was familiar with them (six points) and he used to talk about them from time to time but he never asked for an analysis. In my own mind I think that about four of them were quite easily acceptable and I think I said in a meeting of the cabinet that it would be easily possible to amend the Constitution so as to give effect to most of the Six Points and that would perhaps ease the political situation.[3]

The Commission thought that the government's approach to Mujib's six points was casual. It also observed that Yahya was totally unprepared for talks with Mujib.

On 6 January 1971, General Peerzada, the Principal Staff Officer to General Yahya, called on the Governor of East Pakistan, Admiral Ahsan, and asked him to obtain a copy of the six points programme because he said that on the next day the president would be discussing it with Mujibur Rahman and his colleagues. That at this stage the presidential team did not have so much as a copy of the Six Points programme is in itself a shocking eye-opener.[4]

In the following observation of the Hamood-ur-Rahman Commission one finds confirmation of the hypothesis that Yahya maintained an off-hand attitude towards the six points and had no intention of handing over power to the elected representatives:

...the failure on the part of Gen. Yahya Khan and his advisers to critically examine the Six Points of Sheikh Mujibur Rahman and to permit the latter to campaign on the basis of his said Six-Point programme, declaring that the elections were actually a referendum on the Six Points, seems to suggest that neither the General nor any one of his advisers was ever bothered about what the result of the election would be.[5]

There was no end to the propaganda the regime encouraged to create an impression in Pakistan that the six-point programme was nothing short of a ruse for secession. General Gul Hassan writes in his *Memoirs*:

> The Six Points were concocted soon after the 1965 war....in a nutshell the six points amounted to provinces minding their own business, with the central government being reduced to the status of a referee without a whistle! The 1968 (Agartala) conspiracy may well have been a result of the growing impatience on the part of the Sheikh and India over the non implementation of the Six Point formula.[6]

He gives vent to his strong bias against all politicians, particularly those from the former East Pakistan by averring: 'The Sheikh's avowed objective was to create Bangladesh and his Six Points formula stood unequivocally for the break up of Pakistan...'[7] The people of Pakistan, not given to introspection, accepted this distorted interpretation of events without a critical examination or an objective analysis, failing to understand that these very six points provided the basis for maintaining the integrity of the country.

The third point related to two separate currencies, mutually or freely convertible in each wing or in the alternative a single currency subject to certain safeguards like establishing a federal reserve system with regional federal reserve banks. This point was not immutable and left scope for negotiations. The idea was to prevent transfer of resources from the lesser developed East Pakistan to West Pakistan for the latter's industrialization. Obviously, there was nothing wrong with this demand, more so because independent economists acknowledge that there had been a massive transfer of resources from East to West Pakistan which was one of the causes of ill will between the two wings.

Asking for a separate currency did not amount to a call for secession. It was intended to only guarantee non-transfer of resources from a very poor region to one that was relatively less poor. The people of East Pakistan had full legal and moral right to their own resources and if anything, they were entitled to subsidies on the basis of being more economically depressed than the western wing. It should be recalled that East Pakistan was kept politically and economically in check with the application of the contrived principle of parity. They were not given even half the share in political power and in fact were completely marginalized. Their demand for distribution of resources on the basis of population was stubbornly resisted until after 1971 when the Punjab suddenly found the idea appealing because by then it had emerged as the most populous of the remaining four provinces.

The fourth point related to the fiscal policy which was to be the responsibility of the federating units. The federal government was to be provided funds in accordance with appropriate constitutional provisions to ensure 'that the federal government's revenue requirements are met consistently.' This point envisaged that the federal government should be subservient to the people and receive allocations that were to be determined by the federating units. The demand was based on past experience of the federating units not being allocated their due share of the national resources. This too was an unexceptionable demand not inconsistent with greater autonomy.

It is pertinent to note that the four provinces of post-1971 Pakistan were unable to reach an agreement on distribution of resources for at least ten years prior to 1997 when eventually a caretaker and unrepresentative government imposed an unconstitutional award. The federal government has been encroaching on provincial turf in utter disregard of the Constitution that itself has been mutilated beyond recognition. The federal government now controls even local government elections organized by the chief election commissioner and decides who should be the *nazims* under the much ballyhooed devolution scheme of General Pervez Musharraf. It controls all local and provincial taxes including octroi and doles out charity to the provinces from what little is left after its profligate expenses mostly on mega projects and defence.

The fifth point required separate foreign exchange earnings accounts for each federating unit. This was to prevent transfer of foreign exchange to West Pakistan earned by East Pakistan through export of its jute, jute products, and tea. The point also required entitling the federating units to independently negotiate foreign assistance and trade, and meet the foreign exchange requirements of the federal government 'in accordance with the procedure laid down in the Constitution.' This demand needs to be understood in the context of the usurious interest (18 to 20 per cent) provinces are required to pay for foreign assistance received by the federal government at concessional terms. In recent times a few provinces wished to retire their expensive debts to ease the burden of paying usurious interests but the federal government declined to accede. The fifth point therefore intended to deny unjustified income which the federal government earned by the process of re-lending foreign loans to the provinces on terms substantially higher than those negotiated with the foreign lender. This was also intended to provide relief to the dwindling finances of the underdeveloped regions and give leeway to the federating units to directly deal with foreign lenders and benefit from lower rates of interest. It was clarified that transactions under this clause would be subject to the foreign policy imperatives of the federal government.

The last point concerned the creation of a paramilitary force for the security of each federating unit. At present paramilitary forces like the Rangers, the Frontier Constabulary (FC) and the Coast Guards are the coercive arms of the federal government and operate at its behest. But, for example, the Baloch nationalists consider the 35,000 FC troops as well as an army corps and the auxiliaries in Balochistan to be an occupation force. So this point was intended to safeguard provincial autonomy. All these paramilitary forces are funded by the civilian side of the budget through the ministry of interior or the cabinet division etc. but contrary to the law that regulates their functioning they take orders from the GHQ. In 1996, after the Supreme Court restored the government of Prime Minister Nawaz Sharif he ordered the Rangers to provide coercive support to his nominated governor and chief minister to assume office from the incumbents in the Punjab. The Rangers refused to budge without orders from the GHQ which of course was acting in concert with the conspiring president to undermine a representative government.

NOTES

1. US Department of State (Office of Historian), Foreign Relations, 1969-76, Vol. E-7, South Asia, 1969-72, Telegram from US Consulate General in Dhaka to Department of State, 28 February 1971, Document 121. (http://www.state.gov/r/pa/ho/frus/nixon/e7txt/47238.htm).
2. Gul Hassan Khan, *Memoirs of Lt. Gen. Gul Hassan Khan,* Oxford University Press, Karachi, 1993, Appendix A.
3. *The Report of the Hamood-ur-Rahman Commission of Inquiry into the 1971 War* (as declassified by the Government of Pakistan), Vanguard Books, Lahore, 2001, p. 72.
4. Ibid., p. 77.
5. Ibid., p. 343.
6. Gul Hassan, op. cit., p. 242.
7. Ibid., p. 261.

5

General Elections (1970)

The first general election held in Pakistan on the basis of universal adult franchise and 'one man one vote' was the long awaited step for establishing a healthy tradition in democracy. Were the 1970 elections indeed fair? People generally believe so. A qualified answer would be 'yes'. Given our propensity to manipulate the system, any system, these elections were by and large fair mainly because the machinations of the regime were subtle as opposed to the ham-handed methods adopted by Yahya's predecessors or his military successors. According to Brigadier A.R. Siddiqi:

> (Maj.-Gen.) Umar's outfit had been busy throughout the election campaign. Their main aim was to weaken the Awami League's vote drawing power. Lt.-Col S.D. Ahmad—a Dhaka based Martial Law officer—openly bragged that he had some Rs 5m to play with.[1]

Massive public support for the Awami League and in particular for Mujib acted as a deterrent against any blatant methods of rigging in East Pakistan and reduced the regime's options. Moreover, intelligence prognosis of a split verdict by the East Pakistani electorate provided comfort and assurance to Yahya that he will have ample opportunity to play games after the elections and maintain his stranglehold over power. He had been given to understand by his intelligence staff that no political party would command a majority in the house and demand transfer of power.

In the report on general elections of 1971 the Chief Election Commissioner recorded:

> ...the first general election held in Pakistan on the basis of universal adult franchise and on the basis of one man one vote was the first step for the establishment of healthy tradition in democracy....the conduct of election in a free and impartial manner speaks highly of sagacity and wisdom of the Returning Officers whose responsibility it was to conduct these polls and to

ensure their smooth and efficient conduct with a total strength of 335,890 polling personnel.

The results of these elections demonstrated beyond any shadow of doubt that the people of Pakistan are second to none in the keenness of their response to election urges or in the degree of political sophistication....[2]

It would be naïve to expect the Election Commission to indict itself for failing to hold less than fair and free elections, whether they were the controversial 1977 elections organized by Zulfikar Ali Bhutto or the massive fraud perpetrated in the name of elections by Generals Ziaul Haq and Pervez Musharraf in various referendums and general elections. Ziaul Haq strove to legitimize himself through a referendum based on a convoluted question and a similar effort was made by his less than illustrious military successor. The referendums held by Ziaul Haq and Musharraf were conducted by officers of the judiciary instead of the much-maligned district and civil service officers who had conducted such polls in the past. The first polls conducted by Pervez Musharraf in 2002, believed to be no better than the two earlier referendums, were held under the benign supervision of the judiciary and an 'independent' Election Commission.

Field Marshal Ayub Khan also micromanaged elections including the ones in 1962 and 1964. By rigging elections, Ayub subverted the Constitution he himself had given to the people of Pakistan. Earlier he subverted the 1956 Constitution by imposing martial law and pre-empting elections that were due in early 1959. In doing so, he effectively thwarted the democratic progress and set a precedent for every military commander to aspire to the top political job. He was not alone in this. The then President Iskandar Mirza was worried at the prospects of impending elections and found a more than willing co-conspirator in Ayub to derail democracy.

The 1970 general elections were the culmination of a democratic process ironically set in motion by Yahya whose strong urge to grab power overcame any gratitude he might have felt for Ayub for appointing him Commander-in-Chief.

According to the Hamood-ur-Rahman Commission Report, Pakistan's military intelligence chief, who had taken up residence in the Dhaka Intercontinental Hotel, told a group of foreign correspondents, with a glass of whisky in hand, that the Awami League would get no more than 60 per cent seats in the forthcoming elections. It was this kind of intelligence analysis that emboldened Yahya to hold relatively free elections, secure in the belief that a divided house would pose no threat to his continued hold on power. He would play the puppeteer to the politicians. The Report says:

> In our examination of the events during and after the election campaign we have seen that General Yahya did not support any particular party but rather that he was expecting an election result in which no single party would emerge as a force strong enough to dictate its own terms and that a number of comparatively small parties would be thrown up.[3]

In the words of the Commission:

> Remarkable though it might seem, it appears that at no point of time before the results were in, did the administration anticipate that the Awami League would be returned in such a majority. In fact it appears that in the beginning the thinking was that what was likely to emerge from the elections both in the East and in the West were a number of small parties, say about 8 or 10 in number. It is obvious that if such had been the result not only would the gravity of the Six Points be no longer an important matter to consider but there would be no party or combination of parties who could put itself forward as the proper and legitimate recipient of power.[4]

To ensure the outcome, Yahya Khan used public funds. The Commission made a damning observation on the conduct of elections touted as the fairest by the regime's propagandists:

> During the election campaign Gen. Yahya Khan endeavoured by use of money and other means to influence the results of the elections so that not one or two parties but a conglomeration of small parties should be returned, none being of a size large enough to be in a position to dictate terms.[5]

Yahya did not leave matters to chance. Evidence presented before the Commission established that the director intelligence bureau, N.A.M. Razvi, an officer of Police Service of Pakistan, had been 'indulging in politics, collecting funds from industrialists and others and utilising the same to further the political ambitions of General Yahya Khan and his military junta.'[6]

The general elections were originally scheduled to be held on 5 October 1970, but were postponed on the pretext of the havoc caused by the cyclone even though it had hit only two of East Pakistan's nineteen districts. There were rumours of further postponement which according to newspaper reports prompted Mujib to sternly warn the rulers that such a move would be resisted even if it meant that ten million had to die.

The elections were eventually held on 7 December for the national assembly and on 17 December for the five provincial assemblies. Voter

Table 1: Number and Percentage of Valid Votes Polled: National Assembly[7]

S. No.	Province	Number of seats		Total number of registered votes	Total number of valid votes polled	Political Parties		
		Total	Contested			AL	PPP	PML (Q)
						Number %	Number %	Number %
1.	East Pakistan	162	162	31,211,220	17,193,351 55.09%	12,914,225 75.11%	–	184,154 1.07%
2.	The Punjab	82	82	16,364,495	10,879,416 66.48%	8,089 0.07%	4,532,795 41.66%	589,150 5.42%
3.	Sindh	27	27	5,335,523	3,118,338 58.44%	7,713 0.25%	1,401,660 44.95%	333,694 10.70%
4.	NWFP including Centrally Administered Tribal Areas	25	'24	3,074,217	1,439,720 46.83%	3,170 0.22%	205,599 14.28%	325,924 22.64%
5.	Balochistan	4	4	956,045	373,240 39.04%	3,965 1.06&	8,869 2.38%	40,827 10.94%
	Total	300	299	56,941,500	33,004,065 57.96%	12,937,162 39.20%	6,148,923 18.63%	1,473,749 4.46%

'There was uncontested return from one constituency

Abbreviations: AL = Awami League, PPP = Pakistan People's Party, PML (Q) = Pakistan Muslim League (Council)

turnout all over Pakistan was high with 57.96 per cent of registered voters casting their votes in the national assembly elections. Table 1 presents summarized province-wise data on the number and percentage of votes polled during the 1970–71 National Assembly elections:

It should be pointed out that the enthusiasm of the electorate was markedly higher in West Pakistan than in East Pakistan as can be seen from the turnout in the national assembly polls—63.42 per cent combined for the four provinces of West Pakistan versus 55.09 per cent in East Pakistan. Voter turnout for elections to the provincial assemblies was similarly higher in West Pakistan—14.9 million or 58.24 per cent (combined for all four provincial assemblies)—against 15 million or 48.28 per cent in East Pakistan. Two of the larger provinces in West Pakistan, the Punjab and Sindh, had a voter turnout of 61.5 and 56.99 per cent respectively in the provincial assembly polls, again higher than the 48.28 per cent turnout in East Pakistan.

A total of 1,579 candidates from all over Pakistan contested 300 National Assembly seats, an average of five candidates for each constituency; in fact, many seats were contested by up to three to six candidates. In East Pakistan, a total of 873 nominations were filed for the 162 National Assembly seats of which six were rejected and eighty-seven were later withdrawn. The Awami League won in all but two constituencies from where Nurul Amin Khan, a veteran politician, and Raja Tridev Roy, chief of the Chakma tribe were returned victorious. A summary of the number of candidates who contested the National Assembly elections from East Pakistan and all four provinces of West Pakistan is given in Table 2.

On an all-Pakistan basis the Awami League polled 39.2 per cent votes in the National Assembly elections followed by the Pakistan People's Party which secured 18.63 per cent votes. The remaining political parties and independent candidates polled in the range of 1.58 per cent (Jamiat-e-Ulema Pakistan, Niazi Faction) and 7.04 per cent (Independents). The verdict in favour of the Awami League was overwhelming and unambiguous.[9]

The voting pattern in East Pakistan was instructive. The Awami League secured 75.1 per cent of the votes cast in the province for the national assembly elections while the Jamaat-e-Islami (in spite of being the second largest party in East Pakistan) managed only 6 per cent; the Pakistan Muslim League (Convention), the official league of Ayub Khan, received only 1.6 per cent votes. Yahya's regime created difficulties for the Muslim League by denying the party use of its own funds and showed a preference

Table 2: Constituencies and Nominations: National Assembly[8]

S. No.	Province	No. of general seats, excluding seats reserved for women	Number of candidates				
			Nominated	Whose nomination rejected	Validly nominated after acceptance of appeals, if any	Withdrawn	Contesting
1.	East Pakistan	162	873	6	868	87	781
2.	The Punjab	82	616	7	610	150	460
3.	Sindh	27	227	4	225	55	170
4.	NWFP including Centrally Administered Tribal Areas	25	211	2	211	68	143
5.	Balochistan	4	30	-	30	5	25
	Total	300	1,957	19	1,944	365	1,579

for the Jamaat-e-Islami by supporting it through various administrative means that included providing finances.

There were eight national assembly and fourteen provincial assembly seats in Khulna district which were contested by a large number of parties, some with no popular base. The rules stipulated that the deputy commissioner or additional deputy commissioner be appointed returning officer if a constituency extended over more than one sub-division. But in all of East Pakistan just seventy-nine returning officers were appointed for the 162 general seats; this obviously implied that some officers were responsible for returning election results from more than one constituency. As additional deputy commissioner of Khulna I was appointed the returning officer for one national and two provincial assembly seats.

There was a keen contest in Khulna for all national and provincial assembly seats. The Awami League candidates were mostly little-known people, generally from the lower middle classes, confronting well-known politicians who had blossomed in two martial law regimes. Initially, fifty-five nominations were filed for the eight national assembly seats in Khulna but after a few nominations were withdrawn, forty-five were eventually left in the race. Of the 1.54 million registered voters in Khulna district 955,000 or 59.82 per cent cast their votes with the Awami League securing the highest number of votes (71.72 per cent). The Jamaat-e-Islami was in second place with 12.02 per cent votes followed by Muslim League Convention with 4.32 per cent votes; the remaining parties fared poorly.

A total of 130 candidates filed nominations for the fourteen provincial assembly seats in Khulna district. The Awami League polled 70.45 per cent votes followed by Jamaat-e-Islami (4.5 per cent) and Convention Muslim League (3.45 per cent).

Because general elections in Pakistan are rarely held on a regular basis they excite deep passions whenever they take place. These elections were no different. But based on my personal observation I can say that the elections were largely fair. Polling was peaceful and orderly with no complaints of high-handedness, rowdyism, stuffing of ballot boxes or intimidation by political opponents. Starting with delimiting constituencies to registering voters, establishing polling stations, appointing the polling staff, accepting nomination papers and all the rest—the process was transparent. Dictatorial regimes more than the 'democratic' governments try to rig elections at one or all stages of this process.

On the day of the election I visited a number of polling stations in the city plus a few in the outskirts and saw people queuing peacefully, waiting for their turn to vote. The usual pushing and shoving was completely absent. All voters looked relaxed and showed no signs of fear. One could sense their hope for a peaceful transfer of power from the military to elected representatives; democracy was on the march and it was a great sight to see.

When polling ended by late evening that same day, each polling station started reporting to me the results on telephone which in turn were promptly transmitted to the provincial election commission in Dhaka. A typical result from a polling station in Khulna was 900 votes for the Awami League candidate, three for Jamaat-e-Islami and one for Khan Abdus Sabur (a former federal minister for communication in Ayub Khan's cabinet). The results from all polling stations followed a similar pattern. By about 4 o'clock in the morning the results were fairly obvious. It was a landslide. I decided to stop receiving updates, put the telephone receiver off the hook and went to sleep after informing the election commission that all Awami League candidates in my district were headed for a landslide victory. Not surprisingly the official at the other end did not protest. The outcome had become so obvious. The pattern for the provincial assembly polls held ten days later was similar. By next morning when the actual count of the vote had been completed it became clear beyond doubt that the Awami League had swept the polls.

The election results were a great disappointment to the junta because contrary to intelligence estimates the Awami League received an overwhelming mandate. The impression given out by the regime that voters had been subjected to intimidation at the hands of Sheikh Mujib's hooligans was a deliberate attempt to discredit the Awami League's thumping electoral victory. Considering that the regime earlier declared that the elections had been free and fair, this was clearly a ruse to deny transfer of power to the elected representatives of the people.

Yahya and his crew took some time to recover. Confronted with the situation where transfer of power had become inevitable, the regime started conspiring to thwart the people's demand to get their country back from the praetorian guards. Their machinations had to be put in high gear. They dusted up their contingency plans and started the deadly process of implementation. Yahya travelled to Larkana and stayed as a guest of Bhutto for three days. This was obviously to enlist Bhutto's support for his sinister designs which came to light on 25 March 1971 when the military started its crackdown on the unsuspecting people of East Pakistan. Yahya later visited East Pakistan and the only honour he did to Mujib—the clear winner of the electoral contest—was to grant him an audience and declare that he was the future prime minister of Pakistan.

NOTES

1. A.R. Siddiqi, *East Pakistan: The Endgame*, Oxford University Press, Karachi, 2004.
2. *Report on general elections, Pakistan, 1970-71*, Manager of Publications, Karachi, July 1972.
3. *Report of the Hamood-ur-Rahman Commission*, op. cit., pp. 124-5.
4. Ibid., p. 118.
5. Ibid., p. 342.
6. Ibid., p. 125.
7. *Report on general elections, Pakistan, 1970-71* (Vol. 1), op. cit., p. 202.
8. Ibid., p. 197.
9. *Report on general elections, Pakistan, 1970-71* (Vols. 1 and 2), op. cit.

6

An Engineered Crisis

The elections were now over and the country waited with bated breath for the finale of the democratic process which meant transfer of power back to the people to whom it belonged. In comparison, India held general elections in February 1971 and a new government took office on 1 March. The months following our own elections (January and February) were peaceful but full of suspense and anticipation. The calm was broken by the sub-martial law administrator in Jessore, Brigadier Durrani (who lived in Quetta before he died), when he called a meeting of all the DCs on 28 February at the Khulna Circuit House. There was no formal agenda.

I attended this meeting as acting DC of Khulna. Durrani was vague and enigmatic but had very little to say besides thanking the participants for their help in the conduct of peaceful elections. He did make an intriguing remark though, that we salute any government in power (regardless of its legality) and that it might be Sheikh Mujib's government the next time around. 'But we must be ready for any unforeseen eventuality,' he added. This was an ominous remark but made no sense to me. What was not known at the time was that the very next day, on 1 March 1971 at 1 o'clock local time (12 noon in West Pakistan), Yahya would announce that convening of the National Assembly, which was scheduled for 3 March, was being indefinitely postponed. In reality the decision was made soon after the election results were known when Yahya had gone into secret parleys with Bhutto in remote Larkana. But according to the Hamood-ur-Rahman Commission Report, 'the decision to post-pone the assembly was, however, taken on the 22nd Feb at a meeting of the Governors and Martial Law Administrators at Rawalpindi.'[1] This of course was merely to formalize a decision the chief martial law administrator had already taken when confronted with the shocking results of the 7 December elections.

35

The junta reckoned that if the National Assembly was called into session it would be difficult to prevent peoples' power from sweeping them out of office. The legally elected assembly would certainly demand transfer of power or simply wrest it from the usurpers.

The circumstances in which I was appointed acting DC make an interesting story. Fariduddin Ahmed was one of the three additional DCs in Khulna and was due to leave for West Pakistan on completion of his two-year tenure. However, because of an unfortunate road accident in which the incumbent acting DC, Enam Chaudhry, was injured Farid was told not to leave and assume Chaudhry's office in the interim. But he had already made plans for returning to West Pakistan and had been eagerly counting the days; this was symptomatic of the unhappiness of West Pakistani officers serving in that province, as if they were serving a prison sentence. Another batch mate of mine felt the same way and had started the countdown in hours when there were still a few months left for his repatriation to West Pakistan. But the situation changed and he had to delay his departure, which sent him rushing to stargazers and clairvoyants who reassured him of an earlier than expected return.

Coming back to the story, Farid hit upon a brilliant idea and enlisted me in a conspiracy. On the morning of 9 February 1971, the two of us and an unsuspecting Bengali additional DC sat in Farid's office discussing politics over a cup of tea—something that the Pakistanis have been doing since 1947 and have now refined into an art form. But it had been agreed beforehand between the two of us that Farid would quietly hand over charge to me and leave. We had signed the charge papers in complete secrecy ensuring that no one got wind of this. I saw Farid off before noon as he left for Dhaka in the DC's official Mercedes car. After he left we received a telegram from the chief secretary staying his departure but before he could be physically stopped at Dhaka he had already flown off to Lahore.

Later that evening the acting commissioner (there was no commissioner either) called to ask me the whereabouts of Farid. I told him that he had handed over the charge and left. 'To whom did he hand over charge?' the commissioner asked. 'To me,' I answered. 'But with whose permission?' he demanded. 'Must have been with yours,' I replied. The matter ended there but now Khulna had an acting commissioner and an acting DC.

The decision to postpone the session of the National Assembly triggered an intensely negative response. Dhaka Radio Station broadcast Mujib's call for a public protest in Dhaka on 2 and 3 March in the rest of the province to protest against the postponement. But people were unable to restrain themselves and showed a spontaneous and forceful resentment by coming out in the streets within half an hour of the announcement. I too had listened to the broadcast on the radio in my office and was unsure what would happen next. I felt very upset and let down. About 150 people showed up in my office and respectfully asked me to order the closure of the office because 'their democratic rights had been violated'. I ordered accordingly.

Then followed twenty-five days of a complete shutdown during which supplies were denied to the cantonments housing West Pakistani troops. I recall a cartoon that appeared in an English language newspaper published from Dhaka depicting a PIA flight with chickens peeping out of the windows. They were purportedly being flown from West Pakistan directly to the cantonments.

The anger at the unjustified halt in the process for the restoration of democracy brought forth a spontaneous and immediate outpouring of peaceful marchers on the streets of Khulna. They obviously raised slogans against Yahya and his regime but were fired upon by the military.

I made the following entries in my diary:

- 1st March: Mr Nurul Amin takes over charge of DC (of Khulna). Important event of today, considered from the viewpoint of the violent reactions it has generated, is the postponement of the National Assembly session by the president. Sense of security has further diminished.
- 2nd March: There were processions today. Offices couldn't function beyond 11 a.m. We held offices again at 12:30 p.m. and beyond. A very busy day.
- 3rd March: Eventful day indeed. Thank God it passed off (peacefully for us). The whole trouble was triggered with the military firing on the procession, killing 7 and injuring 29. We (had) feared a mob attack on any of us at any time. But people showed understanding. They directed their resentment against the army alone. There is a deep cleavage between the people and the army. Officers of the police and other departments are clearly identifying themselves with the people. Army is alone on (the) other side. Last hope of understanding between East and West Pakistan is over. Adjournment of National Assembly session was a very foolish act. A day of nerves!
- 4th March: A day of surprise(s). There were processions. But no confrontation. However, they (the Bengalis) mercilessly lynched a civilian and dragged his corpse for a mile and hung it on a tree upside down. A busy day. I was in the office till 6 p.m.
- 5th March: Full of events. In Khulna army fired and killed 9 and wounded 24 civilians. Pathan and Bengali fights also resulted in few casualties.

Meanwhile things in East Pakistan look very bleak. Sheikh Mujib is likely to declare independence on Sunday (BBC). General Yahya is addressing the nation on 6 March. East Pakistan has gone still further in its distrust of West Pakistan. Bengalis look upon the army as a force of oppression and exploitation. Colonel Shams (commanding officer of the unit posted there) was raving (mad) and said few indecent things to the DC. Most disgraceful!

- 6th March: From midnight to 8.30 in the morning in the control room. Things appear better this morning (1130 hrs). Life seems to be returning to normal. President's broadcast fixes 25 March for National Assembly session. Reaction to his speech, I assume, is not favourable here. Sheikh Mujib is making an important announcement tomorrow. It is rumoured that policemen are giving up their duties to protest against the alleged killing of two of their colleagues by the army. God help us. Going fast towards a national disaster culminating in a "civil war"—with fratricidal overtones.

- 7th March (Sunday): Mass movement of people in East Pakistan amply demonstrated their resolve and determination to brave all dangers to humble oppressive forces in the country. Their struggle is just and highlights the bondage they have endured. Repression is no solution. It has never paid. You cannot subdue the people—six crores (60 million) of them by sheer force.

The colonel in charge justified the killings on 3 March on the grounds that people were abusing Yahya. There were no more killings of civilians. It is my hunch that the military operations were to start in early March but had to be postponed to allow time for more troops to be brought in from West Pakistan. In the meanwhile, as a ruse to buy time for the final crackdown, Yahya started a 'dialogue' in Dhaka with all West and East Pakistani political leaders. This finds confirmation in the Hamood-ur-Rahman Commission Report.

The province by this time had slipped out of Yahya's control. He could only look on helplessly at the mess he had created while the Awami League issued detailed instructions for the conduct of all business in East Pakistan. For instance, it was decided that banks would not transfer money to West Pakistan and would not accept any treasury *challans* in favour of the federal government. Similar restrictions were imposed on rail and road transport. No mail would be exchanged between the two wings by the postal department. Rail and road travel was also severely restricted. Not surprisingly there was total obedience. This was peoples' power at its best. Even the treasury officer, who was a subordinate, declined to follow my advice and refused to accept payments into the federal account. Obviously his sympathies lay in the right place and he knew the price of non-compliance.

Yahya invited all West Pakistani political leaders including Bhutto—arguably the most important of them all—to Dhaka to continue his charade of a political dialogue. But there was deep anxiety. It was perhaps on 23 March that I received a telephone call from Qudrat Elahi Chaudhry, a Bengali colleague serving as additional deputy in Rajshahi, to express his joy over a possible deal between Yahya and Mujib. What made him happier though was his information that Yahya had decided to by-pass Bhutto. How convincing was Yahya that perfectly intelligent people like him would fall prey to his shenanigans!

This reminds me of my teacher and friend, the late Shamsul Huda, a professor of Political Science in Government College Mirpurkhas, who had met Mujib during his visit to West Pakistan before the elections. The latter appeared very optimistic about the prospects of transfer of power and when Huda asked him how he could be so sure, Mujib replied that he felt Yahya was different and would deliver on his promises. Unfortunately, Mujib had either not read history or had not learnt from it. Nevertheless, the Bangladeshis blame Bhutto more than Yahya as the former symbolized for them the obduracy of the West Pakistani elite determined to deny power to East Pakistan. People both here and in East Pakistan expected better statesmanship from Bhutto than the dictatorial generals.

NOTE

1. *Report of the Hamood-ur-Rahman Commission*, op. cit., p. 337.

7

Yahya Panics and Postpones National Assembly Session

Yahya had reluctantly fixed 3 March for summoning the first session of the newly elected National Assembly hoping that by then his problems would have gone away. But if not handled sensibly and in time, problems have a nasty habit of compounding, which they did with each postponement. One can only imagine what machinations were taking place in West Pakistan, in particular the GHQ, to subvert the popular will of the people. Contrary to the junta's expectations, the elections had thrown up a single majority party in the National Assembly which wanted its terms to be taken into account. The situation was a disaster for Yahya and not acceptable to him. So in panic and quite contrary to the heightened expectations of the East Pakistani population for a peaceful transfer of power, he announced a *sine die* postponement of the National Assembly session on 1 March 1971.

It was on 1 March that Noor-ul-Islam arrived to take charge as the new DC of Khulna. But it was a sad day for Pakistan. The Commander-in-Chief of the Pakistan Army, who was also the country's president, had cast the die for its eventual break-up with this announcement on national radio and television. I had listened to the radio broadcast in my office and was saddened and stunned at this turn of events. One had expected transfer of power to take place but instead one was confronted with this incredulous decision. The reaction in East Pakistan was instant and negative. An announcement on behalf of the Awami League, who had apparently taken over Dhaka Radio Station, soon followed that of Yahya's to protest against the postponement of the National Assembly session.

I had noted in my diary that 'Sheikh Mujib is likely to declare independence on Sunday (7th March).' As a matter of fact I had heard this on the BBC. On 7 March, Mujib addressed a mammoth rally but did not declare independence. Yahya must have been disappointed as he had probably hoped that Mujib would proclaim independence and thus provide him the justification to arrest the East Pakistani leader. Amongst other things Mujib demanded immediate withdrawal of the military and transfer of power to the elected representatives of the people of Pakistan. These demands were democratic and perfectly legitimate with no element of secessionism. According to Sherbaz Khan Mazari in his book *A Journey to Disillusionment*,[1] Mujib was wary of the ultimate aims of the army and considered Pakistan's politics as politics of conspiracy and intrigue.

Not expecting such a swift reaction, Yahya decided to address the nation on 6 March. Although the protest of the entire population of East Pakistan had been peaceful up till this point, Yahya sensed the possibility of a sharper reaction and heeding some sane advice from the likes of Admiral S.M. Ahsan, the then governor of East Pakistan, he fixed 25 March for summoning the National Assembly session. This was a ruse to gain time as proved by later events, and a charade enacted at the national level as Yahya had no intentions of summoning the National Assembly into session. The date was fixed to synchronize with the planned assault on the Bengali civilians—mark the chicanery of the general who rescheduled the assembly session with his planned crackdown on an unsuspecting population.

On 8 March I noted in my diary that there was a,

> ...temporary lull. Perhaps a precursor to a holocaust. God forbid! President Yahya must accept Sheikh Mujib's terms to preserve the integrity of the country. Otherwise all of us will be taken hostages, and Sheikh Mujib might declare independence, which he is loath to do.
>
> To his credit, Mujib didn't do that to the last until after the army had seen to it that Bangladesh became a reality.

In view of the uncertain situation, Roshan Zamir, (a batch mate posted in Khulna as deputy director Basic Democracies) and I gave up the official accommodation because it was a well recognized place widely known to be occupied by West Pakistani officers and moved into the anonymity of Rupsha Rest House on 13 February. We stayed there until 29 March when we finally left for Jessore, then on to Dhaka and finally to West Pakistan.

Fortunately I kept brief notes of events in a diary even though this wasn't done on a daily basis. On reviewing these notes, I find that after three decades my views and sentiments about those events remain largely unchanged although it is not unusual to feel differently when one has the benefit of hindsight, and thoughts are less burdened with emotions and objectivity is not clouded by immediate concerns. Following are some excerpts:

11th February: 'I met Mr Collins first secretary of the British Deputy High Commission, Dhaka. I have no record of the discussion but guess that the thickening political crisis must have received some attention.'

24th February: 'I had a meeting with Col. Shams of Frontier Force. He was CO of the unit stationed in Khulna and had occupied the whole Circuit House. I have this record of the meeting: "His speech was elaborately punctuated by abuses (not addressed to his interlocutors). Suffers from an inferiority complex. Short (in stature) but friendly."'

11 March 1971: 'Finished reading Nehru's *India's Quest*[2] (Paperback by Jawaharlal Nehru, Reviews). It lacks in literary quality, although it is very revealing as a history of people's struggle for freedom. There are fascinating parallels in situations before independence and (at) present (in) East Pakistan vis-à-vis the army. Army rule must go. Democratic process must be allowed to operate. Sheikh Mujib is controlling everything. Nothing happens contrary to his orders. CSP Association of East Pakistan has declared allegiance to Sheikh Mujib. Foreign missions are evacuating.'

19 March 1971: 'Civil disobedience movement enters its 19th day. I was not feeling like writing the diary for all these days. Started this day with (a) telephonic conversation with Sajid (my younger brother), who is in Bogra. His spirits were slightly low. His company is not very keen on transferring him back to West Pakistan. Narrow-mindedness of (the) Bengalis is manifest in a number of ways. DC also appears to be a victim of this outlook. There is a refugee camp (for Pathans) there, which is being neglected by the DC. The ungrateful Bengalis are ignoring these Pathans, whereas West Pakistan donated 10 times more to the relief during cyclone. How stupid of West Pakistan. Only solution to present deadlock is separation, although people raise their eyebrows at the mention of the idea. But they are myopic, I consider.' (Note: I wouldn't describe the Bengalis narrow-minded now. Their response to the treatment at the hands of West Pakistani rulers is understandable.)

22 March 1971: 'Political climate seemed to have improved. Bhutto is also in Dhaka under heavy security. Some coalition central government formula is in the offing. Quite an impracticable arrangement with Bhutto and Mujib huddled together—a permanent arrangement of a deadlock.'

23 March 1971: 'Pakistan Day today. New flags—alleged to be independent Bengal flags—are visible on rooftops today. Some over enthusiastic Bengalis have drawn out a programme for Pakistan Day today. It includes all things except any concept of solidarity. However the day passed off peacefully. Talks at Dhaka between Sheikh Mujib and Gen. Yahya are keeping the people in

control of themselves. Some optimism prevails regarding the outcome of talks. Other West Pakistani leaders are also available in Dhaka.'

24 March 1971: 'Another day of expectations. No declaration (of a breakthrough). East Pakistan is happy over the expected realization of its aim of maximum autonomy. Talks continue. Met Maj. Gen. Rao Farman Ali (at Khulna). Discussed our problem and pleaded for transfer to West Pakistan. He was very kind and (immediately) offered a ride in his helicopter there and then. (He knew what we didn't. Military operation had to start in the next 24 hours and he was personally delivering orders to his formations. Roshan and I had met him in the Circuit House and after politely declining his offer asked instead to be given official transfer orders).

25 March 1971: 'Another day of expectations. We were playing bridge at the house of Additional Deputy Commissioner, Amin, when I got Col. Shams' message (to see him in the Circuit House). He told me of the failure of talks at Dhaka and (informed me of a decision) of the proposed clampdown by the army. Suggested me to takeover from DC whom he wanted to kill or at best arrest. However, he was nice enough not to insist on (implementing) this idea. Most disturbing news indeed. I rang up Sajid and asked him to come over immediately. While I was still talking the telephone line went dead (just at) the moment I asked him to come over to Khulna (by train). Don't know if he would come.'

26 March 1971: 'A day of (the) greatest anxiety. The train by which Sajid was supposed to come was stopped at Naopara—20 miles from Khulna. I took a military truck and three miles short of the railway station we were prevented from proceeding [further] because of [a] huge roadblock. Telephones [lines] to that station were cut. Finally used WAPDA channel but was informed that Sajid had not been seen for two days. Since it was not true, I repeated my message. Finally it was reported that Sajid was well and plans no trip outside. Naopara railway station reported no first class or ACC (air-conditioned) class passenger having boarded at Ishurdi. I was temporarily satisfied.

27 March 1971: 'A grave situation for the army. Khalispur area of Urdu speaking people was raided [by Bengalis] after constructing roadblocks. Army retaliated ruthlessly [by killing the Bengalis]. A very dangerous situation indeed. Full 'civil war' [has started]. BBC and AIR reported East Pakistan Regiment and Police have revolted. It was immediately contradicted by Radio Pakistan.

28th March 1971: 'A very dull and depressing day because of bad signs of overall situation. Army is optimistic. Late at night, Nawazish Ali Zaidi (a banker friend) suggested that we shift over to Jessore cantonment for safety.

Luckily a military convoy is going tomorrow at 5 a.m. Packing completed. General spirits very low. Sajid is causing worry. No news from him.'

29 March 1971: 'Started in Zaidi's car with the convoy at 5:30 a.m. An eventful journey profuse with all sorts of fire. Three civilians were dragged from their houses and asked to help in the removal of roadblocks. Some roadside huts were set aflame. They are supposed to be harbouring miscreants. Reached at about 9.30 am and were lodged in the Guest House. All officers of the army behaved very decently all along. They looked after our comfort indeed well. I am grateful. Nothing could be done for Sajid's evacuation.'

30 March 1971: 'Went for Sajid's evacuation. [There was no way to do that. All road, rail, sea or air links had been cut]. But the Brigade Headquarters themselves failed [to deal] with the grave situation as a result of Kushtia EPR rising in arms against the solitary company of Major Shoaib. Then suddenly at 9:30 a.m. fire shots were heard inside the cantonment. We were told that (the) Bengal Regiment had mutinied. It was [an] awfully dangerous situation. Our lives are in imminent danger. Luckily rebels were overcome at 2:30 p.m. Families were evacuated. Bengali officers resented the attempts to disarm EBR. Thank God the day passed off. Sajid could not be helped.' (Note: I was trying to seek army help for his evacuation; but with their resources stretched to the limit and all communications broken down they could do nothing to help. They could not help their military colleagues in Kushtia, where everyone was killed.)

31 March 1971: 'This morning troops and ammunition are being airlifted from Dhaka (by PIA Fokker-27 aircraft). All three of us decided to take a lift on its return journey. Sajid could not be helped because [the] army is engaged in Kushtia. Ill luck, however, I and two others reached Dhaka. Met Gen. Rao Farman Ali who was very kind indeed. Put us up in MNA Hostel, which is being protected by [the] army. So long I thought Ishurdi [where Sajid lived] was peaceful. But a brigadier told me that things were not too happy there. Zaidi left for Karachi today. Roshan and I lying in low spirits in MNA Hostel.'

1 April 1971: 'Tried to see Gen. Farman Ali, without success. Met Deputy Secretary S&GAD. Roshan obtained his leave. On our return we found some of our things stolen. Felt helpless. Roshan left for airport (I stayed on to be able to help Sajid evacuate). I discussed my plight with a captain (Army) who advised me to leave for Pakistan, as things were very uncertain. I felt very sick because of Sajid. May he be safe? Took off at 10.00 p.m. and arrived via Colombo at Karachi at 4.30 a.m.'

On return to West Pakistan, the five of us who were members of the civil service and domiciled in Sindh reported to the provincial government as and when we arrived for our posting orders. Four officers were assigned to various posts in the province but I was exiled to Lahore in May 1971 where I stayed until June the following year. I noticed (in Lahore and elsewhere in Pakistan) that there was total lack of awareness of the looming crisis to the extent that on 6 September Lahore wore a festive look. Right up to the Wagah border with India, people were happy and making merry totally oblivious of the imminent dismemberment of the country. When I spoke to people they appeared out of touch with reality and did not comprehend the complex political issues.

NOTES

1. Sherbaz Khan Mazari, *A Journey to Disillusionment*, Oxford University Press, Karachi, 2000.
2. Jawaharlal Nehru, *India's Quest: Being Letters on Indian History from 'Glimpses of World History'*, Asia Publishing House, London, 1963.

8

Military Crackdown, 25 March 1971

Between 1 and 25 March the Awami League controlled everything in Khulna because of which we had nothing to do except follow the slowly unfolding events and ponder over our uncertain future. I spent time playing bridge and on one occasion the session lasted 36 hours. We usually went to our Bengali friends in official jeeps/cars but in order to be in synch with the sentiments of the local population we tied a black ribbon somewhere on a conspicuous part of the vehicle as a mark of protest at the postponement of the National Assembly session. By taking this simple precaution we did not have to fear for our lives—at least not until 25 March. The political situation would invariably come up for discussion and our Bengali hosts would ask whether or not they had the right to rule the country after having won the elections so convincingly. One had no answer. There was absolutely no justification for denying the political process to reach its denouement. One good effect, in personal terms, of these marathon bridge sessions was that I developed a total disgust for the game. I gave up playing bridge for good.

Coming back to the main issue, normal civic life had come to a virtual standstill. Nothing moved in East Pakistan without orders from the Awami League which had also assumed control of the Dhaka radio station. The authority of the federal government had evaporated into thin air. This state of near anarchy could have easily been reversed if power was transferred to the elected representatives of the people. But that was not to be.

On 24 March 1971, Major-General Rao Farman Ali paid a 'surprise' visit to the military units deployed in Khulna. He came by helicopter. Roshan Zamir and I went to meet him. We pleaded with him to have us transferred back to West Pakistan as we had almost completed our mandatory stay of two years and had forfeited our usefulness in the emerging political scenario. Moreover, we were worried for our safety and would be at serious risk in the event of a final showdown between the

46

military and the Bengalis. I for one thought that things wouldn't come to that pass.

The general invited both of us to ride with him in his 'copter back to Dhaka. We were not prepared for such an abrupt acceptance of our request and wanted formal permission from the federal government through the chief secretary, East Pakistan. We respectfully declined. We had no clue about the purpose of the general's visit and were not privy to what transpired between him and his units. The mystery unfolded a day later.

Colonel Shams was in charge of the army unit in Khulna. The following day he called me to the Circuit House where he lived and informed me in strict confidence that in six hours time, that is at midnight between 25 and 26 March, there would be a *pucca* military action—a crackdown—against the Bengalis. It was to be open season. He also informed me that in pursuit of the objectives of the operation he would kill Noor-ul-Islam, the Bengali DC who had arrived only three weeks earlier; and invited me to take over as DC Khulna. I listened to him in total disbelief, but he was dead serious. Realizing the gravity of the situation, I tried to dissuade him from pursuing his deadly plans. The superintendent police of Khulna, Raquib Khondakar, met Shams sometime later and succeeded in convincing him to spare the DC's life. Noor-ul-Islam died of natural causes a few years later. The poor man must have been under tremendous strain.

The night between 24 and 25 was an eerie experience. Khulna, the second largest city of East Pakistan and teeming with people in ordinary circumstances, presented a scene of deathly silence on 26 March. One could even hear the rustling of leaves on the road. At one point on that day I asked the telephone operator to connect me to a number but before doing so he asked me in a tone of mutual confidence if I knew what the military was up to. He must have noticed some unusual movement. One had not seen such things before. I said I knew no better. I then got a call from a friend who was an engineer telling me that some students were outside his house demanding that he hand over his licensed pistol/revolver, and inquired if he should do so. I told him that he seemed to have no choice in the matter and that in any case the district administration was no longer functional.

Sometime after 25 March, Roshan Zamir and I went to the DC's house to ask for a boat to take us to Chalna Port. We thought we might catch a ship sailing for West Pakistan and thus escape this doomed place. The DC had several luxury launches but instead he offered us accommodation in his house which he felt would be safe. He cautioned us against the boat journey because he thought the Bengali crew could get some fancy ideas *en route* to Chalna and would simply dump us in the sea and say that we had safely disembarked at the port. We came back wiser after the encounter, and did not pursue this line of action.

At the Rupsha Rest House we only ate *dal, chawal,* potatoes and *roti* because all markets were closed. One day we had a 'feast' when someone brought *achar* to break the monotony of our daily fare. In this crisis the 'war council' comprising the four of us, the other two being Nawazish Ali Zaidi and Syed Anwar Shah of Union Bank, met daily to review the situation. We concluded that with nothing stirring and the political stalemate showing no signs of getting any better, the only option was to explore all avenues of escape. I had thus far kept my distance from the military so as not to be misunderstood by the people whose trust was critical to our ability to function in the district. But in desperation I rang up Colonel Shams on 28 March, late in the evening, asking for help to extricate ourselves from this situation of near hopelessness. He promptly offered to move us the next day to Jessore Cantonment, a place far more secure being a Brigade headquarter. This sounded too good to be true, so I asked how could that be possible when all roads were closed. He said that the first military convoy after the crackdown had arrived from Jessore at about 9 p.m. that very day and was to return the following morning at 5 a.m. Apparently, the road had been cleared and we could travel safely. We immediately accepted the offer and started very early in the morning in Nawazish's car, attaching ourselves with the military convoy headed for Jessore.

Before leaving Khulna I packed all I had which was not much, resolving never to come back. Roshan Zamir was however determined to return, which incidentally he did. Not fully conscious of the enormity or gravity of the situation I asked my Bengali servant to come along to Jessore to cook for us. But he knew better because all Bengalis were potential victims of the army ire. He only stood mum and didn't say a word.

Before starting off on this potentially hazardous journey we debated on where to position our car within the convoy of heavy military vehicles, and concluded that it was not possible to select a position that would be absolutely safe. So we selected a random position. In the event there was no fire on our convoy throughout the journey. The roadblocks removed by the military the previous day had mostly reappeared and at places full-grown trees had been felled to block the road. There was so much anger at the military operation that everyone seemed to have joined the resistance to create as many hurdles as possible. The convoy took eight hours to clear the road and reach its destination only forty miles away. Thank God, we made it safely without any incident although the military kept firing on both sides of the road if only to keep the Bengali militants away. But we remained anxious throughout our travel through 'hostile' territory. A goat that had strayed onto the road was picked up by the troops for 'violating the curfew'. It went into the preparation of the feast that day.

After many weeks of living in fear we now felt safe because we were in the secure precincts of a cantonment. Our army colleagues provided us the best available accommodation and food. Even otherwise every West Pakistani was implicitly their friend and a Bengali their foe. But two days later our peace was shattered with some intense firing of heavy weapons. This was worrisome and on asking we were told that in the process of disarming the 1st Bengal Regiment stationed in the cantonment, a standoff had taken place. The Bengal Regiment had not been dispossessed of its arms till then because disarming a military unit is always a very delicate operation, more so when this is done without justification. After all, the Bengali troops had not committed any breach of army discipline to warrant this humiliation. Since they had the same weapons as the other army units, it appeared that a showdown was inevitable. The army was worried because the firing from the other side had been intense besides which the rebellious troops were joined by the Bengali police and Rangers who had reportedly surrounded the cantonment. It was now the Bengalis versus the rest. Every Bengali felt that he had to fight for the 'cause' against the 'occupation forces'.

That evening an army captain was recounting the day's exploits. I was saddened to learn from him that they or perhaps he himself had killed our good Bengali doctor, an army colonel. I expressed my horror at the unwarranted murder of an innocent and well-meaning human being who had invariably shown great concern for us. This remark provoked the young captain to point his gun at me because he felt I was defending a traitor; for the Pakistani troops every Bengali was a traitor. Roshan Zamir's timely intervention averted a possible shooting and I must consider myself lucky to be alive. Even though I did not believe he would actually shoot me, I must confess I was scared because it occurred to me that a trigger-happy army captain was capable of taking one more life.

During the next two days reinforcements in men and materials kept arriving from Dhaka and the army succeeded in bringing the situation under control. We heard the drone of aeroplanes and on asking were told that these were PIA Fokker-27 planes transporting arms from Dhaka and perhaps beyond. The roads were closed. This looked like a God-sent opportunity so we asked if it was possible to hitch a ride on their return trip to Dhaka. We were told that we could, and that there would be no charge! On 31 March, finally and mercifully, we were out of Jessore and on our way to Dhaka. All passenger seats in the aircraft had been removed to make space for carrying military cargo so we had to squat on the floor which was dirty. I sat on my handkerchief but Roshan was far more depressed and in a greater rush, and sat down without much ado. Because the aircraft was flying low we could see fires burning in villages all along the route to Dhaka. The troops had torched these bustling villages to vent their frustration at not being able to suppress people demanding their democratic rights.

Once in Dhaka, we had to find accommodation and transport. After some hesitation, I rang up General Rao Farman Ali from the airport, little believing he would take my call but to our pleasant surprise he promptly came on the line. With great affection and generosity he offered us the hospitality of his house; and it was with much difficulty that we persuaded him otherwise. He however promised to send a car which arrived within half an hour along with a lieutenant-colonel who was to be our escort and guide. Since the general had taken my call in full view of the entire staff at the airport they were duly impressed and offered to do whatever was possible to help including providing tickets for Karachi by any flight of our choosing. It should be noted that getting a seat on a flight to Karachi was almost impossible because a large number of people were queuing up to leave. These were times when people were prepared to part with their car keys in return for an early flight to the safety of West Pakistan although the price of the ticket was just Rs225 or Rs250. We were booked on the flight leaving Dhaka the next day, 1 April 1971.

The colonel drove us to the second capital where the National Assembly was to hold its first session. The army was all over the place and the area totally secured, somewhat like the 'green zone' created by the occupation forces in Baghdad thirty-two years later. We were given decent accommodation in one of the rooms meant for the MNAs who were now on the run. We rested for the night and next morning left to see the chief secretary to obtain leave of absence. We couldn't inform the civil secretariat of our presence in Dhaka as we had left our posts without formal sanction. Once outside the safety of the National Assembly complex we asked a traffic constable if it was safe to travel to the city. Dhaka presented a deserted look but he was ebullient in assuring us with a great deal of pride and with a visible sense of satisfaction, his chest thrust forward, that things were very safe indeed because 'we have sorted the [expletive] out'. He had to be a Bihari because he shared with the military in equal measure a pathological hatred for the Bengalis.

We met the chief secretary and requested him for one or two months' leave which he granted before we could even finish making the request; he was probably too scared to say no to two West Pakistani officers. We then went to see Fakhruddin Ahmad, the Bengali deputy secretary of services and general administration department. He was sitting morose and downcast. It turned out that the army had ransacked his house the night before and had slapped his mother. The soldiers appeared to have been in a no-nonsense frame of mind, and relented only when the inmates of the house begged them in the name of Allah and in the name of the Quran to show mercy. The *jawans* were surprised to see the Quran in their home because they had perhaps been made to believe that they were dealing with a non-Muslim (*kafir*) population. The military leadership has a way of conditioning the minds of its troops. It was no secret that West Pakistani leaders, military mostly, wanted everyone here to believe that the Bengalis were unduly influenced by the Hindus in demanding their civil rights and the right to their language. One has to read General Gul Hassan's book to believe it.

A nasty surprise awaited us when we returned to the MNA hostel in the afternoon. Most of our belongings had been stolen. It was unbelievable that this could happen in an area controlled entirely by the military. When we complained to the authorities we were told that it would be difficult to find the thieves because most people were in transit with whom the authorities weren't familiar. This also reminds me of an interesting episode when I needed toilet soap and asked Roshan if he had any. A *jawan* standing nearby promptly offered to help and asked which soap I would like to have. He then opened the palms of his hands and showed two different brands of soap, one in each hand. I took one and was trying to thank him when he cut me short by saying that he had not paid for these but had 'taken them'. This piqued my interest so I asked if he had taken part in any operation, meaning had he killed anyone. He replied in the affirmative but said that since he had not been able to find a male Bengali he had killed a woman instead. He added ruefully that they were under orders not to loot and as such all they could do was break into shops and destroy TV sets or whatever else was there since that was 'enemy property'.

We were booked to leave for Karachi by a PIA flight scheduled to depart at 11 p.m. on 1 April. A stranger, perhaps an airline employee, accosted me at the airport with an apparently innocuous request. He wanted me to carry four tags for baggage already booked on the flight and deliver these to a man in Karachi whose particulars he gave me including a telephone number. He wouldn't describe the nature of the merchandise but I insisted on seeing the baggage. They turned out to be four huge crates which I suspect contained betel leaves (*paan*), if nothing more sinister. Soon thereafter the actual owner emerged, an army officer perhaps of the rank of a lieutenant-colonel. I was anxious and worried over the possible adverse consequences of carrying such a huge consignment of *paan* and afraid in equal measure of refusing a colonel. People were harassed if they carried baggage that exceeded their allowance by even one kilogramme or less. On arrival in Karachi I went straight to the city and called the person from the safety of the town to take delivery of the baggage tags.

I had imagined everyone in Karachi would be furious with Yahya for launching the operation in East Pakistan. But I soon found that this was not the case. On the contrary, almost everyone including some intellectuals I met over the next few days held the view that the crackdown was long overdue and more than was justified. How could the people of West Pakistan be so callous to the plight of their countrymen in the other wing and oblivious of the consequences of denying them their democratic rights? One Rafiq Inayat Mirza, a senior civil servant who was chairman of the National Press Trust, whom I went to meet when I was in Islamabad, and who was busy in our usual chat in the office with some visitors, rued the fact that the Sindhis were clamouring for a Sindhi chief secretary. He was horrified at the thought that 'unpatriotic' people were making such a scandalous demand adding, quite innocently, that Punjabis never made such demands, little realizing that chief secretaries in all the provinces of the country were from the Punjab. Surprisingly, his audience of coffee drinking friends seemed to agree with him wholeheartedly. The absence of any empathy for their East Pakistani brethren was mind-boggling.

9

Mujib's Arrest and Trial

Very few people know that a shaken Sheikh Mujibur Rahman was slapped after he had surrendered to the army team sent to arrest him late in the evening of 25 March 1971.

Brigadier (Retd) Z.A. Khan has given a first-hand account in a careful, cautious and sanitized version of events in his book *The Way It Was*. Politicians are not criminals and don't run away from the law. What emerges from the account is the absolute futility of assembling a huge military force to arrest a political leader who had no intention of absconding or resisting arrest. He was willing to drive down to the nominated place for his intended incarceration. According to Z.A. Khan, when Mujib 'came out of his bedroom totally shaken, after the army raiding team had detonated a grenade in his house, fired a burst of machine gun and a pistol, Havaldar-Major Khan Wazir, later Subedar, gave him a resounding slap on his face.'[1] (Explosives were set off on the ground floor whereas Mujib was on the first floor.) This unwarranted treatment of a man who had already surrendered, and who would have been the country's prime minister, must put the rulers to shame. In apparent appreciation for this act of bravery, the author has included a faded photo of this valiant Subedar in the book. Nothing could be more outrageous!

Although Z.A. Khan gleefully recounts this sordid detail, it needs to be said that the havaldar was under Khan's command and the shameful act of slapping a potential prime minister must therefore be to his eternal discredit. Otherwise respected for his high standards of integrity, the brigadier once seriously suggested the need to 'nuke' India. This was in a private conversation with the writer at a friend's house.

To quote from the book:

I later learnt that...someone had fired a pistol shot into the room where Major Bilal's men were collected, luckily no one was hit. Before anyone could stop him a soldier threw a grenade into the veranda from where the pistol shot had come and followed it with a burst from his sub-machine gun. The grenade burst and the sub-machine fire made Sheikh Mujib call out from behind the closed room that if an assurance was given that he would not be killed he would come out. He was given an assurance and he came out of the room.[2]

That is when this shameful and totally unnecessary act of slapping took place.

Brigadier Khan goes on to say that Mujib told him on his way to prison that 'we had only to call him and he would have come on his own.'[3] But the supremely confident brigadier told Mujib 'that he wanted to show him that he could be arrested'.[4] The irony of not being able to apprehend any of the hundreds of Awami League leaders who chose to evade the army was lost on the brigadier. This entire episode leaves one depressed. For one, Mujib was the majority leader in the National Assembly of Pakistan and as such the country's prime minister-in-waiting. A slap on his face was a slap on the face of the nation. The shabby treatment of an elected representative, particularly a prominent leader like Mujib, by a member of the 'disciplined' armed forces leaves one stunned with disbelief. Mujib's captors should have been taking orders from him and not from a dictator just because he was their commander-in-chief and the custodian of their institutional interests.

The honourable brigadier did not so much as even reprimand the havaldar so that as a very minimum he could distance himself from this disgraceful act. Nor did he show chivalry to a prisoner as is expected from a gentleman officer.

Getting back to the story of Mujib's arrest, it was Brigadier Z.A. Khan who was assigned the responsibility of arresting him. In his own words:

Sheikh Mujib's compound perimeter was secured, it was pitch dark. Mujib's house and the adjacent houses had no lights. The house search party now entered the house; a guard of Sheikh Mujib was escorted out with a soldier walking by his side. After going a little distance from the house the guard pulled out a 'dah', a long bladed knife and attacked his escort, he did not know that he was being covered from behind and was shot but not killed. The ground floor was searched and no one was found there, the search party went upstairs, there was nobody there in the rooms that were open, one room door was bolted from the inside. When I went upstairs someone said that there was some sound coming from the closed room, I told Major Bilal to have the door of the closed room broken down and went downstairs to check if Captain Saeed had arrived and if there was any sign of a crowd.

When I came out on the lane in front of the house I found that Captain Saeed had arrived with the vehicles but in turning the long five-ton vehicles he got them stuck in the narrow lane in front of the house. On the loudspeaker of the wireless set on my jeep I could hear Brigadier Jehanzeb Arbab, later lieutenant general, urging one of his units to use their 'romeo romeos'.

While I was instructing Captain Saeed on how to sort out the vehicles, there was a shot, then the sound of a grenade exploding followed by a burst from a sub-machine gun; I thought that someone had killed Sheikh Mujib. I ran back to the house and upstairs and there I found a very shaken Sheikh Mujib outside the door of the room that had been closed. I asked Sheikh Mujib to accompany me, he asked me if he could say good-bye to his family and I told him to go ahead. He went into the room where the family had enclosed themselves and came out quickly and we walked to where the vehicles were. Captain Saeed had still not managed to turn them around; I sent a radio message to inform the Eastern Command that we had got Sheikh Mujib.

Sheikh Mujib then told me that he had forgotten his pipe, I walked back with him and he collected his pipe. By this time Sheikh Mujib was confident that we would not harm him and he told me that we had only to call him and he would have come on his own; I told him that we wanted to show him that he could be arrested. When we got back, Captain Saeed had the vehicles lined up, Sheikh Mujib was put in the middle troop-carrying vehicle and we started back to the cantonment.[5]

The physical maltreatment of Mujib was a national disgrace and an act of abject cowardice. It also showed the utter contempt of a so-called disciplined army for civil authority. The army's own capability can be gauged from the fact that it failed to apprehend any other major Bengali leader most of whom either went into hiding or crossed over to India. It was only possible to arrest Mujib because he had decided not to hide and instead stand up for his democratic rights. India would have had a field day if Mujib had crossed over to head a Bangladesh government in exile. But Mujib stood for a united Pakistan and did not want to create doubts as to where his preferences lay.

Unfortunately, our military believes it is capable of solving every problem of the country and thus holds civilian leaders in contempt. Bhutto was hanged, Nawaz Sharif was jailed and sent into exile and former chief ministers of smaller provinces were put on trial on trumped up charges. The Constitution which is the source of all laws has been treated in a cavalier fashion to suit individual conveniences. It was not for the last time in 1971 that the country's Constitution was shown such disdain because just five years later another martial law was imposed, this time by General Ziaul Haq. He termed the Constitution a useless piece of paper that he could discard at his whim. We are a people given to breaking laws.

Against all canons of justice, Mujib was tried for treason by a military court which had no jurisdiction because Mujib was not an enlisted man. Brigadier Rahimuddin Khan (later a general) was the court's president. During Ziaul Haq's military rule, Rahimuddin was appointed governor of Balochistan where I served with him. In the very first conversation I had with the governor he talked ceaselessly in Napoleonic terms referring to Balochistan as 'my province' and the Balochis as 'my people'. When the author met him afterwards Rahimuddin fondly recalled his civilian role as governor but omitted to recount any of his military achievements. It is worth pointing out that Balochistan was the only province at the time without a council of ministers even though Rahimuddin was supposedly a very busy military man, concurrently holding command of the Army Corps in Multan.

It was ironic that the person who had the mandate of an overwhelming majority of Pakistan's electorate to be the country's prime minister was being tried for treason by the military subordinates of a usurper who himself was guilty of treason for violating his oath to protect the Constitution. Mujib's only crime was that he had won the elections.

The venue of the trial was Faisalabad which was strange because it was then a small provincial town. But this made perfect sense to the military because it wanted the proceedings to be kept away from the prying eyes of the media. Faisalabad was perhaps chosen because being a relatively small town tucked away in the Punjabi heartland it was easier to keep nosey journalists at bay. The trial was a farce in more ways than one. The military enacted a charade, parading a few witnesses before the elected leader of the nation in a secret trial held inside the Central Jail Faisalabad.

During his imprisonment, Mujib was denied newspapers and radio and had no news of the outside world. His jailors were not allowed to speak to him. According to a story, soon after Bhutto took over as president of a truncated Pakistan, he called Mujib for a meeting. On the way to Rawalpindi, Mujib heard or saw something that prompted him to ask his captors if Pakistan had gone to war with India. Receiving no reply, tears started flowing down his cheeks and he remarked, 'Alas, my Pakistan has been destroyed.' And yet this was the man demonized as a traitor to justify the military crackdown.

Nasim Ahmad, a friend who had been the WAPDA resident engineer in Serajganj, was produced as a witness at Mujib's trial to prove the charge of treason. Nasim had come to West Pakistan as a refugee with his mother, wife and children on 26 May 1971. His mother had miraculously survived gunshot wound(s) that had scraped the top of her skull. The incident occurred in Sylhet where Nasim's mother had been staying with his younger brother who worked for the PIA. Bengali crowds had entered his brother's house and killed him, his wife and left the mother for dead. His frightened children, the eldest being seven and the youngest a baby of two and a half years, scampered for safety to the bathroom or under the bed or wherever they thought they would be safe from the murderous crowd. It was the Bengali *ayah* of the six children who hid them in the bathroom which was at a distance from the bedrooms and beyond the courtyard. When the 'miscreants'—a term given much currency by the military junta to demonize all Bengalis—left, the dazed children emerged from their hiding and sensing that their grandmother was still alive dragged her to a bed and called for help. They placed bed sheets over the dead bodies of their parents. The Bengalis that committed this gruesome atrocity perhaps justify the crime by believing that they had exercised their right to resist aggression initiated by the military on 25 March.

Nasim's mother had to be admitted to the Jinnah Postgraduate Medical Centre in Karachi where she remained under treatment for three months. She lived to be 75 years.

PIA flights between East and West Pakistan normally flew over India but permission was withdrawn by India in the wake of the hijacking of an Indian aeroplane to Lahore. In reality, the hijacking was a drama staged by India to justify denying permission to PIA aircraft from using their airspace for flights to and from Dhaka. As a result the airline was forced to adopt a circuitous and expensive route and had to transit via Colombo. Before the final curtain fell on the saga of East Pakistan, even these flights were discontinued because India opened an overt military front on the East Pakistan borders on 22 November 1971. On 6 December 1971, India recognized Bangladesh. It took another ten days before Bangladesh became a reality symbolized by the formal surrender of 90,000 West Pakistani troops and civilians, including their commander General A.A.K. Niazi.

Getting back to Mujib's farcical trial, one Colonel Abdul Haye visited Nasim at his house in Karachi and told him he was required in Faisalabad on 'temporary martial law' duty. This was strange and amounted to saying that appearing as a witness in a sham trial constituted martial law duty for an ordinary civilian. It was not quite clear what duty Nasim was required to perform. He was given an air ticket. On arrival at Faisalabad he was lodged in a rest house that belonged to the Saigols. All legitimate comforts were provided and the food was particularly splendid—Nasim recalls being served seven-course meals. Colonels Haye and Mukhtar kept the 'witness' constant company but Nasim's request to be shown round the town was firmly turned down.

There were other witnesses too but no one witness knew what evidence the others had given in court. There was Mannan, the deputy inspector general of prisons, and Alauddin, the former commissioner of Dhaka; according to Nasim the latter appeared nervous and agitated, guzzling coffee every half an hour and feeling unsure if he would ever return alive. Nasim was virtually a prisoner between 16 and 29 September and was taken daily to the Central Jail where Mujib was being held.

Mujib refused to recognize the 'court'. He sat in a chair placed at a lower level and turned his face away from the bench as a mark of his refusal to recognize the 'court'. He appeared angry and kept quiet. He stated and rightly so that he was the elected representative of the majority population of Pakistan and as such the legal prime minister. A.K. Brohi was Mujib's defence counsel. But it's significant to recall that the same Brohi had led the prosecution against the accused in the 1951 Rawalpindi Conspiracy case when it was the 'unpatriotic' Huseyn Shaheed Suhrawardy who accepted the defence brief without charging a fee. And a few years after Mujib's trial Brohi was once again the prosecution counsel working for General Ziaul Haq in the farcical case against Bhutto. As best as Nasim can recall there were about five people adorning the court's dais.

Nasim testified in 'court' that he had been taken prisoner along with his family from his official residence attached to the Serajganj powerhouse. They were all then thrown into a jail which had acquired the notoriety of being a slaughterhouse with Biswas Babu, a Bengali magistrate, overseeing the massacre of all non-Bengali residents of the area. People who were not Bengalis fell into the category usually characterized as Biharis irrespective of the fact that they were Sindhis, Punjabis, or Pathans; these 'Biharis' were mercilessly culled by the Bengalis and conveniently dumped into the nearby river Jamuna.

A.K. Brohi did not cross-examine Nasim. There was not much to cross-examine as he said nothing to incriminate his client in any way and Nasim's evidence did not prove the act of treason. The 'accused' was the prime minister elect, and the accusers guilty of high treason. Nasim, however, presented a receipt to the 'court' issued on an Awami League pad by the boys who controlled the town for a licensed pistol and gun they had taken from him. His evidence included a statement that the crowd that 'raided' Nasim's house included boys wearing Awami League caps. That would constitute proof of treason in the eyes of the military junta and its judges because Mujib, who was in custody since 25 March, had allegedly sent these hoodlums to Nasim's house.

According to Nasim's testimony, there were as many as forty Pathans in the jail who, it was reported, earned their living as moneylenders. They were not visible to someone not looking for them keenly. Nasim and his family were in jail for eight hours. Thanks to one of his Bengali assistant engineers, Ayub Ali, a letter of reprieve was obtained from Master Muteeur Rehman, the MNA elect from Serajganj, because of which Nasim was released and restored to his official residence in the power station. The prosecution learnt about the letter from the MNA-elect that saved the lives of Nasim and his family, but did not place it on record because this evidence was considered too inconvenient.

Shamsuddin, my Bengali successor at Serajganj, reportedly organized operations to arrest all non-Bengalis in the district. Later reports suggest that all he did was disappear for couple of weeks fearing the unknown consequences of the military crackdown and reappeared after two weeks. After the military regained control of the area, Shamsuddin was arrested and tortured to death even though an assurance had been given to the then chief secretary East Pakistan, Shafiul Azam, that he would not be harmed. His relatives were not permitted to see his dead body perhaps because it was mutilated beyond recognition.

The proceedings of the 'court' were not made public. However, a former cabinet secretary, in an unguarded moment, told me he had read the proceedings and the verdict therein was 'guilty' but with no supporting judgement. He was told that a military court does not write a judgement or give reasons for its conclusions. Nevertheless, Mujib escaped execution but only because the generals succeeded in forcing East Pakistan out of the federation and creating an independent Bangladesh—there would have been an international outcry if he had been killed.

When Mujib was taken to meet Bhutto soon after the latter had taken over as president on 20 December 1971, he (Mujib) was not aware that Bangladesh had emerged as an independent country. In fact, Mujib suspected that Bhutto too was under arrest and learnt only afterwards that the latter was now the chief martial law administrator and president of the remaining half of the country.

The two discussed critical issues in light of the situation that had emerged. There should be an official record in the archives of the Government of Pakistan on what the two leaders discussed, but this has never been made public. According to one witness, the question of trial by the government of Bangladesh of ninety-two war criminals from

Pakistan came up for discussion. The two leaders privately agreed that there wouldn't be any trial although Mujib said he would make appropriate noises demanding this trial. The two leaders should have realized that it would have been in the interest of both as well as justice and democracy to try senior military commanders of the Pakistan Army for war crimes.

After Bhutto was nominated to replace Yahya as president, the latter reportedly offered to do a favour to Bhutto by executing Mujib before he made over the charge of office. Gul Hassan in his *Memoirs* says it would have been better had Mujib been eliminated during his trial in the Agartala Conspiracy Case.[6] His contention that any impediment in the conduct of smooth military operations ought to be removed implies that by eliminating Mujib the army would have succeeded in resolving the grievances of the entire Bengali nation and that they wouldn't have found another leader to carry forward their struggle. It was the sustained persecution of Mujib that catapulted him into the position of being the only authentic voice and the sole spokesman for the people of East Pakistan.

Transfer of power was another favourite phrase of the times. It must be realized that the military, deeply indoctrinated to believe in its own invincibility, was seriously demoralized after the events of 1971 and this contributed in finally nudging Yahya out. Otherwise he was least impressed with the peoples' verdict because he continued to believe that the vast majority of the Bengalis had been coerced into voting for Mujib.

NOTES

1. Z.A. Khan, *The Way It Was*, Dynavis (Pvt) Ltd, Karachi, 1998, p. 269.
2. Ibid., p. 269.
3. Ibid.
4. Ibid.
5. Ibid., pp. 267-8.
6. Gul Hassan, op. cit, pp. 244, 285.

10

Military and the Constitution

I attended the National Defence College (NDC) course for one academic year and although I did not attend a single class at the Quaid-i-Azam University, Islamabad or take any of its examinations, the university awarded me a M.Sc. degree in Strategic Studies. Anyone who entered the portals of the NDC emerged armed with a master's degree regardless of whether he had previously earned a bachelor's qualification. That this degree was not marketable is a different matter but that is not the issue. What is necessary to point out is that Pakistan's military academies were not degree awarding institutions till the late 1960s; clearly officers who graduated from these academies prior to that—and had risen to the rank of brigadiers when they attended the NDC with me—had no degrees. Attending the NDC was a windfall for such people because they were awarded a Master's degree when they did not even have a bachelor's qualification. Every participant of the course was assessed eligible by the DSs or Directing Staff (serving officers who comprise the faculty) to receive a master's degree and the Quaid-i-Azam University would respectfully award that. The present National Defence College has now been given the charter of a university and awards degrees to its qualifying students.

The NDC enables selected senior officers of the armed forces and civil services to study subjects of national security and defence in preparation for assignments at the policy planning level. The scope extends to studying elements of national power and their relationship with military strength, comprehensive direction and control of national power and evaluation of significant aspects of contemporary international relations; the course aims to develop amongst students an understanding of the problems of higher defence planning and to raise their academic knowledge to post-graduate standard.

The year-long preparation of these officers may make them outstanding foreign service officers, master strategists, economists, administrators or social reformers but does not inculcate in them any respect or understanding of the Constitution. And neither does the course emphasize the responsibility of military officers to defend the Constitution, with their lives if necessary.

Out of the twelve incipient major-generals in our NDC batch only the most unlikely one made it to a general's rank. Pure merit! The Constitution was restored in 1988 but that was the result of Divine intervention when a C-130 aircraft blew up in the sky and facilitated transition to democracy. The 1988 elections provided a split verdict thanks this time to the 'Establishment' which cobbled together a conglomerate of disparate political parties to form the Islami Jamhoori Ittehad (IJI); this was done to deny the Pakistan People's Party (PPP) a clean sweep at the polls, something that had then appeared likely.

The PPP led by Benazir Bhutto still emerged as the single largest party in parliament. Under the Constitution that had been corrupted by the infamous Eight Amendment, President Ghulam Ishaq Khan was required to invite the leader of the party who in his opinion was likely to command a majority in the house to form the government. But rather than asking the PPP to seek a vote in the assembly, the president went into marathon sessions of consultation that extended over weeks and included sessions with political parties that had just one member in parliament, ostensibly as a prelude to forming his opinion. In reality he was providing time and opportunity to the establishment's favourite, Mian Muhammad Nawaz Sharif, to buy or coerce enough MNAs into supporting him.

While this farce was being played out on the national political scene, the class at the NDC could not remain un-involved in the day-to-day progress of events. Its vision was of course coloured by the preferences of the establishment and it shared the extreme anxiety at the unwelcome prospect of the PPP forming the government. During a discussion on the situation, a brigadier remarked that Benazir was very ambitious because she wanted to move up the political ladder and become the prime minister without having worked at the grass-roots level. Even when he was told that it was the simple arithmetic of election results that entitled her to legitimately claim the mantle of office, the brigadier was not persuaded.

There was some outpouring of grief from the military brass at the C-130 'accident'. The burial of General Ziaul Haq or whatever was left of him within the precincts of Islamabad's Faisal Mosque drew some crowds, most of them Afghans who formed the constituency of the dead chief of the army staff (COAS). He spent his eleven and a half years in power fighting for the rights of the Afghans and tried to help them get a government of their choice. That the people of Pakistan could not enjoy similar rights did not present a dilemma to him. The brigadier was convinced that the late COAS was a popular man as could be seen by the crowds at his burial, and sought my endorsement. When I said it was not possible for me to comment by just watching visuals of the burial on TV, the brigadier complained that I was being difficult and should know better having once been a commissioner. I had to tell him being commissioner was not the same thing as being an election commissioner; it is the latter who oversees elections that determine the popularity of a leader. Another civilian officer attending the course with me was confronted with a similar question but his reply was different. He countered by asking why then did the late COAS avoid holding free, fair and transparent elections if the brigadier thought he was so popular.

On another occasion, there was a discussion on the subject of differences in service prospects of the civil service and the military. A brigadier complained that as against a civilian who retired at the age of 60, a military officer retired at a much younger age. I told him that in Pakistan this rule had been suspended and military officers continued to serve way beyond 60, albeit in civilian jobs. Besides they could start their careers at the age of 18 when their counterparts in civil service were still in college. He then said that under the Constitution the armed forces had a 10 per cent reserved quota for jobs in the civil but complained they rarely got their due share. When told that this was only an administrative instruction of the government and not part of the Constitution, the man did not understand and persisted in his argument. The distinction between the Constitution and an ordinary administrative instruction did not register with him till the very end.

The sprawling NDC Complex in Islamabad contains a huge ornate library. I once went there to become a member as an alumnus. I looked for a copy of the Constitution but failed to find one. I asked for help but soon found that in fact this document was not held by the library. I should add however that they did have a little known copy of a commentary on the Constitution. While economics, even Islamic economics, Islam, politics and psycho-socio-political subjects are taught at the NDC, the Constitution or causes of the 1971 military defeat are religiously avoided.

While visiting the Army Staff College in Quetta, our class of NDC was given a video presentation by a lieutenant-colonel during which he proudly recounted the achievements of the alumni of the college saying that Ayub, Yahya, and Ziaul Haq had gone on to become presidents of the country. When I suggested that hopefully that was the last time such a thing happened, the lieutenant-colonel replied with some bravado, 'Of course not. There would be more.'

Disregard for the Constitution is nothing new for the military mind. During the Quaid-i-Azam's first and only visit to the Staff College, Quetta, he advised the officers thus:

> One thing more. I am persuaded to say this because during my talks with one or two very high ranking officers I discovered that they did not know the implications of the Oath taken by the troops of Pakistan. Of course, an oath is only a matter of form; what is more important is the true spirit and the heart.......I want you to remember and if you have time enough you should study the Government of India Act, as adapted for use in Pakistan, which is our present constitution....[1]

Ayub Khan was present in that assemblage but did not heed the advice of the Father of the Nation and abrogated the Constitution in 1958, just months before the long-awaited elections under the 1956 Constitution were to be held. As a matter of fact, rumblings had started much earlier and the Rawalpindi Conspiracy Case was a clear manifestation of things to come.

There is another reported incident when Jinnah, soon after independence, chided a young army officer who complained against important posts being entrusted to British officers. The Quaid cautioned the officer not to forget that the armed forces were the servants of the people. 'You do not make national policy; it is we, the civilians who decide these issues and it is your duty to carry out these tasks with which you are entrusted.'

NOTE

1. Mohammad Ali Jinnah, *Speeches and Statements 1947-48*, Government of Pakistan, Ministry of Information and Broadcasting, Directorate of Films and Publications, Printed by Elite Publishers (Pvt.) Ltd, Karachi, 1989, pp. 264-5.

11

Inevitable Happens (April and December 1971)

Bangladesh emerged as an independent nation on 16 December 1971. The ordeal of the people of East Pakistan was finally over. They had endured much suffering at the hands of our armed forces for nine months, and had been denied their fair share of political and economic power for twenty-five years. The jubilation at getting rid of the army was spontaneous and widespread. With Mujib and his constituency out of the way, Bhutto was now strategically placed to demand transfer of power from a discredited Yahya. The latter reluctantly acceded to this demand four days after the shameful surrender of 16 December 1971.

Bhutto, however, showed great magnanimity and retired Yahya honourably so that he could draw a pension from the treasury of a country he had helped to dismember. He also retired all the top generals with the exception of General Niazi. Here was an opportunity for Bhutto to cut the army to size but because of his grandiose ambition he decided to retain a large and powerful force with whose help he could preside over the destiny of a truncated Pakistan for as long as he wished. In the end this window of opportunity for Pakistan to free itself from Bonapartism, a term Bhutto was wont to use, was shut for all times to come.

To drive home the point that military rule was an unmitigated disaster, Bhutto hurriedly screened on national television the film of the surrender at Paltan Maidan, Dhaka. The Bengalis were so resentful of the military that a man in the crowd at the surrender ceremony rushed to hit the Pakistani general with his shoe. Most West Pakistanis, however, were ignorant of the situation and wanted to know what the reality was. It was announced that the footage of the surrender would be telecast again the following day but that day never came. The screening of the film was withheld because Bhutto was concerned about the army's reaction or perhaps, if Gul Hassan is to be believed, the 'reaction' had already been conveyed to him. He also appeared to be anxious about the proposed war-crime trial of ninety-two military officers alleged to have committed various atrocities.

On taking over power, Bhutto moved at full speed. There was not a day when he did not announce one reform or the other. He claimed that Pakistan had emerged stronger after the debacle which made little sense as it implied that further trimming of an already truncated Pakistan would make it even stronger. But he spoke in populist terms and did give voice, howsoever feeble, to the poor.

Yahya Khan pretended to be punctilious about constitutionality and the legality of the transfer of power, but the contradictory nature of his actions exposed this facade. Earlier, before the crisis got out of hand, he had refused to accept Mujib's proposal to withdraw martial law and transfer power to elected representatives at the provincial level on constitutional grounds, and yet he didn't fuss about any legal nuances while forced to hand over the charge of chief martial law administrator to Bhutto. He only knew and understood the language of force. He forced Ayub to quit and he quit when forced in turn, although he had believed he would survive the secession of East Pakistan and was therefore preparing to give the nation an Islamic constitution.

In the event, Yahya Khan very reluctantly surrendered power on 20 December. Yahya's plans to announce an Islamic Constitution, which had nothing Islamic about it, and would have given him unchecked authority including the power to override the constitution and the parliament, got derailed. We now have the much maligned and severely mutilated Constitution of 1973 which is thought to have survived two military dictators.

The belief that Gul Hassan was responsible for nudging Yahya out of office, a myth that Gul Hassan himself demolished in his book, is still held to be true by some people. It was the totality of the situation resulting from the abject surrender in East Pakistan that perhaps influenced the thinking of the armed forces who then felt that Yahya could no longer be supported or sustained. It is the institutional interest of the army more than the personal welfare of its chief that ultimately influences its collective decision to either lend or withdraw support to or from a usurper. Thus, it was not a newfound commitment to the concept of democracy that persuaded the army to withdraw its support from Yahya but the belief that allowing him to remain in power would have disastrous consequences for the institution.

A ceasefire with India was accepted by Yahya Khan after the fall of Dhaka. The proposal to appoint Bhutto deputy prime minister under

Nurul Amin, a Bengali politician as prime minister with just his own seat out of the 162 seats in East Pakistan, became redundant with the secession of East Pakistan. Bhutto had to be reluctantly accepted both by the military and Yahya not only as the president of Pakistan but also its chief martial law administrator. The latter appointment was made to overcome some 'legal' difficulties that the usurper claimed to have confronted. He forgot that when he took over the reins of the country in violation of the Constitution that he was under oath to defend, these 'legalities' presented no such difficulty. In reality, such difficulties only arise when power is being transferred from the military to the people and their representatives.

Bhutto enjoyed immense power because the army's stock amongst the people of a demoralized and truncated Pakistan was then at its lowest ebb. If he had so wished, Bhutto could have downsized the military in his populist style by abolishing superfluous posts of generals without having to touch the bulk of the army itself. But his sense of history was not as sharp as he claimed because he relied on strengthening the military and weakening the democratic forces in the vain hope that the army would sustain him in power as its benefactor. In the event, at the first sign of trouble they overthrew him, sent him to jail and finally hanged him through a farcical trial. The judiciary must also accept responsibility as a collaborator in the crime. A former judge of the supreme court who later became chief justice acknowledged on a private TV channel long after he had retired that he was wrong in convicting Bhutto. But then he justified his pusillanimous decision by saying that judges have children too. He was the only judge brave enough to have restored a government, in this case that of Nawaz Sharif after it was dismissed by Ghulam Ishaq Khan. That he first checked with the then COAS is yet another matter.

Bhutto did not put Yahya on trial nor did he make public the latter's machinations in overthrowing Ayub or his role during and after the 1970 general elections. Bhutto ought to have stood with India and Bangladesh in putting all the generals responsible for the disaster on trial. This would have exposed all the conspiracies of the ruling generals, and perhaps ushered democracy in Pakistan. But then this would have also exposed Bhutto's own role which was far from laudable.

In Lahore during the 1970s one had no choice but to read the *Pakistan Times* because this was then the only English language newspaper published from that city. Z.A. Suleri was its editor. It carried GHQ press releases and endorsed them unquestioningly and never once demanded handing over of power to the people or wrote a thing on behalf of the

Bengalis. Its editorials as far as I can recall were nauseating. When Bhutto took over, one of the first things he did was to dismiss Suleri. I called Suleri on 17 December and said that since the armed forces of Pakistan had finally surrendered the least he could now do was write the truth. Little did I know that he had already been dismissed!

In early December 1971, I went by car on an official tour to Dera Ismail Khan and made a night stop at Jhang. I met Paracha, the DC, who had a great reputation for honesty and integrity. Over a cup of tea in the evening we discussed the current situation but he was upset with me for saying that East Pakistan was going to 'secede' and become an independent country. When this actually came to pass, a few weeks later, he came looking for me in Lahore to ask what else the future held for him as he believed I could foretell events correctly.

On 16 December I was playing tennis in the lawns of the Civil Service Academy in Lahore with Sheikh Abdul Hameed, a deputy director at the academy, when Indian air force jets constantly hovered overhead causing everyone a great deal of anxiety. We stopped the game and walked over to Hameed's residence on the campus. Since I was keeping myself up-to-date and was not in denial, I believed most BBC reports and told Hameed that it was a sad day because we had lost East Pakistan. He chided me for saying such a foolish thing. How myopic can one get! When we reached his house he asked for tea to be served and tuned into Radio Pakistan for the 5 o'clock news. The broadcast broke the news that we had received a 'small' setback in East Pakistan—it was then that the truth finally dawned on Hameed that East Pakistan was lost forever.

12

Sajid and his Escape

My younger brother Sajid was in East Pakistan during those crucial days. He had passed his engineering examination from Sindh University but was without a job for almost a year. Things were different in East Pakistan. There were not many engineers and numerous positions were vacant. I suggested he come to East Pakistan and though he was initially reluctant, he eventually agreed. He landed a good job courtesy my dear friend Nomani who worked for the East Pakistan WAPDA—the organization had split into two entities prior to a similar division of the country. Nomani knew someone in the Imperial Electric Company—a West Pakistan based enterprise which built high-power generation grids and related infrastructure.

The political climate in East Pakistan thickened after the elections and very soon the country was faced with a full-blown crisis. Sajid was working in Bogra but had his headquarters at Ishurdi, a place considered relatively safe because of its sizable non-Bengali population. It was a railway junction and railways were largely manned by the Biharis. Sajid had rented a portion of a house from an elderly Bihari gentleman, one Mr Sharfuddin, who showed fatherly concern for Sajid. Sensing the emerging political crisis I feared that things might get out of hand and Sajid could find himself in a very frightful situation. I tried to use my influence to have him transferred to West Pakistan but failed.

Because of the backlash caused by the postponement of the National Assembly session travel in East Pakistan had become a risky business. These were the days when the Awami League had assumed total control of everyday life and passions of the populace were running high. It was foolhardy for West Pakistanis to expose themselves to the public and be caught at the wrong place. This situation lasted until 25 March but things up till then remained ominously quiet. People were pinning hope on some settlement as a result of the marathon discussions Yahya was holding with Mujib and others. But things got out of hand after the 25th, when talks abruptly broke down and a full military operation was launched.

When I learnt a few hours in advance that the military had decided to crack down on the insurgents at midnight of 25 and 26 March, I started worrying for Sajid because he was likely to be easy prey for an agitated mob. He was then in Ishurdi. I asked him to come to Khulna by the next train but didn't tell him why. He kept insisting that I give him a reason but I refused to do so. The telephone lines were disturbed and I suddenly lost the connection leaving me unsure if Sajid had finally accepted my advice. It later turned out that Sharfuddin did not permit him to venture out or board a train. In the end it was a very wise decision because Sajid would not have survived the journey travelling through a countryside infested with enraged Bengalis.

Not knowing his decision and assuming that he had boarded the train I got up early next morning to receive him at the railway station. But the situation on the ground had changed dramatically. There was deathly silence in the bustling town of Khulna as the Bengalis had blocked all the roads with trees or other obstacles. It was so quiet one could hear the rustle of dry leaves. I called the army and was informed that the train from Ishurdi had been halted some ten miles from Khulna. This did not portend well for Sajid's safety as he would be a sitting duck for the angry mob. Any travel to the place was dangerous if not impossible. But I couldn't give up. I insisted and the good Colonel Shams of the Frontier Force ordered a military platoon to accompany me. We started off but could go no further than three miles before coming up against tree trunks blocking the road. I insisted on trying to go further but the platoon captain wisely pointed out that we would not be able to go beyond a few more metres and might get ambushed by a hostile population.

I gave up with a heavy heart but from then on every moment was a period of trial and torture, not knowing if Sajid was on the train or in Ishurdi and if so was he alive or not. Telephones had stopped working and normal life had come to a standstill.

I then planned my own escape. When I reached Dhaka, as narrated in an earlier chapter, I was more worried about Sajid than anything else. I refused to leave for West Pakistan until such time I could evacuate my brother to safety. But I was advised by military officers to return to West Pakistan and hope for the best because under the circumstances there was nothing that even the military could do. Its writ was restricted to just major towns and that too during the day time. I travelled back to West Pakistan a very depressed and worried man. Every waking moment was a torment and the night would bring greater anguish because I couldn't sleep for more than a few hours due to my worry about Sajid's safety.

I would keep awake at night thinking of him sometimes in the present tense and sometimes in the past. It was not unnatural for morbid thoughts to assail me. I would mourn over his possible loss so early in life when he could have done so much for his family, for the country and for himself. I went into deep depression.

In desperation I turned to my friend Dr Asif Jah Karwani. He claimed to be a medium able to contact and communicate with spirits of the dead. During the 1965 Pakistan–India war most of us believed that we would soon wrest Kashmir from India, but a ceasefire was announced in just seventeen days of inconclusive fighting. The country generally felt let down because everyone believed that our army had been ascendant and victory was just around the corner. Dr Karwani—he was then the principal of Government College, Nawabshah, and I a lecturer—perhaps in an attempt to cheer me up said that he had 'spoken' to the Quaid-i-Azam who had informed him that the ceasefire would not last long and Pakistan would eventually achieve its objectives. He was obviously off the mark on that occasion but conducted a séance on my request and said that Sajid was safe and in military custody in East Pakistan. But that didn't make much sense because only the Bengalis were being apprehended by the military. Why would the military arrest a patriotic West Pakistani?

I returned home from this 'psychic' experience dejected and forlorn. But lo and behold, what do I see? Sajid. He was standing right there in person. I cannot describe my sense of relief and joy. This was an emotional meeting. He had finally arrived. He had his wits about him and had not neglected to buy a small packet of pans on the advice of his friends which he sold for some profit on arrival at the airport.

This is what he had to tell me. After my critical call to him on 25 March asking him to come to Khulna where I thought we would both be safe, an agitated and spontaneously assembled group of Bengalis interrupted our conversation. He ran for his life to his home nearby which is why I could not gather if he had agreed to my proposal to board the next train. Because telephones those days were rare there was no way I could now communicate with him. Sharfuddin was very kind and told him not to heed my call as it was too dangerous to venture out. Even otherwise travel was out of the question since all transport had been suspended some twenty-five days back. He then asked Sajid to move into his house with his family.

Having great faith in CSP camaraderie I made the near fatal mistake of asking the DC of Pabna, in whose jurisdiction Ishurdi fell, to take care of Sajid. I gave him his address and all the other details. But the Bengali

DC had other ideas. He gave Sajid's address to the rampaging Bengalis, who were acting at his behest and under his command, and they came asking for Sajid. Sharfuddin hid him under the bed and pretended that he had left already, and thus saved Sajid's life.

From 25 March onwards Sajid stayed a prisoner in Sharfuddin's house. On 10 April he heard that the military had arrived and went out to verify this. As soon as this was confirmed, the Biharis who had been in fear for their lives over the past two weeks emerged from hiding and took charge of the city. From being frightened chickens cooped up in their homes they let loose their pent up anger on their helpless Bengali neighbours. One such unfortunate incident witnessed by Sajid was the attack on a young Bengali engineer who was brutally and savagely beaten with staves, sticks and stones and left to die a slow death. The attackers were the victim's former friends and classmates. Sajid's pleas for mercy went unheard. The battered body of the victim was left at the doorstep of Sajid's tenement and lay there for a day or two until Sajid asked the boys to remove it. They obliged but only after they were paid a rupee for the favour.

Sajid didn't see any military around but heard that they were garrisoned at the airport. He decided to walk several miles to the airport along with his few possessions, sharing the burden with his domestic help, a diploma engineer whom Sajid had employed because the man was desperate for a job. He paid him way above the normal wage. The poor fellow showed little regard for his life because if he had been caught by the military he would have been a dead duck. But he was lucky and was not noticed. The moment Sajid was sighted by our military they moved menacingly towards him and he had to quickly introduce himself as being a West Pakistani. Their attitude changed and they took care of him, putting him in a PIA Fokker aircraft returning empty to Dhaka. Of course, he didn't have to buy a ticket because these flights were returning to Dhaka anyway and had been commandeered by the military for transporting troops and ammunition.

Once in Dhaka he went straight to his company's head office but it was closed as everyone, including his bosses, had already left for the safety of West Pakistan. Most of the company employees were West Pakistanis which, of course, was not unusual. But his employers had acted thoughtfully—they had left behind an air ticket for each employee who had not been able to leave East Pakistan till then. Sajid had a ticket waiting for him. Had his employers a better understanding of the evolving crisis they would have transferred all West Pakistani employees before 25 March. But then even West Pakistani intellectuals thought that the crisis would soon pass and they would once again control the destiny of East Pakistan.

Part II

PART II

13

Hamood-ur-Rahman Commission Report

The much talked about Hamood-ur-Rahman Commission Report was finally published in India and then in Pakistan during General Pervez Musharraf's rule. It suffers from a large number of infirmities. General Gul Hassan in his *Memoirs* terms the Commission a 'non-starter', perhaps because Bhutto and not the military initiated the inquiry. But generals do not ordinarily appoint a commission of inquiry—it wasn't done for the 1965 war or later for losing Siachen to India or the explosion of the Ojhri Camp ammunition dump that created havoc in the twin cities of Islamabad and Rawalpindi or for the unsuccessful Kargil operation. Generals mostly suppress the truth that might reflect poorly on them.

In the absence of any other objective report besides the self-serving accounts of some generals, the Hamood-ur-Rahman Report is all one has to make sense of the events that resulted in the break-up of Pakistan. At a time when the continued existence of the report was still the subject of some speculation I was posted as additional secretary in the cabinet division (1995–96). One of the items in my charge was the joint custody with a deputy secretary of the report which was kept in the cabinet library located in the basement. I was excited at the prospect of being able to read the report which very few people had even seen and about which it was rumoured that all its copies had been destroyed. I wanted to see and touch this much talked-about report. To the credit of this deputy secretary, who was my subordinate, he turned down my request to take the report home but allowed me to spend as much time in the basement as I liked. The report comprised a large number of dusty volumes placed haphazardly in the shelves. I hastily read some of the conclusions where the Commission had recommended action against the generals. This report wouldn't be there had Bhutto not been in power and there had been a military ruler instead.

A Commission of Inquiry was appointed with terms of reference (ToR) that charged it with the duty of 'inquiring into the circumstances in which the Commander, Eastern Command, surrendered and members of the armed forces of Pakistan under his command laid down their arms,' and secondly to inquire into the ceasefire ordered 'along the borders of West Pakistan and India and along the ceasefire line in State of Jammu & Kashmir.' The ToR did not even touch the core issue. What, for instance, led to the delay in transfer of power after the 1971 general elections? Surrender by the armed forces was peripheral to the fundamental question of transferring power to those who had won the mandate of the people of Pakistan.

Too many questions were left unanswered. Why was the National Assembly session not convened? What was it that Yahya discussed for three days as a guest of Bhutto at Al Murtaza (Bhutto's private residence) in Larkana—and that too soon after the election results had been announced? Why wasn't a similar visit paid to Mujib who was the leader of the majority party? What games was Yahya playing when he orchestrated the charade of dialogue in March in Dhaka pretending to serve as an honest broker between two major political parties? What events took place on 25 March 1970 before Yahya stealthily left Dhaka and ordered the military operation to be launched when he was safely in West Pakistani airspace? If the talks were indeed continuing till the 25th then what was General Rao Farman Ali doing visiting army units a day before if not delivering orders for a crackdown? When was the conspiracy hatched not to transfer power when the election results were so clear? And a host of other such questions that go to the heart of the problem.

The Commission was headed by Justice Hamood-ur-Rahman and had as members Justice Anwarul Haq, Chief Justice of the Lahore High Court and Justice Tufailali Abdur Rehman, Chief Justice of the Sindh and Balochistan High Court. Justice Anwarul Haq later presided over the Supreme Court that handed down a split decision to execute Bhutto on a murder charge that by judicial standards had not been proved.

The Commission examined a total of 213 witnesses that included:

Army:
Serving personnel 61
Retired personnel 27

Air Force:
Serving personnel 39
Retired personnel 9

Navy:
Serving personnel 14
Retired personnel 7

Political leaders: 23

Civil servants:
Serving 17
Retired 6

Journalists: 3

Members of public: 10

The conclusions of the Commission are based on limited terms of reference and on the evidence of 213 witnesses along with the documents they chose to produce. But views of the people of Pakistan's former eastern wing—their demand for democratic rights, the grief brought on them by the army's onslaught and the larger grievance of being denied their due share of power over twenty-five years—were neither solicited nor recorded in the report.

With evidence obtained from mostly military officials (157 out of 213) whose accounts were necessarily self-serving, the conclusions of the Commission could neither be objective nor would represent the views of the general populace. Only ten members of the public, three journalists and a score of civil servants were examined. No one from the erstwhile East Pakistan was invited to testify unless of course the likes of Nurul Amin, Mahmud Ali, and chief of the Chakma tribe, Raja Tridev Roy, are considered representatives of the Bengali people. It appears that press reports of debauchery which became a favourite fare as soon as Yahya was removed swayed the Commission although it was an issue that strictly speaking was not within its mandate. Profusion of tales of the lascivious life of the generals and their cohorts only helped to make the report a readable item for those with a prurient taste. Unfortunately many of those named in the report have died in the past thirty-five years during which time the report remained a secret document. The report also contains chapters on democracy and its numerous benefits.

With the ToR so narrowly focused on the surrender by Eastern Command, and a preponderance of witnesses from the armed forces, the Commission's report is no more than an intellectual diversion. Surrender was only the culmination of a process that was evident even to a person of the meanest intelligence. It started with the military operation launched on 25 March 1971 but the real genesis of the problem lay in denying genuine Bengali leadership their due share of power from the day Pakistan came into being. Rabindranath Tagore's Bengali was declared a regional language while Urdu was imposed as the national language of both wings of Pakistan. Then in 1954, following the rout of the official Muslim League in the provincial elections, A.K. Fazlul Haq was reluctantly allowed to form the provincial government in East Pakistan. But this lasted for just a few months and Iskandar Mirza was installed as the all-powerful governor of East Bengal.

It took Pakistan nine years from the time it gained independence to frame a Constitution but when it was finally adopted in 1956, elections were interrupted because of a conspiracy hatched by Iskandar Mirza. He manipulated himself into the position of president and in cahoots with Ayub Khan imposed martial law in 1958. This was the first of a series of martial laws that the country has since endured. But Ayub deposed Iskandar Mirza just three weeks after martial law was imposed and through a dubious referendum in 1960 was elected president. His own decade-long rule finally ended when Yahya seized power in 1969 and instantly promised to hold the country's 'first fair and free elections.' What he didn't say was that he had no intention of following through on his promise or the results of the promised elections.

East Pakistanis were denied their democratic rights from the day the country won its independence. The West Pakistani establishment shunned Huseyn Shaheed Suhrawardy, a respected and popular Bengali leader who finally died in Lebanon in 1963 under mysterious circumstances. Even a man of Quaid-i-Azam's statesmanship declared at a public meeting in East Pakistan in 1948:

> But let me make it very clear to you that the state language of Pakistan is going to be Urdu and no other language. Anyone who tries to mislead you is really the enemy of Pakistan. Without one state language, no nation can remain tied up solidly together and function.[1]

This statement quite naturally inflamed the passions of the Bengalis and a few students were killed in the ensuing riots. In memory of those who died, *Shaheed Minars* were built all over East Pakistan, even in small towns, and the day is commemorated every year on 21 February with rallies in which people walk barefoot.

The framing of the Constitution was delayed deliberately to deny East Pakistan its share in power. When the late Jam Ghulam Qadir Khan of Lasbela—a member of the Constituent Assembly—was asked by the author why it had taken them so long to adopt a constitution, he admitted quite candidly that it was to keep the Bengalis out of power.

The Commission observed that martial law was a curse and the character of the military the source of all our problems. A great part of the report is devoted to detail the depravity and moral degeneration of Yahya—as many as sixteen pages (pp. 296-312) describe the ladies that visited the President's House both in Rawalpindi and Karachi. Yahya's sojourns in Dhaka were also known to be less concerned with matters of state and more with indulgence in sexual dalliance at state expense with the helpful connivance of all around him. This part of the report did not, except perhaps by implication, address the ToR which was to determine the circumstances of the surrender:

> After analyzing (sic) the evidence brought before the Commission, we came to the conclusion that the process of moral degeneration among the senior ranks of the Armed Forces was set in motion by their involvement in Martial Law duties in 1958, that these tendencies reappeared and were, in fact, intensified when Martial Law was imposed in the country once again in March 1969 by General Yahya Khan, and that there was indeed substance in the allegations that a considerable number of senior Army Officers had not only indulged in large scale acquisition of lands and houses and other commercial activities, but had also adopted highly immoral and licentious ways of life which seriously affected their professional capabilities and their qualities of leadership.[2]

The moral degeneration of Yahya is emphasized in many parts of the report. In Chapter 26 under the title 'The Moral Aspect' and subtitled 'Effect of Martial Law Duties' the Commission observed:

> The evidence before the Commission shows that the processes of moral degeneration among the senior ranks of the armed forces was set in motion by their involvement in Martial Law duties in 1958. Army officers were for the first time, much more so that in the limited martial law of 1953, exposed to the temptations inherent in direct contact with the various sectors of civilian

life and administration. They were called upon to deal with Big Business, influential industrialists, foreign exchange racketeers, pimps and prostitutes, and other criminal elements of society. They came to wield tremendous power over the lives and liberties of the people by presiding over Military Courts and otherwise regulating the conduct of civilian affairs. Many of them ended up by not only becoming arrogant but also corrupt.[3]

Things have only gotten worse since then and another Hamood-ur-Rahman Commission may be on the cards because we refuse to learn from history. But more relevant is the question if these observations of the Commission enlighten a reader as to why the surrender occurred.

The Commission noted that the events surrounding the imposition of marital law by Yahya on 25 March 1969 confirm the belief that he did not take over the country in order to restore normal conditions or re-introduce democracy but to acquire power for its own sake. The Commission recorded:

> General Yahya Khan, General Abdul Hamid Khan, Lt. Gen. Gul Hassan, Maj. Gen. Umar and Maj. Gen. Mitha should be publicly tried for being party to a criminal conspiracy to illegally usurp power from F.M. Mohammad Ayub Khan, if necessary by the use of force. In furtherance of their common purpose they did actually try to influence political parties by threats, inducements and even bribes to support their designs both for bringing about a particular kind of result during the elections of 1970, and later persuading some of the political parties and the elected members of the National Assembly to refuse to attend the session of the National Assembly scheduled to be held at Dhaka on the 3rd of March, 1971.[4]

This aptly summarizes the manipulation by Yahya and his colleagues in furtherance of their common design to remain in power indefinitely. One may wholeheartedly agree with the analysis but the indictment has nothing to do with the causes of surrender, except perhaps again by implication.

The results of the 1970 general elections which gave a commanding majority to the people of East Pakistan in the National Assembly were not acceptable to Yahya and the military that stood by him. They showed little regard for the possibility that this could lead to the dismemberment of the country. This is not to suggest that if the majority party had been from West Pakistan, Yahya and his coterie would have rushed to transfer power; but then an East Pakistani majority was an absolute anathema. The army generals found it easier to comport with West Pakistani feudal

politicians but it was extremely difficult for them to live with the middle-
or lower-middle-class leadership of East Pakistan. After all, they needed
to safeguard their financial interests. What the generals and their
collaborators had planned and wished for was a splintered National
Assembly which could then be manipulated into playing a subservient
role—an art that has been perfected by the military and carried forward
into the twenty-first century. The election results defied DS solution
(a DS solution is the 'ideal' answer and a benchmark against which a
student's response to a given problem is assessed by the students at the
NDC).

India's victory was inevitable. With 75 million Bengalis fully backing
Mujib in his struggle to get them their democratic rights, and a hostile
India surrounding East Pakistan, our own military stood no chance of
winning the war. In fact it is surprising that it took India so long to
engineer the defeat of the Pakistani forces in East Pakistan, more so when
the former enjoyed the support and sympathy of the local population.
The suffering of the civil populace could have been shortened had India
intervened earlier and perhaps some lives might have been saved. But
going to war is no child's play and India worked hard to create a global
environment to justify armed intervention in East Pakistan.

The reference by the Commission to counter-insurgency measures in
East Pakistan since March 1971 assumes that there was a rebellion by a
handful of people. In reality the conflict was tantamount to the army
rebelling against the people of East Pakistan because after winning the
elections they were the legitimate rulers of that province, if not the entire
country. Since the primary premise of the Commission was incorrect,
inferences that followed were bound to suffer from serious flaws. The
situation in East Pakistan on 25 March 1971 was not that of an insurgency
but of a heightened state of expectancy and hope. Having won the
elections convincingly, the people of that province wanted a peaceful
transfer of power. But Yahya was not prepared to do that and was
determined to hold on to power at all costs including, as it turned out,
by losing half the country.

The Commission committed a serious error by introducing some
preconceived notions in their analysis. To quote:

It is necessary that this painful chapter of the events in East Pakistan be looked
at in its proper perspective. Let it not be forgotten that the initiative in
resorting to violence and cruelty was taken by the militants of the Awami
League, during the month of March 1971, following Gen. Yahya Khan's

announcement of the 1st of March regarding the postponement of the session of the National Assembly scheduled for the 3rd of March 1971.[5]

This observation reflects a strong bias which is clearly the result of preconceived notions held by the honourable members of the Commission. I was in Khulna during the crucial months of 1970–71, and was a witness to the situation before and after the military action. There was no militancy whatsoever and there were no Awami League militants. When Yahya made that fateful announcement on 1 March 1971 at 1:00 p.m. East Pakistan time, the reaction was sharp and swift. Within minutes there was an announcement from Radio Dhaka, which was instantly changed from Radio Pakistan to 'Baitar Kindro Dhaka', that in protest against the unjustified postponement of the National Assembly it had been decided by the leadership of the Awami League that a strike would be observed in Dhaka on 2 March and in the remaining districts on 3 March. The Commission ought to have unequivocally condemned Yahya's action of postponing the long delayed National Assembly session and launching an unwarranted military operation. There was no insurgency; the Bengalis merely organized a civil protest—it was just people's power resisting an unjust diktat.

The Commission, however, rightly observed that Yahya was masquerading as an honest broker: 'We have also touched upon the negotiations, which Gen. Yahya Khan was pretending to hold during this period with Sheikh Mujibur Rahman on the one hand and political leaders from West Pakistan on the other.'

The Commission made another error in stating that: '...there is reliable evidence to show that the miscreants indulged in large-scale massacre and rape against the pro-Pakistan elements in the towns of Dhaka etc.' It named almost all the towns of East Pakistan—Dhaka, Narayanganj, Chittagong, Chandragona, Rungamati, Khulna, Dinajpur, Dhakargaon, Kushtia, Ishurdi, Noakhali, Sylhet, Maulvi Bazaar, Rangpur, Saidpur, Jessore, Barisal, Mymensingh, Rajshahi, Pabna, Sirajganj, Comilla, Brahmanbaria, Bogra, Naogaon, Santapur—and several other smaller places where these massacres and rapes were perpetrated.[6]

To reach this conclusion on the testimony of a few witnesses from West Pakistan who had a marked lack of compassion for the Bengalis detracts from the report's objectivity. The Commission found reliable evidence to show that during this period the 'miscreants'—a term applied to the local Bengali population, in particular those involved in resisting the military—perpetrated large-scale massacres and rape against pro-Pakistan elements.

These elements were the non-Bengalis, many of whom collaborated with the Pakistani forces to fight against the local population and joined vigilante groups known as Al Badar and Al Shams. Both these groups were used by the army to do their dirty work at places where they dreaded to go. Throughout the Bangladesh crisis Pakistani military officers referred to the Bengalis as 'miscreants', and any civilian expressing concern for human rights in the eastern wing of the country was branded a traitor. How can one term the entire population of the province 'miscreants'?

Instead of protecting the minorities, the state was perpetrating acts of religious persecution. The Commission refers to the allegation that General Niazi ordered his subordinates to exterminate the Hindus. When Niazi would visit an operational area he would make it a point to ask his troops how many Hindus they had killed. In May, Brigadier Abdullah Malik of 23 Brigade issued an order in writing to kill Hindus while R.P. Saha, a Hindu philanthropist, was picked up along with his only son and both murdered in cold blood. The Commission recorded:

> There was a general feeling of hatred against Bengalis amongst the soldiers and the officers including the generals...There were verbal instructions to eliminate Hindus. In Salda Nadi area about 500 Hindus were killed.

> ...innocent people were killed by us during sweep operations and it created estrangement amongst the public. [Lt. Col. S. M. Naeem (witness No. 258) CO 39 Baloch]

> A Bengali who was alleged to be a Mukti Bahini or Awami Leaguer was being sent to Bangladesh, code name for death without trial, without any detailed investigation and without any written order by any authorised authority. [Lt. Col. Mansoorul Haq (witness No. 260), GSO I, 9 Division][7]

Sending the Bengalis to 'Bangladesh' after they had suffered virtual occupation for the previous twenty-five years was a cruel mockery of their political aspirations.

There is an impression that the Bengalis started killing the non-Bengalis before the military crackdown, something that even the Hamood-ur-Rahman Report seems to believe. But accounts of such killings are exaggerated. For want of direct evidence the Commission relies on second-hand accounts like the one given by Qutbuddin Aziz, 'a renowned journalist of high standing' in his book *Blood and Tears* (United Press of Pakistan, Karachi, 1974). Since the Commission didn't visit Bangladesh to obtain first-hand testimony, it refers to Aziz'z book in recalling the harrowing tales of inhuman crimes committed on the helpless Biharis, West Pakistanis, and patriotic Bengalis living in East Pakistan during that period. 'According to various estimates between 100,000 and 500,000 persons were slaughtered during this period by the Awami League militants.'[8]

Non-Bengalis were certainly worried after the landslide victory of the Awami League as they had all voted against that party and some, of course, were killed and harassed but all this happened not before but after 25 March as a direct reaction to the military crackdown. The Bengalis obviously chose soft targets of a defenceless community and only occasionally succeeded in claiming a few military casualties in guerrilla-style attacks. How many Biharis were killed, maimed, or raped is difficult to estimate.

NOTES

1. Ibid., p. 183.
2. *Report of the Hamood-ur-Rahman Commission*, op. cit.
3. Ibid., pp. 285-6.
4. Ibid., pp. 537-8.
5. Ibid., p. 507.
6. Ibid.
7. Ibid., p. 510.
8. Ibid., pp. 507-8.

14

Anecdotal Accounts of Atrocities

Bengalis have recorded many accounts of atrocities committed by our armed forces in East Pakistan, but reliable accounts by West Pakistanis have been few and far between. There is, however, a great deal of anecdotal evidence here that could provide a glimpse of what might have occurred. One hears, mostly overseas, exaggerated accounts of barbarities committed by the military which are discounted in Pakistan as being motivated by traditional Western malice. Thus there was all the more reason to have constituted an international tribunal to determine the truth so that unfounded allegations, if any, could have been dismissed and culprits on both sides brought to book.

Major Mumtaz Khan, a friend's brother, told me that on arrival in Dhaka from West Pakistan he was sent straight to his assigned operational area. This was after the military operation against the Bengalis had already been launched. On the very same day, still a stranger to the area and its people, he accompanied his troops on a routine patrol of a village. The sun was about to set and the villagers were preparing to have dinner. Suddenly the Pakistan Army swooped upon them and shot every one of them—men, women, and children. The only survivor was a baby, crying plaintively. The major couldn't bear to see this heartrending sight and begged his colleagues to finish off the baby too. This they refused to do because according to them the baby deserved to die a slow death. The major was disgusted at the atrocity but did not challenge the institutional bias of his colleagues; this could not have been a stray incident. One did not hear of any conscientious objectors anywhere.

Tasneem Siddiqui was additional deputy commissioner of Mymensingh and he too was caught in the middle; he could not leave the place as all traffic from Mymensingh to Dhaka had come to a halt after 25 March. We talked to each other on the telephone until 25 March and naturally discussed the looming crisis. I was fearful for my personal safety because of the emerging situation and expressed a desire to move to a place where we could all be together. He famously remarked: '*Patthar apni jaga bhari hota hai.*' After 25 March he went missing and was untraceable for a good two months. Because I arrived in Karachi earlier than the rest, his brothers and friends asked me about his welfare. But since everyone stranded in East Pakistan was inaccessible I had no means of knowing any better than those in West Pakistan. Some thought that Tasneem might have been killed because Mymensingh was hardly the place from where a non-Bengali could come out alive. But Tasneem is a tough man with a great sense of humour which helped him survive to tell the tale. I had kept my faith and did not allow pessimism to take hold.

Tasneem finally made it. His escape was narrow. With him were two West Pakistani officers, one of whom was from the police. They survived by moving on a daily basis from one place to another. At one point while travelling in an official jeep they were almost caught by the Bengalis but luckily Tasneem was not recognized as a West Pakistani. He was wearing a Bengali outfit, a *lungi* etc., to pass as one and sat at the back of the jeep.

Tasneem narrated the occasion of General Niazi's first visit to Mymensingh, where he addressed his troops thus: 'Comb the area, flush the jungles and improve the race.' This from a general who was ruling the 'colony' of East Pakistan! Can one expect to see a worse specimen of a general officer from a disciplined army?

Biharis ostensibly enjoyed the patronage of the military and were classified as pro-Pakistan elements. They were collaborators in the eyes of the Bengalis who were fighting the occupation forces. And yet they too were not spared. Some of them complained that the jewellery they had so painstakingly collected over the years as dowry for their daughters had been stolen by the troops during raids on their houses. But even worse, the military was accused of raping young girls. The complaints lodged by the Biharis were never investigated because such incidents were dismissed as collateral damage.

The grievances of the Bengalis did not even merit a hearing. When a few of them—the bearded ones nominated on peace committees formed to serve as a bridge between the military and the besieged population—complained against the troops descending on their localities in the evening to prey on their womenfolk, the allegations were dismissed as pure nonsense. The Bengalis at great personal risk caught a couple of *jawans* while they were molesting Bengali women and handed them over to the authorities. Action was not taken as that would have demoralized the troops.

Another batch mate, Anwar Mahmood, was sub-divisional officer in Tangail in the same district. He was not so lucky because there were no troops deployed in the outlying areas. He and his wife were taken away by a Bengali mob but were fortunately rescued by the military that arrived some days later. During the time they were prisoners, Mahmood was made to dig his own grave but a few decent people amongst his captors prevented the rest from killing him. A few village women reportedly asked the hot-headed Bengali youngsters not to harm the two prisoners because they had taken Anwar's wife as their daughter and would not allow any harm to come to her. Anwar finally made it along with other prisoners of war but he was completely shaken by the experience, both physically and emotionally.

Tariq Saeed Haroon of the civil service was posted in Comilla district where he witnessed the killing and secret burial near the airport of the Bengali DC and a few others. He told me that many years later whilst he was serving as private secretary to Raja Tridev Roy, then a minister in Bhutto's cabinet, a Bangladeshi delegation visited Roy and inquired about the Bengali civil servants killed in Comilla and tried to determine the location of their burial. To the good fortune of the visitors Tariq routinely walked into the minister's office—and quite by coincidence the Bengalis found the man who could give them accurate information. Up until that point Tariq had not shared this knowledge with anyone but decided that the incident was now history and there was no harm or risk in letting the Bangladeshis know where their dear ones lay buried.

Poor people living along the railway lines were bayoneted and their flimsy shacks set on fire. French Consul General Pierre Berthelot and his wife felt such great empathy for the people of East Pakistan that they carried munitions for the Mukti Bahini—the Bengali militia fighting the Pakistani forces—in their car which had diplomatic immunity.

Archer Blood, the US consul general in Dhaka, openly supported the Bengalis. Henry Kissinger, Nixon's national security adviser and later secretary of state, punished him for his dissenting views by giving him a dead-end appointment in the State Department. In a conversation with Nixon, Kissinger characterized Blood's actions as 'rebellion' and referred to him as 'this maniac'.[1]

NOTE

1. US Department of State, op. cit., Conversation among Nixon, Kissinger, and Keating (the US ambassador to India) 15 June 1971, Document 137 (http://www.state.gov/r/pa/ho/frus/nixon/e7txt/48553.htm).

15

A Typical General's View of the Disaster

Most accounts of the disaster written by people from West Pakistan are self-serving and represent a provincial, narrow and jingoistic attitude that proceed from preconceived notions to foregone conclusions. One such account is *Memoirs* by Lieutenant-General Gul Hassan Khan. He has blamed everyone for the disaster but himself or his institution. He scapegoats a large number of people who according to him were singly or jointly responsible for the disaster, and includes people such as Mujib, Bhutto, General Niazi and some officers at the martial law headquarters, but not the C-in-C of the army who had usurped power and was running the show.

In his self-serving account, Gul Hassan laments the fact that Mujib was allowed to go free, firstly in the Agartala Conspiracy Case and later in the 1971 trial. He thinks that had Mujib been 'eliminated', the army would not have faced the ultimate humiliation at the hands of the Indians. They could have 'pacified' East Pakistan. He forgets that there would have been someone else to voice the sentiments of the Bengalis because they, unlike their brethren in this part of Pakistan, do not meekly submit to the demands of the oppressors. And who is to say that Mujib's successor might have been a less formidable foe or a more uncompromising nationalist than Mujib, who, according to all indications was ready for a compromise till the fatal end. Mujib was a populist leader who voiced the sentiments of his people.

Various declassified documents of the US government pertaining to the 1971 crisis in South Asia show that the charge of secession levelled by Yahya and his military junta against Mujib was simply not true. There is overwhelming evidence to prove that the accusation was a concoction meant only to justify the refusal to transfer power. Had Mujib won less than an absolute majority, the military wouldn't have had to launch the crackdown and would have instead played ducks and drakes with the politicians without having to transfer power.

Mujib was released only after Bangladesh had become a reality. It was his people who sacrificed their honour, property, and life to attain freedom from an oppressive army. He remained in jail for as long as Yahya held on to power. When he landed in London after being released by Bhutto he welcomed the creation of Bangladesh. His detractors in West Pakistan cite this as proof of the real intention he had harboured all along. But what else could the 'father of the nation' say in his first public statement after his country had come into being following a traumatic conflict?

Gul Hassan is, however, candid while referring to the 1965 war and the 1971 crackdown on the unfortunate people of East Pakistan, saying frankly 'we failed miserably in both these undertakings'.[1] This is the same man who, according to Brigadier Iqbalur Rehman Sharif, deposing before the Hamood-ur-Rahman Commission, asserted that he (Gul Hassan) would ask troops during visits to formations in East Pakistan, 'How many Bengalis have been shot?'

Gul Hassan confesses that 'Our commitment to Martial Law was total in 1971',[2] a clear negation of what constitutionalism represents. While referring to Yahya, the perpetrator of the highest act of treason, i.e., breaking the country, besides organizing a coup to topple Ayub Khan in violation of the 1962 Constitution, Gul Hassan says that he 'was professionally, competent, exuded confidence, and carried a good head on his shoulders.'[3] Some good head indeed!

The charge of conspiracy hatched by Yahya and his cohorts is dismissed by Gul Hassan as 'irresponsible talk about how we took over from Ayub Khan.' According to him Ayub Khan was a sensible man and did not wish to preside over the disintegration of Pakistan. So he passed this assignment (of presiding over the country's disintegration) to his successor Commander-in- Chief. Gul Hassan says, 'I found him [Yahya] competent, decisive, broad-minded, easy in manner ... and above all ... a remarkable memory and a high IQ,'[4] while the Hamood-ur-Rahman Commission characterizes Yahya as a debauch and a drinker, who barked like a sergeant-major. It may not be possible to reconcile these apparent contradictions.

Brigadier A.R. Siddiqi also compares Yahya to a sergeant-major at a parade ground because he barked like one.[5] But one remembers his grunts on the TV and radio which one had to endure frequently during the three years he remained in office.

Referring to the many grievances of the people of East Pakistan against their fellow citizens of the western wing, Gul Hassan is generous in saying that 'there was an element of truth in these accusations, but no one had apprised them (the Bengalis) that development in the West was not as considerable as they were led to believe.' If it were that simple why did the generals and their cohorts not use their monopoly of power and complete control over their propaganda machinery to inform the people of East Pakistan accordingly. Obviously propaganda cannot be a substitute for facts on the ground or erase perceptions that had taken hold.

Gul Hassan blames the political leaders for not displaying the same resolve to come to the rescue of Pakistan when its break-up looked imminent as they were in slipping the noose off Mujib's neck after his release from the Agartala Conspiracy Case.[6] If the release of Mujib was such a catastrophe, it was Ayub and not a civilian politician who was to blame. It was the military that brought the country to such a pass by pursuing a course of self-aggrandizement. The generals were part of the problem. Gul Hassan has a fertile imagination—he reaches the startling conclusion without an iota of evidence that 'there is little doubt that India was instigator of the Agartala conspiracy and perhaps also the author of the six points.'[7] One could as well argue that the Agartala conspiracy was a plot hatched by the generals. As for the 'six points', they have been analysed in a separate chapter. Such asseverations are the stock in trade of Pakistani generals, Gul Hassan being no exception.

Gul Hassan makes no distinction between the Awami League and the Indians—both were enemies because they had indoctrinated the Bengalis against Pakistan. But he shows great sympathy for the non-Bengalis and more for the other ethnic groups for detesting the Awami League. What other ethnic groups, unless he is referring to people of the Aryan stock from the Punjab and NWFP performing their colonial duty? Or did he only have the Biharis who collaborated with the occupation army in mind?

While completely disregarding the Bengali majority represented by the Awami League, Gul Hassan shows selective concern for the Biharis. How phoney this affection is can be gauged from their plight decades later as they wait in Bangladesh to be repatriated to Pakistan. They continue to live in miserable conditions in camps in Dhaka. The military used them as cannon fodder to fight a genocidal war in East Pakistan—the Razakars, Al Badar and Al Shams were outfits comprising the misguided youth of the Bihari community who were deployed as the vanguard in the army's fight against the Bengalis. Yet the same army has been in power for nineteen out of the thirty-six years since 1971 and have chosen to disregard them.

In giving full vent to his spleen against Mujib, Gul Hassan makes an unsubstantiated claim that Mujib's avowed object was to create Bangladesh and his six-point formula stood unequivocally for the break-up of Pakistan. He calls him a traitor and holds all the politicians responsible for the events that followed the crackdown. To quote:

> Some of those politicians who had attended the Round Table Conference were unequivocally responsible for the tragic events which overtook the country shortly after. They had pleaded for the release of a traitor, against proven evidence that Ayub Khan had produced before them, and discarded the advice of some of the East Pakistani leader that the Sheikh was a dangerous and unreliable character. It was they who had let the genie out of the bottle, but could not influence him to show some temperance where the disintegration of Pakistan was looming ominously over the horizon.[8]

Nothing could be further from the truth. Mujib did not once speak of the separation of East Pakistan. He is widely reported to have questioned as to why the majority would secede; the Bengali population was indeed larger than the combined population of all the four provinces of West Pakistan. While East Pakistan was in the throes of its worst crisis, Mujib was languishing in a West Pakistani jail just as the military was busy creating a new country.

Gul Hassan pays tributes to the British who as the colonial power in India dispensed justice to the people and learnt the native language. 'We, on the other hand, had done nothing of the sort.'[9] He thus equates himself and his cohorts with the British and implicitly views himself as the colonial power in East Pakistan. But in reality, except for developing a taste for the finest Scotch whisky, our generals learnt nothing else from the British. One assumes that the author of this self-serving account did not learn the language of the people whom he so clearly despised. As for dispensing justice this was perhaps not even a remote concern as he was fully occupied in keeping the politicians at bay.

He claims that he is not a bloodthirsty hound and cites as proof the temporary and tactical withdrawal of troops to the barracks after 4 March 1971.[10] When the people of East Pakistan gave vent to their fury at the postponement of the National Assembly session scheduled for 3 March 1971, the military operation was deferred. According to Gul Hassan, 'On 4 March there was yet another bombshell from HQ Eastern Command: the troops deployed in Dhaka were ordered back to barracks, despite the explosive situation.'[11] So the postponement of the National Assembly session was right but the protest wrong? Punishment for the protest, the general believes, should have been instantaneous and the accursed tactical withdrawal a 'bombshell'. The tactical withdrawal by the military was not motivated by a love for democracy or concern for the people but was guided by an implicit admission of inadequacy to deal with the united opposition of civil society. The military needed reinforcements and the time between 4 and 25 March was effectively used to fly in as many troops as the security on the western borders would permit without jeopardising it.

Allowing the governance of East Pakistan to its people was, according to Gul Hassan, 'like leaving a virgin in the care of a habitual rapist.'[12] Mujib has thus been termed a 'rapist' and the people 'virgins'. Only a man of Gul Hassan's calibre is capable of such a sublime thought! Donald Rumsfeld, former US secretary defence, equated the return of Iraq to the Iraqis with the handover of Germany to the Nazis. Great minds think alike or conversely fools seldom disagree.

The crimes committed by his troops completely escape the general's attention. He accuses the Americans of being Mujib's 'possible sponsors'[13] although the United States firmly stood by Yahya's genocidal regime and tried its utmost to prevent India from interfering. As the declassified American papers show, President Nixon and Henry Kissinger were busy contriving a position on the crisis that would not upset Yahya. The US administration cannot be accused of ever siding with the democratic aspirations of people from Third World countries. Their imperialist interests guide them generally to nurture, cuddle and sustain in power military dictators and authoritarian regimes.

Gul Hassan's ire is not just directed at Mujib. Referring to Colonel M.A.G. Osmany, a retired officer of the Pakistan Army and an Awami League MNA-elect who was appointed commander of the Bangladesh liberation forces, Gul Hassan contemptuously accuses him of harbouring ambitions of attaining the rank of field marshal.[14] That is a sardonic remark, implying that only the author deserved that signal honour. He accuses Osmany of large-scale slaughter of West Pakistani officers but does not substantiate the claim with evidence. Osmany ultimately became minister in Bangladesh whereas Gul Hassan was unceremoniously retired and as a sop given a diplomatic mission abroad by Mr Bhutto whom he loves to revile.

And instead of being grateful to Bhutto, Gul Hassan shows scorn for the man. While accusing Bhutto of considering his electoral victory equal to that of Mujib's, the general forgets that it was the military which treated Bhutto not only at par but at a level higher than Mujib by acceding to

Bhutto's demand not to transfer power to Mujib, the undisputed leader of the majority. It was Bhutto's advice that the military sought even if this required the commander-in-chief to travel to Larkana.

Admiral S.M. Ahsan resigned as governor of East Pakistan on 7 March 1971 because he opposed the planned military crackdown and favoured the transfer of power. Not a single judge in East Pakistan was prepared to administer oath of office to General Tikka Khan who was appointed in Ahsan's place; later Tikka was to acquire the sobriquet of the 'Butcher of Bengal'. In Gul Hassan's opinion Tikka Khan 'was dealing with the complex situation which was beyond his comprehension.'[15] So who was responsible for putting him there? Not the people of Pakistan or their representatives—the responsibility lay squarely with the military and its high command.

Gul Hassan refers to the carnage of the West Pakistanis and Biharis between 4 March and 25 March 1971. What carnage? He has absolutely no idea what happened in East Pakistan during those three weeks. Gul Hassan appears totally oblivious to the possibility that others might see things differently. Except for the standstill of all public life that the Awami League ordered, no acts of violence were perpetrated and there was certainly no carnage. It is important to note that the massacre followed the 25 March action and did not precede it. Even the Hamood-ur-Rahman Commission was misled into believing that the carnage preceded military action. Correct sequencing casts a different light on the military operation. Brigadier A.R. Siddiqi in *East Pakistan: The Endgame* chronicles 'Acts of Violence and Lawlessness' but except for a few entries relating to Pabna and Chittagong all such acts according to him were perpetrated post 25 March 1971.[16] Yet the military junta and its hired propagandists succeeded in convincing the credulous West Pakistani elites that the sequence of events was the other way around.

Gul Hassan blames General Niazi for dealing with the East Pakistan crisis as a military problem rather than a political one. He also criticizes Niazi for dissipating his forces in an attempt to secure all East Pakistan from Indian intrusions rather than concentrating resources to protect just the cantonments and saving lives of both East and West Pakistanis. Gul Hassan believes that had his plans for the defence of Dhaka been adopted the subsequent disaster could have been averted. This is a speculative hypothesis which was not tested, and would have in all probability failed. It was not a classical war between two countries. It was an assault on a civilian population by its own military.

Ironically, Gul Hassan claims that if there had been more troops in East Pakistan the military crackdown could have been avoided, as if to imply that he thought that the Bengalis would be browbeaten into submission or perhaps he lamented the loss of Bengali lives that occured. The reality is that additional forces were needed by the army not to prevent loss of innocent lives but to escape the ignominy of surrender which in the end forced the army to give up power, first to the Bengalis helped by the Indians and eventually to Bhutto in the remaining half of the country. He also assumes that additional forces would have succeeded in suppressing the Bengalis with brute strength, compelling them to give up the fight for their democratic rights and meekly submit to the military might.

General Gul Hassan projects himself not only as a political sage who could foresee political events but also a military genius who could think clearly with several years' hindsight. About General Niazi, the author asserts that he did not have a clue of what was going on around him. Niazi asked the Indian general to whom he cheerfully surrendered in front of the entire world, 'How have I fought?'[17] How pathetic can one get?

The argument that by securing Dhaka and vacating the rest of the country might have made it possible to avert surrender shows Gul Hassan's complete lack of understanding of political and military realities. The Bengalis had risen as one man to protest against the postponement of the National Assembly session and denial of their democratic rights. They were rewarded appropriately by our military with a ruthless crackdown. Even if the entire army had cocooned itself in Dhaka, the city would have eventually capitulated because Indian forces would have laid siege and cut off all food supplies. The idea that Dhaka could have been defended through Gul Hassan's untested strategy is far fetched.

A CIA study dated 12 April 1971 (SNIE 32-17: Prospects for Pakistan) said that if India were to support or intervene in a Bengali rebellion (in East Pakistan) it could 'provoke Islamabad into launching an attack on Western India' but added that 'in the 1965 war the Indian military showed itself more then (sic) a match for the Pakistanis. The Indians are now much better equipped than in 1965, and face forces weakened by transfer of Pakistani units to East Bengal.'[18]

Gul Hassan acknowledges that the GHQ knew little about happenings in East Pakistan. If the GHQ was in the dark then it should have stayed away from meddling in politics and playing with the destiny of the nation. He concedes that the General Staff (GS) Branch was engaged in confusing the Eastern Command.[19] A confused command and a scheming GHQ—

a fatal brew! The architect and head of this intricate system of governance was Lieutenant-General S.G.M.M. Peerzada, the principal staff officer to the president. According to Gul Hassan, Peerzada was allergic to making decisions howsoever trivial. He identifies Yahya and General Abdul Hameed Khan, Yahya's chief of staff, as the principal actors in the tragedy as if all other generals had no hand in sustaining these two in power. With people like Tikka, Niazi and Peerzada et al. in command positions it was no surprise that Pakistan had to surrender in East Pakistan. Gul Hassan generously acknowledges 'our own blunders' for losing half the country but omits to specify what those blunders were or how they might have been avoided. 'I do not absolve myself of the blunders committed. I mentioned these and I share the responsibility.'[20] This tongue in cheek admission is a convenient device to deflect closer scrutiny of the generals' responsibility. He squarely places responsibility for the disaster on politicians but is unable to decide if the debacle was military or political or both. The fact is that the generals were in charge of both Pakistan's military as well as its politics.

Only someone like Gul Hassan can have the gall and gumption to describe the disaster in terms like 'the recent loss of East Pakistan, ostensibly attributed to blunders committed by the Army,' as if to say that forces besides the Pakistan Army were rampaging in East Pakistan. This assertion echoes Bhutto's hilarious comment that the dismemberment of the country had made Pakistan more manageable.

Gul Hassan admits that the army could not bail out East Pakistan once it was attacked by India. This negates the strategy he so painstakingly advocates for General Niazi to have adopted. East Pakistan was always militarily indefensible and should have been rescued before India attacked it instead of waiting for the attack to come. Why were the generals deluded into believing that with millions of refugees streaming into India, the latter would quietly stand by and allow them to get away with murder? The interest of a traditionally hostile India to exploit the situation in East Pakistan was abundantly clear for all to see. The Indian prime minister had been visiting world capitals to lobby for pressure to be brought on Pakistan to make a political settlement with the Awami League so that India could have a friendly government on its eastern border. Even otherwise, one was always made to believe that Pakistan had to sustain an unbearable expenditure to support a huge standing army in order to keep India at bay. And yet the army failed to prevent India from interfering in East Pakistan. The generals belatedly opened a front with India in West Pakistan but in the end, as Nixon and Kissinger would have us believe, they had to be saved by the Americans before losing the rest of the country.

Gul Hassan ruefully refers to the PIA plane sent by Yahya after the ignominious surrender in Dhaka to bring Bhutto back from Rome, a man he would much rather never have seen. His account is full of contempt for Bhutto in particular and all politicians in general. He then talks of an intriguing demand for additional troops made by the Quartermaster General (QMG), Major-General A.O. Mitha, to augment the Special Services Group (SSG) for an undisclosed mission. Brigadier Ghulam Muhammad, the SSG commander, rushed to Gul Hassan and told him that the QMG wanted a company of the SSG moved to Rawalpindi as soon as possible for the protection of the president.[21] One may infer from this that regardless of the loss of one half of the country, the military still wanted to hold on to power and planned to conduct an East Pakistan-style military action in West Pakistan. In the event this did not happen—for the next five years at least till they struck again on the night of 5 July 1977.

Gul Hassan believes that discontent in the barracks due to the loss of East Pakistan endangered the very existence of the army which in turn jeopardized Pakistan's survival.

> On 20th December, I awoke from a none too restful sleep...first the turbulent atmosphere at the COS's talk, later, the visit of the two officers from Gujranwala; and later still, what Brig Ghulam Muhammad...had divulged to me. All these were alarmingly ominous happenings, putting the very existence of the army in jeopardy, and hence whatever remained of Pakistan.[22]

He was referring to unrest amongst junior officers in Gujranwala Cantonment who had challenged the conduct of the war by the generals. Clearly, the higher echelons of the army have a greater priority in Gul Hassan's estimation than the country itself.

Gul Hassan takes pride in the fact that he disobeyed his political bosses. He acknowledges that in the aftermath of the Dhaka surrender the standing of the army was at its lowest ebb. According to him this was not because the army had lost the war in East Pakistan but because the country was governed by politicians. He claims that when he was the COAS he refused to comply with the order of the prime minister to deploy troops in Karachi to curb labour unrest. He says that on another occasion he went to Bhutto with a proposal to set up an armed forces bank, which envisaged all ranks contributing a certain sum throughout their service so that on retirement the bank would pay to each the difference between the pension and the pay last drawn. According to Gul Hassan, Bhutto raised 'umpteen spurious objections to it (the proposal), despite the fact that I informed him that the practice was already in vogue in Iran.'[23] If the proposal had been accepted the general thought 'the morale of the armed forces would have rocketed sky high.'[24] It is difficult to understand Gul Hassan's logic of linking the establishment of a bank with the morale of the armed forces. In some strange way real estate and setting up of banks and industry has a salutary effect on the morale of the army, read the generals. Incidentally in every educational institution of the country which is not run by the military itself a fixed number of seats are reserved for the children of *shaheed*, retired and serving military personnel. Since the *shaheed* are very few, the retired and the serving reap the benefits.

During Bhutto's administration there was a proposal to have military officers screened by the police or intelligence agencies before appointing them to certain key positions. This proposal may have stemmed from the need felt by Bhutto to determine the political affiliations of the officers in order to check Bonapartism. Gul Hassan claims to have opposed the proposal because 'I did not wish a police constable to control the destiny of my officers.'[25] But the general did not find anything wrong in the overt screening of civilian officers at every stage of their career by JCOs of the Pakistan Army, a practice overtly introduced during the military rule of General Pervez Musharraf.

Gul Hassan talks of the Yahya, Mujib, and Bhutto meetings (plural) and emphasizes that such meetings were held without anyone else present. He obviously wants to convey that he should have had a part to play in such meetings. However it's not true that all three leaders met together except on one occasion when Yahya called both Mujib and Bhutto to Dhaka. But they (Mujib and Bhutto) were never allowed to get out of Yahya's sight. Had they met as often as Gul Hassan claims things might have turned out differently.

NOTES

1. Gul Hassan, op. cit., p. xi.
2. Ibid.
3. Ibid., p. 238.
4. Ibid., p. 289.
5. Siddiqi, op. cit., p. 14.

 6. Gul Hassan, op. cit., p. 285.
 7. Ibid., p. 241.
 8. Ibid., p. 244
 9. Ibid., p. 340.
10. Ibid., p. 265.
11. Ibid., p. 262.
12. Ibid., p. 266.
13. Ibid., p. 270.
14. Ibid., p. 271.
15. Ibid., p. 275.
16. Siddiqi, op. cit., p. 243.
17. Gul Hassan, op. cit., p. 329.
18. US Department of State, op. cit., SNIE 32-71: Prospects for Pakistan, 12 April 1971, Document 131. (http://www.state.gov/r/pa/ho/frus/nixon/e7txt/50127.htm).
19. Gul Hassan Khan, op. cit., p. 304.
20. Ibid., p. xi.
21. Ibid., p. 343.
22. Ibid., p. 346.
23. Ibid., p. 358.
24. Ibid., p. 368.
25. Ibid., p. 360.

16

The Tragedy—A Politician's View

In his book *A Journey to Disillusionment*, Sherbaz Khan Mazari, a highly respected politician, analyses the events of 1971 from the point of view of a committed democrat. He unequivocally asserts the right of Mujib and his party to govern Pakistan on the basis of the majority they won in the general elections. He quotes Akbar Bugti who met Mujib on 10 February as telling the latter as being 'extremely conciliatory towards West Pakistani politicians in general' (of course, with the exception of Bhutto).[1]

Mazari attempts to absolve Yahya of much of the blame because 'he was found to be inept for the task in the end. He totally lacked the political wiles to deal with the conundrum posed by the Awami League and East Pakistan.'[2] One would also disagree with Mazari's observation that Yahya was indecisive because of the growing pressure from the junta's generals; Yahya was the architect of our national shame and was very much part of the sordid drama. He was very decisive when it came to advancing or protecting his personal ambition. Even from Mazari's account—which is as close to the truth as one can get—it is clearly evident that the army was determined to keep power through the person of its commander-in-chief.

Mazari apportions responsibility for the disaster on Bhutto and Generals Hameed and Peerzada. Surprisingly Yahya finds no mention in this 'Hall of Shame'. He believes that Bhutto acted at the behest of his uniformed benefactors in adopting an aggressive attitude towards Mujib. He considers it fair to state that although the leading generals and Bhutto reached an understanding vis-à-vis Mujib, their motivations remained distinctly different. Mazari contradicts himself in claiming that Bhutto was acting at the behest of the generals. Bhutto was too smart to be a pawn of the scheming generals. He saw an opportunity of a lifetime to encourage two powerful antagonists to destroy each other leaving him as the sole survivor of this triangular contest so that he could pick up the pieces of what was left. Bhutto did not appear to have much interest in East Pakistan.

The generals wished to safeguard their interpretation of 'national integrity', writes Mazari, while 'Bhutto continued to be haunted by his pursuits of personal power.'[3] Because of Yahya's visit to Larkana soon after the elections Mujib suspected Bhutto to be conspiring with the military junta.

When Shaukat Hayat Khan, a veteran politician and elected MNA in the 1970 general elections, met Mujib in Dhaka in January 1971 the latter told him that Bhutto was in league with the generals. According to Richard Sisson and Leo E. Rose in *War and Secession: Pakistan, India, and the Creation of Bangladesh*, Mujib was convinced that Bhutto had become the junta's stalking horse.[4] Mujib felt that Bhutto was creating conditions to provide an excuse to the junta not to transfer power. At the same time Bhutto was trying to muster support from the smaller political parties in West Pakistan to emerge as the sole spokesman for the western wing in dealings with either the junta or Mujib.

Mazari claims that although Mujib had become hostage to the hardliners in his party and his own six-point programme, he (Mujib) perhaps felt that he would be able to overcome opposition from within his party once he was elected the prime minister. To quote: 'If one wishes to give him the benefit of doubt, it is possible to surmise that once the Assembly met, Mujib felt that his position as prime minister would prove sufficient to overawe the extremists within his own party.'[5] My own view is that Mujib commanded enough clout to overcome any intra-party opposition once power was transferred to him. He stood very tall amongst politicians of the Awami League and it would not have been beyond him to convert party hardliners to his own line of thinking. Major-General Rao Farman Ali Khan, then adviser to the governor of East Pakistan, was present at a meeting called on 28 February 1971 to inform Mujib of the decision to postpone summoning of the National Assembly session. Rao says Mujib exclaimed 'for Gods sake get me a new date for the assembly meeting. Even now I can control some of my people.'[6] But that was not to be.

Mujib invited Yahya to his house for a meal during the latter's visit to Dhaka in January 1971 but Yahya declined the invitation.[7] Yet on the other hand Yahya invited himself to be Bhutto's personal guest for three days in Larkana after having earlier turned down the invitation to be Mujib's guest. Yahya then had the audacity to invite Mujib to Islamabad, an invitation he initially declined but eventually accepted, agreeing to come to Islamabad on 19 February. However the meeting between Mujib and Yahya did not take place. According to Mazari, Mujib's initial refusal to visit Islamabad provoked a message from Yahya threatening Mujib with serious consequences. Better sense prevailed and the message was not read out to Mujib.

Mazari writes that in reply to Yahya's bluster that 'I will fix…Mujib' during General Rao Farman Ali's visit to Islamabad on 20 February 1971, the latter advised him that locking up Mujib would not solve anything.[8]

On 17 February 1971, Bhutto made a provocative statement declaring that a National Assembly meeting in Dhaka would be a slaughterhouse for the West Pakistanis.[9] Soon thereafter Yahya invited Bhutto and according to Mazari 'chided Bhutto for his refusal to attend the Assembly.'[10] One finds no evidence to suggest that Yahya was sincere in convening the National Assembly. When viewed in an overall context, this exchange with Bhutto, if at all might have been part of Yahya's charade in furtherance of his conspiracy to deny power to the people. It is a lie to claim that Yahya ever insisted that Bhutto attend the assembly. All Yahya had to do was summon the assembly, debar the membership of those refusing to attend and take to task any person threatening to 'break the legs' of those who tried to attend. But obviously this was not so. The reality is Bhutto was a partner in this conspiracy and both were acting in concert.

Long after his humiliating removal from office Yahya is reported to have self-servingly blamed Bhutto's refusal to attend the assembly session as the single most contributory factor in the break-up of Pakistan. These comments were made six years after Bhutto had consistently ignored an out-of-power Yahya and kept him virtually confined to his residence.

The conspiracy not to transfer power finds further proof in the hasty amendment incorporated on 20 February 1971 in Yahya's Legal Framework Order. This was done so that the resignations Bhutto had gathered from his party's MNA-elects could take effect before the Assembly met. Without the amendment it was not legally possible for resignations to be effective prior to the Assembly sitting in session. Commenting on the amendment that was followed in quick succession with resignations by MNA-elects of Bhutto's PPP, Mazari writes that 'the coincidence was too obvious.'[11] In fact, the amendment to the LFO was part of Yahya's strategy to create a stalemate by confronting Mujib with mass resignations from the largest single party in West Pakistan, and thereby perpetuate military rule.

Mujib was the last person to know about the impending and abrupt postponement of the Assembly session. Governor S.M. Ahsan had no part in the junta's machinations and had advised Yahya against the postponement. He was presented with a *fait accompli* but still did not give up efforts to avert a crisis, and sent a telex to Yahya asking that a fresh date be announced for convening the Assembly session. In the end, when his advice was ignored, Ahsan resigned in protest. To quote Mazari the 'pretext' for the postponement was that 'as the majority of West Pakistan Assembly members would not be attending the assembly session, there was a little point in holding the meetings of the assembly.'[12] Such machinations were not the acts of an indecisive or an inebriated Yahya; instead they were orchestrated by a cunning Yahya in full control of his faculties for intrigue.

Yahya's directive to Ahsan to meet Bhutto and try convincing him to turn up at Dhaka was only a cunning ploy and a smokescreen. One cannot agree with Mazari that the generals of the junta were with Bhutto and not with Yahya. One has to read Gul Hassan to find that out. The army generals were all united against the politicians or the people they represented. Their rancour was evenly focused on Mujib and Bhutto, the plan being to target Mujib first with Bhutto's help and then to deal with the latter when he was left alone in the field.

Having seen the sharp reaction in East Pakistan to the postponement of the Assembly session scheduled for 3 March 1971, Yahya announced that the Assembly would now be convened on 25 March. But this was a ruse as Yahya had other plans. Mazari describes Bhutto's delight at receiving news that the Assembly would not after all be called into session. This happened when Mazari was with Bhutto for dinner at 70 Clifton (Bhutto's Karachi residence) on 2 March 1971, four days prior to the announcement that the assembly session would be convened on 25 March. During the course of the evening Bhutto left to receive a telephone call from Major-General Ghulam Umar, Yahya's national security adviser, and returned with 'a smug expression on his face' to inform Mazari to forget about travelling to Dhaka for the assembly session. Mazari thinks, and rightly so, that Bhutto had been informed in advance of Yahya's plans for a military crackdown in East Pakistan. Bhutto's subsequent visit to Dhaka before 25 March was part of the ruse enacted by him. In the meanwhile, a dialogue was initiated ostensibly to resolve the imbroglio but in reality to gain time to fly in more troops to East Pakistan. According to Mazari two brigades were sent to East Pakistan between 27 February and 2 March.

A number of meetings took place between the Awami League and the army leadership. Bhutto arrived in Dhaka on 22 March to take part in these meetings but he refused to even look at Mujib. According to Mazari, Yahya had to chide both politicians for their childish behaviour.[13] It's true then that military commanders treat the peoples' representatives as no more than children or adolescents. Bhutto refused to acknowledge the basic principle of majority rule by declaring that, because the two parts of the country were geographically separated, this principle could not be applied. In effect he devised his own definition of democracy. On 24 March the Awami League met Yahya's team and was assured by General Peerzada that he would arrange one final meeting with all key players; this meeting never materialized because the next day, on 25 March, Operation Search Light was launched. But Yahya kept insisting till then that 'he was committed to the transfer of power, the final details would have to be agreed upon by all interested parties including the PPP.'

On 3 March Mujib demonstrated his statesmanship and leadership by counselling people at a mass rally to cease all acts of violence and instead launch a Gandhi-style *Satyagraha*. He also spoke of communal harmony between the Bengalis and non-Bengalis and between Muslims and Hindus. On 7 March, while addressing a mammoth rally in Dhaka where the BBC had speculated he might announce the independence of Bangladesh, Mujib made the following four demands: withdrawal of martial law, return of all military personnel to their barracks, inquiry into the recent shootings and killings in East Pakistan, and the immediate transfer of power to the elected representatives of the people. These were perfectly legitimate demands from an elected leader of Pakistan.

Yahya never intended to let go of power and criticized the Awami League for allowing destructive elements into the streets to destroy life and property. He did not cite any evidence in support of his accusation. He warned that he would not allow a handful of people to destroy the homeland of millions of innocent Pakistanis. But the 'handful of people' that ultimately destroyed Pakistan were the generals who comprised Yahya's inner coterie. He declared that it was the duty of Pakistan's armed forces (where did he get this, in the Constitution?) to ensure the integrity, solidarity and security of Pakistan, a duty in which they had never failed. Quite to the contrary, the armed forces have consistently failed, in both the 1965 and 1971 wars, and earlier in 1960 when Ayub signed the Indus Basin Water Treaty to hand over to India three rivers that had flowed through our country for centuries. And since then, it has been the loss of the Siachin heights and the failed Kargil adventure.

It was averred that there were legal difficulties in transferring power to Mujib, partly as a result of Bhutto's insistence that such a step would create a legal vacuum, yet abrogating the Constitution presented no such difficulty to Yahya. Bhutto was only playing the part he accepted in the conspiracy to deny power to Mujib. As Mazari says, Bhutto's role as 'a premeditated last minute spoiler of the negotiations cannot be discounted.'[14]

NOTES

1. Sherbaz Khan Mazari, op. cit., p. 186.
2. Ibid., pp. 214-5.
3. Ibid., p. 184.
4. Richard Sisson, Leo E. Rose, *War and Secession: Pakistan, India, and the Creation of Bangladesh,* University of California Press, 1991, p. 186.
5. Mazari, op. cit., p. 188.
6. Ibid., p. 201.
7. Ibid., p. 188.
8. Ibid., p. 191.
9. Ibid., p. 190.
10. Ibid.
11. Ibid., p. 192.
12. Ibid.
13. Ibid., p. 210.
14. Ibid., p. 196.

17

Who is to Blame?

The historian branch of the State Department held a two-day conference on 28 and 29 June 2005 on US policy in South Asia between 1961 and 1972, inviting scholars from India, Pakistan, and Bangladesh to express their views on the declassified US documents. A report on the seminar quoted Professor Sarmila Bose, a Bengali academic belonging to the family of Subhash Chandra Bose, as saying 'that no neutral study of the conflict has been done and reports that are passed on as part of history are narratives that strengthen one point of view by rubbishing the other.'[1] The report said that Bose 'also spoke about the violence generated by all sides.'[2] She elaborated this by adding:

> The civil war of 1971 was fought between those who believed they were fighting for a united Pakistan and those who believed their chance for justice and progress lay in an independent Bangladesh. Both were legitimate political positions. All parties in this conflict embraced violence as a means to the end, all committed acts of brutality outside accepted norms of warfare, and all had their share of (in) humanity.[3]

After being denied economic and political parity for twenty-five years by the ruling cliques of West Pakistan, culminating in the aggression launched by the Pakistani military and its generals, East Pakistan was literally forced out of the federation. Even otherwise a majority province doesn't choose to opt out of a federation.

As early as November 1969, a US diplomat had warned of the dangers and had this to say to Washington: 'In East Pakistan, one also senses a growing undercurrent that beyond some intangible point, the West Pakistan landlord-the civil service-military elite might prefer to see the country split rather than submit to Bengali ascendancy'.[4] In present day Pakistan, stronger secessionist undercurrents can be discerned in Sindh, Balochistan, and NWFP.

The impasse was between the military and the politicians because the former believed it had the right to rule. Politicians were a mere inconvenience who had to be removed or embedded in a military-led political dispensation. The motions of going through the elections, confident that the results could be 'managed', were only meant to deflect public pressure. But elections howsoever manipulated can still spring surprises. Intelligence estimates had ruled out the possibility of the Awami League winning an overwhelming majority in the general elections. Resultantly the army was not prepared for such an eventuality and reacted badly, without reason or logic. The pity is that the military as an institution continued to support Yahya and his junta throughout the escalating crisis until Pakistani troops were forced to surrender. Was there no one in the army who could stay the hand of Yahya and save this country?

A US government document titled 'Contingency Study on Pakistan: East Pakistan Secession' (prepared in response to NSSM-118, 3 March 1971)[5] warned that 'as a result of Yahya's postponement of the Assembly, the crisis has reached a critical juncture. Unless a compromise formula can be devised, secession by the Bengalis or separation of the two wings of Pakistan by mutual consent have become real possibilities.' Part I of the paper traced the immediate background of the East Pakistan political crisis and assessed the outlook for East and West Pakistan if they became two independent states.

History is only an opinion. Most Pakistanis believe that it is in the nature of the Bengalis to rebel against authority and that they themselves were responsible for their sad plight including the military operation against them. That they received wholehearted help from 'Pakistan's eternal enemy, India' was fortuitous. The Bengalis I met long after the creation of Bangladesh passionately blame Bhutto for the events leading to the 'secession' of East Pakistan. Yahya, according to them, was a debauch and a drunk and as such incapable of any independent action. It was Bhutto who was providing him all the guidance. Surprisingly, I came across well-informed people in India sharing the same opinion. Without denying that one's opinion is coloured by one's background, education, and experience, I would squarely hold the generals responsible. This is one conclusion that was also reached by the Hamood-ur-Rahman Commission.

I have devoted an entire chapter to argue that Bhutto cannot be labelled as the primary culprit for breaking the country into two. He may be an abettor, an accomplice or an unwitting conspirator but he certainly was not in the driving seat. Those who were in control relied on his advice because that was the advice they were seeking. It is the principals and not the advisers who ultimately must take the blame.

Pakistanis accuse Mujib of being a 'traitor' but he cannot be blamed because his only crime was to win elections, that too with an overwhelming majority and then logically demand transfer of power. From the time the military crackdown was launched in East Pakistan on 25 March till the surrender of the Pakistani forces at Dhaka on 16 December, Mujib was in jail and didn't do anything to deserve opprobrium. He was safely locked up in a West Pakistani jail and was in no position to break-up the country.

India too cannot be blamed because the crisis was of Pakistan's own making. Had the generals transferred power to Mujib and not launched an operation that triggered an outflow of refugees to India, the latter would have had no excuse to intervene. And it is to the credit of India that it waited nine months for the generals to see sense and reach a settlement with their East Pakistani compatriots. But the generals refused to heed the advice of saner elements including that of Leonid Brezhnev, the general secretary of the Soviet Communist Party, to seek a political settlement. Even though the generals like to quote the phrase made famous by Bhutto that 'it was not a military defeat but a defeat of the system', it needs to be said that even if the system is blamed that too was devised and run by them.

The generals wish to erase the memory of the surrender at Dhaka. In the highest military training institution of the country, the National Defence College, which is now a degree-awarding university, no discussion of the events of 1971 was permitted. If ever someone raised the question during an academic discussion, he would be abruptly silenced. So much for academic freedom in the military's highest training institution!

The late Z.A. Suleri was invited to deliver a lecture to our class in the National Defence College. Without mentioning Bhutto by name, Suleri alleged that 'someone' (implying Bhutto) took over power (in the aftermath of the country's break-up) without holding fresh elections. Having declared in the earlier part of the same lecture that the 1971 tragedy was the direct outcome of the general elections I asked how he could be critical of 'someone' for not holding fresh elections when he held the view that elections were the cause of separation of East Pakistan. He evaded an answer and denied having said any such thing. He was an acolyte of the generals, first Yahya and then Ziaul Haq. When Yahya very reluctantly made way for Bhutto, I felt pleased and called Suleri urging him to stop blaming the Bengalis for their misery and extolling the armed forces for defending the integrity of the country. He had printed so much nonsense against the people of East Pakistan and in praise of the military that one felt sick. I had not known then that he had already been dismissed by Bhutto in one of the first acts of his administration.

It was on 22 November that India formally attacked East Pakistan. On 6 December it recognized the Bangladesh government in exile. By then things had started to become tense on the West Pakistan border with India. The regime appeared worried at India's military intervention but continued hoping until the end that China or the US or both in concert would come to its rescue by standing up to India. But each country has her own national interests to defend and should not be expected to pull someone else's chestnuts out of the fire.

In the days just preceding the war on the western front, work was at a standstill in government offices. I was serving in Lahore as director finance of the West Pakistan Small Industries Corporation. The chairman of the corporation was a retired Brigadier named Iqbal, from Talagang. He was a farsighted man who did not share the optimism of his erstwhile military colleagues and thought that Lahore might fall to the Indians. He once confronted me with an anonymous letter that had accused me of being anti Pakistan because I was always critical of the military action in East Pakistan. In my presence he tore that letter and threw it into the dustbin. He didn't let me read the letter. Because of his worry that the Indians might reach Lahore and a quick escape might become necessary, he had three cars topped up and parked, one each at his office, residence, and the other side of the River Ravi.

Rather than staying idle I decided to undertake a tour of far-off areas in Dera Ismail Khan. The chairman tried to dissuade me because he thought I might get caught in an aerial bombardment. I countered by asking if I was any safer in Lahore. Obviously he didn't have an answer.

Several months passed during which I took little interest in my diary until things started getting hot towards the end of the year. And this is what I recorded in my diary for the latter period.

Friday, 3 December 1971: Finally Pakistan has responded to Indian aggression in East Pakistan. Air raids have started. Action of 25th March has led to this. Pakistan is at war with India. Emergency has been declared.

Saturday, 4 December 1971: Fierce day of battle on ground as well as [in the] air. Pakistan seems to have gained air control.

Sunday, 5 December 1971: Night was exciting. The whole night, air raids were repeated. Pakistan claims to have shot down 49 planes so far. Important turning point is the meeting of [the] Security Council convened at the request of USA. Indian delegate traced the present war to incidents following 25th March, and said that the present crisis in East Pakistan constitutes an act of aggression by Pakistan. He cited a long list of crimes committed by [the] Pakistan Army. Girls of 19, 16, 17, and 13 and below were systematically raped, he said. People were butchered on a large scale, and 10 m [million] refugees were forced to seek shelter in India and so on. He said President Yahya used filthy language against their Prime Minister. US accused India of violating [the] UN charter and committing an act of aggression against Pakistan.

Indian pressure on East Pakistan is mounting. Fight might be halted within a day or two with the intervention of [the] United Nations.

Note: (Those who hold Bhutto responsible for the break-up of the country blame him for tearing up the Polish-sponsored UN Resolution which they believe would have prevented the disaster that was to occur a week or ten days later. Here was a chance which the regime did not seize. It was in a state of denial and could not foresee the end.)

Monday, 6 December 1971: Left Lahore at 11.00 a.m. Reached Jhang 5.00 p.m. Stayed the night at a rest house. On my way I had tea with deputy commissioner of Jhang, Mr Paracha [He was widely respected for his integrity]. East Pakistan was the natural choice of discussion. I was convinced right from 25th March 1971 that East Pakistan would separate. And, therefore, while expressing my opinion I said as much but upset my host. He was convinced that the military would be able to keep East Pakistan in occupation. DC was very helpful [in terms of ensuring normal courtesies relating to my stay at the rest house].

Situation in [sic] war front is not clear. India seems to be pressing on to East Pakistan. Indian P.M. formally declared recognition of 'Bangladesh' in Indian Parliament amidst enthusiastic applause. The decision has far reaching implications, none of them suitable to Pakistan.

Tuesday, 7 December 1971: India made substantial progress in East Pakistan. Jessore is reported to have fallen. This is the death knell of East Pakistan. BBC reported that the Pakistan army left in such a rush that they left their lunch uneaten. Indian recognition has given the emerging entity a realistic shape. It shouldn't be difficult to capture the entire East Pakistan. Syed Nazrul Islam [MNA Awami League] has been declared Acting President of Bangladesh. Bhutto has also recognized that the BD situation seems pretty desperate. East Pakistan seems to have been lost to us with far reaching implications.

Wednesday, 8 December 1971: Situation seems to be slipping away fast. East Pakistan has almost certainly been lost. Yahya announced Nurul Amin and Bhutto as our Prime Minister and Deputy Prime Minister. [He has finally transferred power but doesn't seem interested in letting go. He wishes to hang on. Neither the PM nor the DPM were transferred power. They were only designated. So was Mujib before the crackdown. How shameless can one get?] This so-called representative Government will take over on 27th December. What a demonstration of sense of urgency? What will have happened between now and then? Pakistan has made no substantial gains on West Pakistan [front] except capturing Chhamb. Ceasefire will be accepted by India as soon as East Pakistan falls. West Pakistan will be left with no choice but to accept the reality of the situation.

There is a horrifying possibility of Russian intervention from the north leading to a world war. General Assembly of the United Nations has recommended immediate ceasefire. By Friday or Saturday ceasefire may have been accepted. Our troops in East Pakistan have no hope of receiving further reinforcements and are likely to surrender *en masse* to India. I think, Yahya is going [into oblivion] within a day or two.

Thursday, 9 December 1971: India claimed more successes in East Pakistan. They said they are within 30 miles of Dhaka. I pity those West Pakistani civilians or military men who face virtual extinction. They have to fight to survive. They might start surrendering *en masse* within a day or two. Pakistan has not made any substantial progress in Kashmir. It seems bargaining position will be too bad. Ceasefire expected by tomorrow or day after. What a misery we have brought upon to us! I hope the criminals are duly punished. [A vain hope to this day]

Friday, 10 December 1971: Left DIK at 9.00 a.m. Reached Leiah 1.00 p.m. Halt for the night. News about East Pakistan was very discouraging. India is planning to take over East Pakistan in *blitzkrieg* but our troops have put up a tough resistance. China has warned India of consequences in case she refuses to accept ceasefire. [No reinforcements that our generals had hoped for arrived though.] India has however made tall claims about victories in East Pakistan. She has immediately succeeded in severing East Pakistan from the rest of the world. Our troops must be in a very sad plight. God help them. [Well, this did not happen!]

Chinese actual intervention will bring to an end the era of short-lived freedom Pakistan and India have enjoyed. May both the countries see sense and shed off their blindfolds of prejudice. It will then become a real disaster for the subcontinent.

Saturday, 11 December 1971: No substantial change in [the] situation of East Pakistan. India has made very little progress, in spite of all advantages on her side. We ought to recognize Bangladesh and enter negotiations with India regarding ceasefire. Otherwise, it might be too late!

Sunday, 12 December 1971: Political situation has not improved. India is narrowing down the strangulation of East Pakistan. Time is on her side. The plight of troops in East Pakistan is highly vulnerable.

Wednesday, 15 December 1971: My birthday coincides with the most severe crisis, the nation has faced. Situation in East Pakistan awfully grim.

Thursday, 16 December 1971: East Pakistan falls. Lt. Gen. A. A. K. Niazi Commander of East Pakistan Forces signs unconditional surrender. Most humiliating situation West Pakistan has had to face. This is culminating point of events, the course of which was charted by Yahya Khan, motivated by his personal desire to stick to power. His ambition is too great [even] for Ayub to match. He had the cheek to address the nation and admit our defeat. Blackest milestone in short history of Pakistan. Mujib who is alleged to be a secessionist is locked in. Yahya accomplished this task perfectly.

Friday, 17 December 1971: Punjabis are realizing their mistaken trust in the Army. Their sense of shock and despair is manifesting itself in their faces. In spite of his [Yahya] speech less than 24 hours earlier to fight to the end the brave man has accepted ceasefire on Indian terms. This acceptance of ceasefire has outraged Punjabi sense of nationalism & patriotism. He will meet the most ignoble end [which he didn't].

I wish the new nation of Bangladesh prosperity and real freedom!

Sunday, 19 December 1971: People are completely dazed like Bengalis in Dhaka on 25 March 1971 as a result of loss of East Pakistan. Their anger is directed against Yahya and his coterie.... Bhutto's arrival is awaited most anxiously, who is coming back from New York after a thorough briefing from [President] Nixon.

Monday, 20 December 1971: Finally Yahya has given up. With him comes to an end the ignominious period of military rule started in 1958. Z.A. Bhutto takes over as Chief Martial Law Administrator and President. He addressed the nation on radio at 10.00 p.m. He only announced two sensible decisions: the retirement of seven generals and the lifting of the ban on the National Awami Party [NAP]. He plans to have coalition with NAP in the NWFP and Balochistan.

He is basically a cunning man. He promised sweeping land and labour reforms and perpetual contact with people. I only pray that he sticks to his promises. We have no option but to support him. At least he represents the people. I hope a new era of freedom ushers in. I hope he does not keep Martial Law too long and becomes Prime Minister soon enough, to allow Nurul Amin to be the president. He stands committed to parliamentary system in spite of his inclinations to the contrary. Because of his obvious collusion with Yahya against Sheikh Mujib he is likely to avoid a public trial of Yahya and his coterie. His stand on AL [Awami League] should have also been just and honest.

If he does not try Yahya and allow the people to know the deep conspiracies against Mujib and Pakistan, he will have to pay dearly some four or five years later. Military will come back again and people will not hesitate to accuse him too like they are doing Yahya now. [But] If he tries Yahya, people will condemn his collaboration.

Wednesday, 22 December 1971: Bhutto is settling down to his job. He is not entirely inexperienced, but so far he has taken only administrative decisions, which is not sufficient. He must do three things: give land reforms, release Sheikh Mujib and withdraw emergency as well as Martial Law—all at once. Otherwise his promises are likely to be misinterpreted.

Monday, 27 December 1971: Things have not shown any radical change. Set up remains the same. Only the actors have changed. Something substantial is required.

Tuesday, 28 December 1971: Bhutto has finally talked to Sheikh Mujib, who is not likely to be of any help under the changed circumstances. He might be set free within a week or so. I understand he has virtually been set free inside the annex of presidential house in Rawalpindi. No major reforms have so far come about, although everybody is talking about them.

Wednesday, 29 December 1971: The year ended after all. It was a year full of thrills. I was in East Pakistan at the beginning of the year along with Sajid. The year had started with my relief duty in Bhola. I was acting deputy commissioner, Khulna too. There I saw full month of March marked with civil disobedience all over East Pakistan. Then my escape from Khulna, and my being a witness to EBR's 'rebellion' in Jessore and final escape to West Pakistan.

NOTES

1. Anwar Iqbal, *Dawn*, 7 July 2005 (http://www.dawn.com/2005/07/07/nat3.htm).
2. Ibid.
3. Ibid.
4. Ibid.
5. US Department of State, op. cit., Contingency Study on Pakistan: East Pakistan Secession (NSSM 118), 3 March 1971, Document 123. (http://www.state.gov/r/pa/ho/frus/nixon/e7txt/47239.htm).

18

Polish Resolution

Apologists for usurpers and the institutions that sustain them have attempted to create an impression that East Pakistan would not have been lost or at least the shameful surrender by the armed forces would not have become inevitable had the Polish-sponsored UN Resolution been accepted by Bhutto who was Pakistan's representative to the United Nations. This Resolution had been presented in the Security Council on 15 December 1971, bearing in mind that Niazi, the general who had earlier vowed that the Indians would only cross into East Pakistan 'over my dead body', had already sent a message of surrender on 9 December.

East Pakistan was as good as gone. In a meeting on 9 December 1971 between President Nixon and Henry Kissinger, the president's Assistant for National Security, Nixon said that they ought to look at the realities of the Pakistan crisis. 'The partition of Pakistan is a fact,' Nixon said and reiterated this by saying: 'We know that.' Kissinger agreed.[1] An alibi is sought to be created by those responsible for this national ignominy by blaming someone or the other, in this case Bhutto, for not accepting the Polish Resolution.

Yahya reportedly called Bhutto and asked him to accept the Resolution but Bhutto pretended not to have heard him and walked out of the Security Council after condemning the United Nations for not acting promptly enough. According to Sisson and Rose, Yahya related this account of the episode in an interview in 1979:

Yahya had been talking to Bhutto—who was at the UN meeting in New York—by telephone about several matters. At one point Yahya said that he was far away, of course, but the Polish Resolution looked good, and 'we should accept it.' Bhutto replied, 'I can't hear you.' Yahya repeated himself several times, and Bhutto kept saying, 'What? What?' The operator in New York finally intervened and said, 'I can hear him fine,' to which Bhutto replied, 'Shut-up.'[2]

In *A Journey to Disillusionment* Mazari also subscribes to the view that the surrender of 16 December could have been avoided if the Polish Resolution had been accepted. In order to clear the confusion it is necessary to look at the Polish Resolution that reads as under:

The Security Council:

Gravely concerned over the military conflict on the Indian subcontinent, which constitutes an immediate threat to international peace and security, having heard the statements by the Foreign Minister of India and the Deputy Prime Minister of Pakistan, decides that:

In the eastern theatre of conflict, the power will be peacefully transferred to the lawfully elected representatives of the people headed by Sheikh Mujibur Rahman, who would immediately be released;

Immediately after the beginning of the process of power transfer, the military actions in all the areas will be ceased and an initial cease fire will start for a period of 72 hours;

After the immediate commencement of the initial period of cease fire, the Pakistan Armed Forces will start withdrawal to the preset positions in the eastern theatre of conflict with a view to evacuation from the eastern theatre of conflict;

Similarly, the entire West Pakistan civilian personnel and other persons from West Pakistan willing to return home, will be given an opportunity to do so under the supervision of the United Nations, with the guarantees on the part of all appropriate authorities concerned that nobody will be subjected to suppressions;

As soon as within the period of 72 hours the withdrawal of the Pakistani troops and their concentration for that purpose will have started, the ceasefire will become permanent. As soon as the evacuation of West Pakistan armed forces would have started, the Indian armed forces will start their withdrawal from the eastern theatre of military operations. Such withdrawal of troops will begin actually upon consultations with the newly established authorities organized as a result of the transfer of power to the lawfully elected representatives of the people headed by Sheikh Mujibur Rahman;

Recognising the principle according to which territorial acquisitions made through the use of force will not be retained by either party to the conflict, the Government of India and Pakistan will immediately begin negotiations through appropriate representatives of their armed forces with a view to the speediest possible implementation of this principle in the western theatre of military operations.

A careful reading of the resolution leaves no one in doubt that power had to be transferred to Mujib but only in East Pakistan. That would leave Yahya hanging on to West Pakistan. Yahya was in a state of denial and remained convinced that his troops would eventually succeed in containing the crisis in East Pakistan. He made light of allegations that Pakistani troops had raped Bengali women. He refused to accept the advice of foreign friends including that of the Chinese and the Russians. The military dictator turned down Brezhnev's advice to make a political settlement because that would have meant talking to the Awami League— something he was loath to do. The generals preferred talking to Indian General Jagjit Singh Aurora rather than with Pakistani politicians! The sole saving grace in this resolution was that the Pakistani armed forces were not required to surrender to the India–Bangladesh Joint Command. This humiliation could perhaps have been averted. But the question remained if India would have allowed that to happen. The resolution was in the form of a draft and had to be debated and then adopted before it could take effect. All this would have taken a few more days unless the five veto-wielding powers had previously reached an accord on an agreed draft. Poland was not a permanent member of the Security Council and the resolution therefore represented the view of a smaller state. As the US government papers now reveal, the Americans were not sure till the end what it was that Yahya wanted and whether the Polish Resolution enjoyed his support.

At that point India might not have been agreeable to give up its military gains and lose an opportunity to publicly humiliate its arch enemy. There is some lack of understanding amongst those keen to pin the blame on Bhutto to the exclusion of all others. India had invested heavily both politically and militarily to ensure the break-up of Pakistan and would have accepted no less than the emergence of an independent Bangladesh. Besides, a UN resolution was not a guarantee that India would have complied if the resolution failed to fully satisfy its own political aims. India continues to be in violation of a UN resolution to hold a plebiscite in Kashmir sixty years after it was passed and there seems to be little hope that it would comply in the foreseeable future. And one must also note that there are multiple UN resolutions that Israel violates or ignores with impunity. The point I am making is that the military likes to cite Bhutto's rejection of the Polish Resolution as a major cause for the debacle which is to imply that its acceptance would have saved Pakistan from the consequences of the questionable policy of denying democracy to the people.

A settlement under the Polish Resolution was to be based on three elements: instituting an immediate ceasefire, restraining India from further aggression against Pakistan, and achieving a political settlement in East Pakistan. Kissinger thought that talks between the Awami league and Yahya would have been difficult to arrange but the Soviets were still prepared to allow Yahya Khan to have dialogue with Mujib from the point where this was broken off on 25 March 1971. In a conversation between Nixon and Kissinger on 10 December, the president remarked that India would not agree to negotiations on East Pakistan, to which Kissinger replied, 'But the Russians have already agreed to it. So what will happen, let's be realistic, what will happen is that the representatives of East Pakistan will demand independence. And in practice I think that is what West Pakistan will then agree to.'[3]

There appears no way that international politics, which is devoid of morality and justice, could have dissuaded India from its pursuit of an outright victory even if the Polish Resolution had been adopted—and that is a big 'if'. Even if it is assumed that had India accepted the Polish Resolution, Pakistan's military may have averted a humiliating surrender and stayed on in power, that would have been a great calamity as it would have left the generals ruling the roost. It was the Falkland's adventure and the Cyprus misadventure that rid Argentina and Greece of their ruling generals. The surrender in East Pakistan was necessary to force the generals to let go of their stranglehold on the country's political power—but sadly while democracy in those other countries is alive and well, in Pakistan it is still a different story.

Yahya was not prepared to talk to Mujib and yet this was an important element of the Polish Resolution. Then there was the letter from Soviet General Secretary Leonid Brezhnev that Yahya spurned contemptuously. Brezhnev advised Yahya to settle his differences with Mujib through dialogue but he was obviously not aware that Yahya did not want a settlement. All Yahya wanted was to be in charge at all cost and not allow the politicians anywhere near the seat of power. He might have even continued as president had some generals not nudged him out and was rather keen to execute Mujib during his watch before he reluctantly ceded power to Bhutto. As for restraining India, there was not much restraining left to do with only two days left for the final act of the sordid drama.

Kissinger too agreed with the contents of Brezhnev's letter and reported to Nixon that he had told the Pakistani ambassador (to the US) that they should agree to negotiate with the Awami League. But Kissinger was not certain if Pakistan would accept this advice and said 'they could be totally obstinate and say that it is their country' adding that if Yahya did not agree (to negotiate with the Awami League) 'then we may have to do without him...(or) we may have to let him get raped.'[4]

On 7 December, when the crisis was fast approaching a denouement, Kissinger met Nixon with Deputy National Security Adviser General Alexander Haig and Press Secretary Ron Ziegler present. While strategizing ways to deal with the deteriorating situation, Nixon abruptly questioned Kissinger: 'Henry, what do you want to have come out of it?' Kissinger responded: '...to show first of all, that in action we showed enormous concern. That in practice we've made major efforts to bring about a political settlement. In fact, the only political movement that has occurred (in EP) has been at our (US) urging.'[5] What movement did Kissinger have in mind is not clear. There were no political, diplomatic, or military moves for all these months. The entire elected leadership of East Pakistan was either in jail or on the run in India, and a political settlement was nowhere in sight. Only the rulers in West Pakistan appeared oblivious of the unintended consequences of their follies.

NOTES

1. Ibid., Conversation between Nixon and Kissinger, 9 December 1971, Document 168 (http://www.state.gov/r/pa/ho/frus/nixon/e7/48539.htm).
2. Sisson and Leo, op. cit., pp. 306-7.
3. US Department of State, op. cit., Conversation between Nixon and Kissinger, 10 December 1971, Document 172. (http://www.state.gov/r/pa/ho/frus/nixon/e7/48542.htm).
4. Ibid., Conversation among Nixon, Kissinger, Matskevich, and Vorontsov, 9 December 1971, Document 169. (http://www.state.gov/r/pa/ho/frus/nixon/e7/48540.htm).
5. Ibid., Conversation among Nixon, Kissinger, Haig, and Ziegler, 7 December 1971, Document 163. (http://www.state.gov/r/pa/ho/frus/nixon/e7txt/48561.htm).

19

Yahya Khan—The Architect of National Shame

A general impression appears to have been deliberately created by vested interests in order to indemnify Yahya of all responsibility by claiming that he was a drunkard, a womaniser, and a lightweight with no ambitions, interested only in gaiety etc. In the words of the Hamood-ur-Rahman Commission:

> Witnesses have told us that he drank heavily and even to excess but nobody has said that he was drunkard in the sense that he was ever found bereft of his senses because of his drink. Apparently the general is capable of taking his drink very well indeed...
>
> There is plenty of evidence to indicate that the general was far from being an austere man sexually. The number of women with whom he had illicit relations is unfortunately all too large.[1]

And quite contrary to popular belief deliberately engendered by his apologists, Yahya was a scheming man and a calculating conspirator. He manoeuvred Ayub out of office and once in power was scheming to perpetuate himself at all cost including if necessary by breaking up the Quaid's Pakistan.

Altaf Gauhar, federal secretary of information in Ayub's regime and one of his closest advisers, writes that Ayub felt isolated and looked to Yahya for help when in the first week of November 1968 agitation spread across the country like wildfire in the wake of a single incident in which a student was killed during a clash between the police and a crowd of Bhutto supporters.[2] Instead of attempting to calm the situation Yahya told Ayub that the problems he faced were essentially political in nature and had to be resolved through political means. This was tantamount to a point-blank refusal to deploy the army to save Ayub's rule and according to Gauhar was a 'veiled threat' from a loyal subordinate. Yahya continued to play his cards with great deftness and repeatedly professed loyalty to Ayub. 'He is like my father,' was Yahya's favourite expression in expressing fealty to Ayub. But in the meanwhile some ministers and senior civil servants started to meet Yahya and other ranking military officers during the last days of Ayub's rule. Yahya had army intelligence generate a report that the opposition was planning to impeach Ayub. According to Gauhar this was 'another turn of the screw by Yahya Khan to convince Ayub that he must rely on the Army even for his own security'.[3]

Gauhar accuses Yahya and his intelligence chief in Dhaka for the mysterious killings of two Agartala under-trial prisoners in Dhaka to frustrate the Round Table Conference of the opposition parties Ayub had called for a dialogue.

In the days just before his ouster, Ayub called an emergency meeting of the cabinet on 19 February 1969. According to Gauhar, Yahya walked into the cabinet room along with his chief of general staff and spoke to Ayub with authority—by then Yahya had dropped his subservient manner—telling him that 'things are moving towards a climax.' Ayub was now convinced that martial law was the only answer to the crisis and that Yahya would be the best man to impose this.

A round table conference of all political leaders from both West and East Pakistan was held in Rawalpindi on 26 February 1969 but instead of resolving contentious constitutional issues, the meeting adjourned till 10 March. According to Gauhar, Yahya had all the time he needed to complete his preparations for the take over. Yahya wanted Ayub to serve as the target that would keep the agitation boiling and would eventually facilitate a popularly backed coup.

The scheming and planning for the take over also finds ample evidence in the Hamood-ur-Rahman Commission Report which in its Summary and Recommendations has observed that:

> ...from the manner in which the plans had been made in advance to take over the governance of the country by the Commander-in-Chief and his army Headquarters, the way in which they continued to hedge the proposal for the introduction of regional Martial Law [at the instance of Ayub Khan to control violence that marked his last days in office], the unusual interest displayed by the Commander-in-Chief in the political affairs of the country during the Round Table Conference by meeting individual political leaders, one cannot avoid the inference that Gen. Yahya did not take over the country in order to merely restore normal conditions and re-introduce the democratic process. He did so with a view to obtaining personal power and those who assisted him did so with full knowledge of his intentions.[4]

Brigadier Siddiqi quotes General Peerzada as saying: 'We should be mentally prepared for Martial Law.' It was on 14 March 1971, a little over a week away from Yahya's take over, that Major-General S.G.M.M. Peerzada, then the Adjutant General, asked Siddiqi to see him. They discussed the political situation in the country till at one point the general remarked that the army might be forced to act and that 'martial law seems inevitable', adding for good measure that 'We can't allow things to get completely out of hand.'[5] Siddiqi got the impression that the senior generals were conspiring to overthrow Ayub and would sabotage any understanding with the politicians at the Round Table Conference. What intrigued Siddiqi most was that in the days preceding Ayub's removal the daily briefings given by Admiral A.R. Khan, the interior minister, continued to paint disturbed conditions in East Pakistan when actually things had started getting better.

Some senior army officers particularly General Peerzada were in close contact with Bhutto and encouraged him to stay away from the Round Table Conference. According to Gauhar most ministers in Ayub's cabinet were acting as Yahya's informers and agents. Ayub had pretensions of having a cabinet that comprised people of high quality, but unfortunately opportunism was their guiding principle.

In his *Diaries*, Ayub presents a very poor picture of Yahya and refers to his depraved character. He writes it was shameful to read in *Time* magazine a foreign diplomat saying that 'Pakistan is a drowning dog, India does not have to push its head under.' He also refers to an article on the 'Private Life of Yahya' published in a *Newsweek* issue (21 November 1971) which was banned in Pakistan. The article talks of Yahya's ten girlfriends, their doings and the influence they commanded.[6]

Ayub refers to a house Yahya built in Peshawar Cantonment financed by the Alvi Brothers of Standard Bank. Its opening ceremony was followed by several days of orgy, drinking and womanizing.[7] Standards of honesty have since steeply declined and our present rulers would rank among the wealthiest in the land.

Yahya was putting on a lot of weight because of excessive drinking and keeping late hours with women. But he had lost both in prestige and respect and Ayub noted that General Peerzada had started addressing Yahya as an equal.[8] Ayub also refers to disturbing statements made by responsible and knowledgeable people about Yahya's conduct and lack of adequate attention to state affairs, adding that Yahya would reach office late in the morning and leave by 1 p.m. to spend the rest of the time 'in drinking, womanizing and some sleep'.[9]

Yahya Khan was irked when Ayub's law minister and information secretary Altaf Gauhar took to him some proposals for resolving the ongoing political crisis. He remarked 'that the situation was far worse and that the new governors could not work miracles nor could constitutional changes calm the situation. Yahya said that he would carry out his duty to the country thus making it clear as to what he was heading for.'[10] Ayub was left with no choice and was forced to hand over to Yahya on 22 March 1969.

In an entry made on 2 April 1971, Ayub writes:

> Yahya successfully cheated us. We could not tell his real intentions till the last minute. In reality he, Lt. Gen. Hamid, Lt. Gen. Peerzada and Razvi, the director, IB (Intelligence Bureau), had planned the take over after my illness in 1968 and General Yahya had been encouraging some politicians to start agitation for my removal—and yet he kept on assuring us that he would destroy any element that opposed me. That was all a bluff. If it was not for his treachery the agitation could have been controlled.[11]

Everyone is wise after the event. Ayub must have selected Yahya for the job of commander-in-chief after careful consideration. He must have been a poor judge of character because his army chief and ministers conspired against him.

On one occasion Gauhar went to see Yahya in the GHQ under orders from Ayub and was told to wait as Yahya was in a confidential meeting with the ministers of law and defence and the federal defence secretary. When Gauhar finally got to meet Yahya the situation became tense with the latter threatening 'to do my duty' by going to Peshawar and sitting at home while the country burnt. Gauhar reminded him: 'General, you cannot interpret your duty according to your wishes. Your duty is laid down in the constitution and the rules of business and you cannot go beyond that.' Had Ayub cared for the constitution of 1956 when he abrogated it in 1958?

On 24 March, Ayub addressed a letter to Yahya requesting him to take over in view of the rapidly deteriorating law and order situation. Ayub wrote:

> I am left with no option but to step aside and leave it to the defence forces of Pakistan, which today represent the only effective and legal instrument, to take over full control of the affairs of this country. They are, by the grace of God, in a position to retrieve the situation and to save the country from utter chaos

and total destruction. They alone can restore sanity and put the country back on the road to progress in a civil and constitutional manner.[13]

Yahya ensured that the speech Ayub made to abdicate was retained by him (Yahya). A colonel in dark glasses walked in the moment Ayub left after making his last speech as president and seized all the equipment and the tape recorder. According to Gauhar, Yahya and his co-conspirators prepared the plan with great care. Yahya was nervous and worried that if one brick happened to fall out of place the whole facade would come crumbling down.

On 25 March, hours before the coup was to be formalised and arrangements for recording Yahya's broadcast to his fellow countrymen were being finalized, Brigadier A.R. Siddiqi arrived at the GHQ and reported to Brigadier Ishaque, the C-in-C's private secretary. After warmly greeting Siddiqi, Ishaque said: 'This is how history is made Abdul Rahman.'[12]

Ayub ought to have followed his own Constitution. The Hamood-ur-Rahman Commission noted:

He could and should according to the 1962 constitution, if he wished to quit the scene immediately, have handed over to the Speaker...There was, therefore, apparently no reason why the President should not have gone on to amend the constitution (to be able to do what he did) What then induced him suddenly to hand over the government of the country to General Yahya as he did on the 25th? The reason, it seems to us, is primarily to be found in the attitude of General Yahya who had made it plain that he would not agree to come to the aid of civil power. The Field Marshal had ever been contemptuous of the ability of the politicians to govern the country in a democratic fashion with success. That General Yahya's opinion was not very different is shown as much by his conduct after he took power as his evidence before us and he was, in any case, motivated by his own desire to come to power.[14]

Ayub Khan had indeed been forced to step aside. But he had a remarkable memory lapse when he forgot that as per provisions of the 1962 Constitution crafted by him the speaker of the National Assembly was required to step in if the president for some reason was incapacitated or unable to perform his duties. He also forgot that the army could not be an effective or legal instrument to form a constitutional government. It appears that even a former general and a self-styled field marshal was as helpless before his own army chief as an elected politician. Those are the dynamics of power that guide the rider on the horseback. Yahya took over and proudly proclaimed that he wore four hats—the C-in-C, the chief martial law administrator (CMLA), supreme commander and the president—in that order.

Roedad Khan describes Yahya as a true hedonist who believed that the art of life was to crowd as much enjoyment as possible into each moment. He was ill-suited both by experience and temperament to defend the country against external aggression and prevent internal disorder.[15]

In *Diaries* Ayub Khan calls Yahya a cheat, realizing only after his own ouster that appointing Yahya C-in-C was a great blunder. Rulers fail to understand that a chief of the army staff quickly realizes that he has the power to take over the country. If circumstances present themselves, no army chief in Pakistan would let the opportunity pass. Ayub showed them the way. The history of this country might have been different if Ayub had not intervened and allowed the first general elections under the 1956 Constitution to take place as scheduled in February 1959.

In any case Ayub's decline was inevitable for he had been in the saddle for far too long. And just that no one forgot, Ayub reminded the people of his prolonged stay by celebrating his so-called Decade of Development, an exercise that proved a public relations disaster. It is generally believed he lost his sheen by rigging his presidential contest against Fatima Jinnah in the 1964 elections. He was further debilitated by the 1965 Indo–Pakistan war and whatever little credibility survived evaporated after the Tashkent Declaration which required both Pakistan and India to return to the *status quo antebellum*; many Pakistanis blamed Ayub for surrendering the gains of a war they thought they had won. His fate was sealed and this became more apparent after he suffered a stroke. Bhutto, whom Ayub made the mistake of dismissing from his cabinet, proved to be a formidable foe, the proverbial last straw on the camel's back. He stirred up West Pakistan and brought popular sentiment to a boil.

With the streets in ferment, Yahya saw an opportunity to fulfil his ambition. He refused to deploy troops to sustain the tottering regime of his benefactor. He started secretly talking to politicians directly or through emissaries. He was meeting all kinds of opposition leaders. Bhutto was Yahya's Trojan horse who was keeping the cauldron of West Pakistan on the boil. Perhaps in the belief that Ayub could not be removed without the military's help, Bhutto became Yahya's secret ally. Although they were collaborating at cross-purposes, this was not the only occasion when the two colluded for a more sinister design. Bhutto pursued his narrow ambitions and could not rise above his Machiavellian manipulations. Yahya positioned his trusted men in khaki at the president's house to control and monitor access to Ayub. There is a great volume of evidence attesting to the designs of Yahya to promote himself contrary to the belief that he was too inebriated or to indifferent to plan such moves.

Towards the end of Ayub's rule there were hush-hush meetings of top generals. The sudden breakdown of law and order mostly in East Pakistan could not have been without purpose and appeared to have been orchestrated by an alliance of dark forces. Ayub called an all-parties Round Table Conference and reached an agreement on the restoration of the political rights of the people, but Bhutto stayed away having earlier declined to attend simply by saying that 'we would put pressure from outside.' All other opposition leaders attended. The battle on behalf of the people had nearly been won because Ayub had conceded to all the demands of the opposition which included instituting a parliamentary form of government, adult franchise, one-man-one-vote, etc. But that was not to be and the military intervened to derail the democratic progress. We were once again saddled with yet another sinister dictator. People lost and conspirators won. Air Marshal Asghar Khan, a latter day democrat, did not protest at Yahya's *coup*, and perhaps may have even encouraged it.

Siddiqi in *East Pakistan: The Endgame* chronicles the planning and preparations by the military high command and gives an eyewitness account of events preceding the 1969 *coup*. On 19 February, a little over a month before the disastrous take over, Siddiqi was in Karachi when he was summoned to Rawalpindi. He arrived in the afternoon and was asked to report in the evening to Ghulam Umar's office, then brigadier and director military operations. Coincidentally Admiral Ahsan, then the Navy chief, travelled with Siddiqi from Karachi on the same flight and on arrival went straight to Yahya's house. Umar was waiting for Siddiqi and after a cup of tea and a cigarette said that 'the old man (Ayub) had already put his hands up. He is ready to quit. So where do we go from here? What are you going to do about it...?' Umar continued: 'We have to do our staff work...but the Army can't just sit on its haunches while the whole country burns...the politicians can never make it...I have never seen a more divided lot.'[16] Umar then went on to detail the future course of action, taking care to explain that this was just a 'temporary affair', adding that Yahya would not move into the president's house but would continue to operate from the GHQ. However, Umar emphasized that 'Ayub must step aside. There is no question of helping him to stay on.'[17] Siddiqi sensed that martial law was in the offing and suggested that if that be the case, it should be accomplished with a quick, surgical strike. Siddiqi tentatively raised the question about the Constitution, to which Umar countered 'What about the Constitution? You cannot reconcile the Constitution to martial law.'[18] This implied that the Constitution had to go.

Arshad-uz-Zaman, the first Bengali to have joined Ayub's personal staff, narrates the conversation he had with Peerzada at the latter's house in Islamabad during the last days of Ayub's rule. On that occasion Peerzada smugly remarked that the Government of Pakistan 'will fall in our lap like a ripe fruit.'[19] He was referring to the turmoil in East Pakistan and urban areas of West Pakistan.

The Hamood-ur-Rahman Commission names four generals that include Abdul Hamid Khan, S.G.M.M. Peerzada and Ghulam Umar as conspirators who made elaborate preparations to grab power including drafting the martial law orders. Obviously they were acting at the behest of their army chief.

Yahya, who loved power and all its trappings, and not having outgrown his churlish, narcissistic tendencies therefore had thousands of his photographs in military uniform taken, mailed and delivered—all at state expense—to the remotest corners of the country. One such photograph arrived at Serajgang, only a sub-divisional headquarter. Akhtar, my Bengali personal assistant, who did not know the difference between a major and a lance-naik's uniform, hung the picture without obtaining my permission. He thought that it was the obvious thing to do. When I saw the picture, I quietly took it down. Thinking that someone else might have inadvertently removed it, Akhtar put it up again. I had to tell him then that it was my decision to take the picture down. This was the best I could do to express my distaste for an illegal regime.

As soon as Yahya took over, the situation suddenly and quite unsurprisingly settled down and the streets became mysteriously quiet. For the first time after ten years of quasi martial law Yahya allowed full freedom of speech as long as the military was kept out of it. Anyone bringing the military that included a *jawan* into disrepute could go to jail for seven years. Obviously he was not as worried about the *jawan* as about protecting the ruling generals. The device was meant to silence all criticism of the military.

Yahya permitted full political activity from 1 January 1970 and fixed elections to be held by the end of the year. This appeared a deliberate and cunning ploy. By allowing such a long campaign time he hoped the politicians would sling as much mud on one another as possible and in the process thoroughly discredit themselves.

Mujib launched his campaign with the slogan that 'Pakistan had come to stay and no power on earth could destroy it.' But Yahya had his own favourites, people like Khan Abdul Qayyum Khan who would rubbish sincere politicians popular amongst the masses. There is evidence that his favoured politicians were amply funded by the regime. At the end of this long period of political activity, elections were finally held after being postponed earlier on the pretext of the cyclone that devastated East Pakistan. He reluctantly allowed the polls to go ahead on the adjourned date after getting an assurance from his military intelligence that no single party would command a majority in the house and that the Awami League would only be able to muster a plurality of 60 per cent of seats in East Pakistan. He hoped he would then be able to play one political leader against another. But then his calculations went awry. The moment it dawned on him that he had lost the gamble, Yahya rushed to Larkana, stayed as Bhutto's personal guest for three days and hatched a conspiracy against Mujib and the people of Pakistan.

O.M. Qarni, the DC of Larkana at the time, told the author he was officially asked not to concern himself with the presidential visit. Bhutto did however ask Qarni to stop one of Yahya's numerous girl friends from leaving Karachi to join him at Larkana but it was too late; she had already left. The Hamood-ur-Rahman Commission puts a gloss over this crucial undertaking of Yahya. It concludes: 'To say, however, that the general and Mr Bhutto were in close concert with each other is not, we think, justified.'[20] This is no more than a surmise which contradicts overwhelming evidence of the two principal actors conniving to deny the fruit of democracy to the winner. Besides, Bhutto was in power when the report was being written.

In an attempt to postpone his day of reckoning Yahya did not announce the date for convening the National Assembly as promptly as he should have. After reluctantly fixing 3 March 1971, Yahya subsequently rescinded these orders and announced a *sine die* postponement. Roedad Khan says that Bhutto reacted sharply when the announcement of the date for convening the National Assembly was made on 13 February, warning that unless there was prior understanding between him and Mujib on the fundamentals of the Constitution, he would not allow the Assembly to meet. Khan distinctly recalls that when asked how could Yahya wriggle out of this commitment, Bhutto replied: 'A law and order situation could be easily created in Dhaka resulting in tear gassing and firing, etc., a few dead bodies and that would more than justify postponement of the National Assembly session'.[21] Obviously people who had waited twenty-five years to get their right to rule the country were not amused—not the Bengalis. Their reaction was swift, furious and predictable. Within hours they were out on the streets.

Yahya's Legal Framework Order was designed to ensure a deadlock. This was virtually the constitution under which Yahya was running the country. He contrived a stalemate by requiring the new National Assembly to frame a constitution within 120 days or stand dissolved; in doing so he overlooked the fact that it took the politicians nine years after independence to produce the first constitution in 1956, and this too was aborted before the first general elections could be held under it. Yahya also retained the power to authenticate, amend or reject the constitution so framed. Yahya loved power and concentrated every bit of it in his person—he was no reluctant 'saviour' pushed to the top by sheer circumstances.

After having 'lost' East Pakistan to the Awami League in the general elections, Yahya prepared a draft constitution that he was to announce on 20 December 1971 but his plans were interrupted because Bhutto assumed power in West Pakistan. His 'constitution' made a mockery of the people and their representatives as all powers including the power to reject any bills passed by the assembly were vested in the person of the president. This is what the Hamood-ur-Rahman Commission had to say:

> The mental unreality of the world in which General Yahya was then living is further provided by the fact that even on the 18th of December after the ceasefire on the Western front, the General announced that his constitutional plans had not been impaired in the slightest and that he intended to proceed with his time table.[22]

Yahya considered the secession of East Pakistan a minor setback which he thought he could survive and continue to hang on to power. He went on air to announce that we (Pakistan) had only lost a battle and that the war in the West (Pakistan) would go on. But Roedad Khan writes that Yahya asserted he was not going to endanger West Pakistan 'for the sake of Bengalis.'[23] Only when the 'minor setback' refused to disappear did the army surrender power to the people and their representatives but only to take it back five years later.

In the words of the Hamood-ur-Rahman Commission:

> We have detailed above a number of circumstances which reflect upon the motivation of General Yahya. The manner in which he took power including

the preparation that he made in anticipation of the event, the procrastinating steps that he took towards summoning the National Assembly, the manner in which he collected and utilised funds for political purposes to negotiate with various parties and finally his future schemes of things as reflected in his draft constitution, have left us with no manner of doubt that the General imposed martial law with the object only of personally seizing and retaining power.[24]

During the entire period of the crisis the United States did not waver in its support for Yahya and his regime. Pakistan had served as a bridge between the US and China, a service for which the Pakistani rulers took great pride; Nixon and Kissinger were both grateful to Yahya for providing a convenient logistical support. Writing about the invitation he received from Zhou Enlai on 2 June 1971 to visit China, Nixon quotes Kissinger as describing it 'the most important communication to an American President since the end of World War Two.'[25] In dealing with other countries, in particular those from the developing world, the American leadership has always overlooked principles and disregarded the concept of democracy. In return, Pakistani military rulers have consistently proved their fealty to the US by carrying out their dirty work either by assisting the *mujahideen* in the war against the Soviets or by fighting the same *mujahideen* in the war against terror.

The impasse between the military and the politicians was a result of the former's belief that it had the right to rule the country. For the military, politicians were a mere inconvenience who had to be removed. The motions of going through the elections were meant to fool people both here and abroad. Siddiqui quotes Yahya telling his regimental officers in an address that 'we must be prepared to rule this (unfortunate) country for the next fourteen years or so.'[26] Following in the footsteps of his erstwhile C-in-C, Ziaul Haq said the same thing when addressing senior civil officers of Balochistan including the governor and the chief secretary a few days ahead of his fraudulent referendum in 1984. I was present at that meeting. He asked them to support him so that the two together could rule for as long as they liked. The ordeal in both cases ended only when the internal dynamics of the military required its own general be sacrificed in the larger interests of the institution.

A CIA analysis lent support to the generally held view in the outside world that the regime's 'talk of enlisting loyalist Bengalis in any significant numbers was wishful thinking.'[27] And about Yahya, a Paper prepared by the National Security Council's Interdepartmental Group for Near East and South Asia charitably said he 'may not fully understand the seriousness of the country's current economic conditions.'[28] But for that matter neither did he fully comprehend the political or military situation. The same Paper correctly noted that the people of West Pakistan were not informed of the situation in East Pakistan. Anyway, which government would want its citizens to know the whole truth?

NOTES

1. *Report of the Hamood-ur-Rahman Commission*, op. cit., p. 122.
2. Altaf Gauhar, *Ayub Khan: Pakistan's First Military Ruler*, Sang-e-Meel Publications, Lahore, 1993.
3. Ibid.
4. *Report of the Hamood-ur-Rahman Commission*, op. cit., pp. 335-6.
5. Siddiqi, op. cit., p. 9.
6. *Diaries of Field Marshal Mohammad Ayub Khan 1966–1972* edited and annotated by Craig Baxter, Oxford University Press, Karachi, 2007, p. 500.
7. Ibid., p. 493.
8. Ibid., p. 377.
9. Ibid., p. 329
10. Ibid., p. 308.
11. Ibid., p. 472.
12. Siddiqi, op. cit., p. 13.
13. Ibid., p. 14.
14. *Report of the Hamood-ur-Rahman Commission*, op. cit., pp. 65-6.
15. Roedad Khan, *Pakistan—A Dream Gone Sour*, Oxford University Press, Karachi, 2000, p. 59.
16. Siddiqi, op. cit., p. 4.
17. Ibid., p. 5.
18. Ibid.
19. Arshad-uz-Zaman, *Privileged Witness: Memoirs of a Diplomat*, Oxford University Press, Karachi, 2000, p. 85.
20. *Report of the Hamood-ur-Rahman Commission*, op. cit., p. 81.
21. Roedad Khan, op. cit., p. 31.
22. *Report of the Hamood-ur-Rahman Commission*, op. cit., p. 122.
23. Roedad Khan, op. cit., p. 31.
24. *Report of the Hamood-ur-Rahman Commission*, op. cit., p. 122.
25. Richard M. Nixon, *In the Arena: A Memoir of Victory, Defeat, and Renewal*, 1990, p. 16.
26. Siddiqi, op. cit.
27. US Department of State, op. cit., SNIE 32-17: Prospects for Pakistan, 12 April 1971, Document 131 (http://www.state.gov/r/pa/ho/frus/nixon/e7txt/50127.htm).
28. US Department of State, op. cit., Paper prepared by the National Security Council's Interdepartmental Group for Near East and South Asia for the Senior Review Group, undated, Document 132 (http://www.state.gov/r/pa/ho/frus/nixon/e7txt/50130.htm).

20

Bhutto's Role

Bhutto willingly served the diabolic designs of the ruling clique without regard to his own credibility or place in history and thus emerged as a favourite scapegoat for the crimes committed by the generals. Gul Hassan, for instance, blames Bhutto for the surrender at Dhaka and accuses him of sending 'the whole of East Pakistan for a six.'[1] He laments the fact that Bhutto refused to attend the National Assembly session in Dhaka which caused additional confusion. The confusion was only 'additional' so he impliedly admits that the generals had already muddied the waters. But this, the 'additional confusion', is precisely what they desperately wanted because it provided them an excuse for not transferring power to Mujib. The closest Gul Hassan gets to acknowledging the military's responsibility is in admitting that: 'We had lost half the country owing to our own blunders (blunder: only a stupid or careless mistake, hence perfectly pardonable). Here I do not mean only the military, which was in power, but also our political leaders, who cannot evade responsibility for the break up of Pakistan.' The general wonders if those who pleaded for the release of Mujib at the Round Table Conference ever regretted their responsibility, and then answers the question himself: 'I doubt it.'[2]

Other charges against Bhutto point to his threats to break the legs of those West Pakistani leaders who attended the Assembly session in Dhaka, or his slogan of *'udher tum, idher hum'* and his statement that he was not prepared to ever sit in the opposition during his lifetime. In Gul Hassan's estimation all this makes Bhutto responsible for the break-up of Pakistan. But it was for the generals ruling the country to ensure that every West Pakistani member of the National Assembly was provided adequate protection to enable him or her to attend the session; they should have threatened to break Bhutto's legs if indeed he was serious in carrying out the threat. In any case, Bhutto's utterances were part of a show orchestrated by the military dictator to provide a pretext for not transferring power to Mujib. The holding of the assembly session would have created its own

131

momentum for democracy which the generals found unacceptable and wanted to prevent at all costs.

Bhutto is the favourite whipping boy of Pakistan's ruling classes, precisely the people responsible for the country's disgrace. Everyone, particularly in the Punjab, blames Bhutto for this tragedy. Surprisingly so do the Bangladeshis. Rao Farman Ali quotes Tajuddin Ahmad, a senior leader of the Awami League whom he met on 4 March as describing Bhutto as the number one killer of Bengalis. They seem to regard Yahya with contempt for being a drunkard and a buffoon who was more interested in his nocturnal revelries and therefore not culpable for his crimes. On the other hand they argue, Bhutto was shrewd, urbane and charismatic and must therefore have been responsible for the ultimate tragedy, particularly the military crackdown that started it all. I met an Indian intellectual in Chandigarh in 2006 who also held Bhutto responsible and lost his cool when I argued against this view. Indians are irked by Bhutto's vow to fight India for a thousand years, a promise he recanted only after the Simla Accord. Bhutto is, perhaps, easy to hate.

Mujib thought much less of Bhutto or his foreign policy which was abhorrent to him because of Bhutto's 'love for Communist China and his intransigent position vis-à-vis India.'[3] A CIA assessment made on 9 December 1971 on 'Implications of an Indian Victory over Pakistan' said that 'West Pakistan's principal civilian political figure, Z.A. Bhutto is a Sindhi, and though the recipient of a heavy electoral mandate in December 1970, has never been permitted to take office by the Punjabi military.'[4] Unless East Pakistan was gone the question of Bhutto taking over simply did not arise. So it seemed that the separation of East Pakistan offered the only option to serve Bhutto's narrow political ends. Yahya would have been happy if the crisis had simply continued or disappeared or even better, if he had triumphed. But India would not allow that.

To support the claim of Bhutto's culpability in the break-up of the country, reference is often made to his remarks following the military action on 25 March: 'Thank God Pakistan has been saved.'[5] Military rulers as well as ordinary West Pakistanis enthusiastically welcomed this statement. No one appeared to recognize that a military solution was being sought to an artificial political crisis created by Yahya and his refusal to transfer power to Mujib. Bhutto spent the night of 25 March at the Intercontinental Hotel Dhaka and was taken around the city in an army jeep the next morning. The real disaster, the military crackdown, had already taken place so the argument that this statement of Bhutto was responsible for the eventual break-up of the country is both facile and misplaced. In fact it was a series of actions, most of them foolish or criminal, culminating in the military operation which resulted in the break-up of Pakistan. If Bhutto is to be blamed for his complicity with the military government, then the main party to the conspiracy would still be the military. Putting the blame solely on Bhutto is not right but has one great advantage—it exculpates everybody else, particularly the military.

Yahya felt he was right in insisting on some understanding between the two political leaders before the assembly session could be convened. On 25 February 1971—a month before the military operation—Joseph S. Farland, the US ambassador in Islamabad, sent a report to the secretary of state on his meeting with Yahya. He said that Yahya 'spoke in a tone of despair of "Blood and Chaos" which might ensue' if the impasse between Mujib and Bhutto was not broken. Yahya also told the ambassador that he was 'considering deferral for a week or two of the National Assembly session' and urged the ambassador to talk to Mujib who had twice declined to meet him. Yahya also referred to the 'widespread suspicion that the US favoured separation of East Pakistan.'[6]

Following up on Yahya's request Ambassador Farland met Mujib at 0900 hours on 28 February at the latter's Dhaka residence. Mujib received the ambassador when he alighted from his car and escorted him inside. Farland reported that in Mujib's opinion 'the political impasse was not due solely to the machinations of Mr Bhutto.' Mujib said that Bhutto could not have acted on his own and that 'without the help and leadership of certain West Pakistani military officers, Bhutto's position would be untenable'.[7]

Having met Bhutto soon after the elections and staying with him as his personal guest, Yahya had obviously hatched a conspiracy. And similarly by not visiting Mujib who had emerged as the majority leader Yahya's designs were becoming clear. He should have called the National Assembly into session and compelled the two parties to adopt democratic norms. But he chose not to. Even if a stalemate had occurred in the National Assembly it could have been resolved by Yahya using his influence. He could have cajoled and coerced or used plain bluster. But his military operation was certainly not the answer. Left to themselves, the politicians could perhaps have reached some working arrangement.

Nixon and Kissinger regarded Bhutto with both contempt and concern. On 9 December—a week before the surrender—the two met in the evening for over half an hour. Kissinger informed Nixon that Bhutto was coming (to the US) as Pakistan's Representative to the UN, which prompted Nixon to use explicit language against Bhutto.[8] Kissinger overlooked the epithet and continued with his briefing saying that Bhutto's instructions were to offer a settlement very close to what the US had suggested and had been putting to the Pakistanis. Nixon said he had read the (State Department's) assessment 'that Yahya may be setting him (Bhutto) up to make a sell out in order to [unclear].'[9] The recording of the latter part of the sentence is unclear but it could well have been '... Yahya may be setting him (Bhutto) up to make a sell out in order to *escape personal responsibility*.' (Italics added) To the extent of Bhutto being set up to take the blame for Yahya's policies, the speculation might have been right. But Nixon's dislike for Bhutto was so strong that he would keep coming back to the man and give expression to his low estimation. This is what Nixon thought of him: 'He's a bad man.'[10]

In a meeting among Nixon, Secretary of State William Rogers and Kissinger on 24 November 1971 to discuss the implications of the crisis in South Asia and the approach to be taken in dealing with India and Pakistan, Rogers expressed the view that Yahya was going to be forced to do something and there was a possibility that 'he would turn over to Bhutto, which would not be a good development.'[11] Horrified at the prospect Nixon shouted: 'Bhutto? Turn over to Bhutto?' He characterized Bhutto a 'leftist' and his actions during the crisis 'disgusting'. Secretary Rogers termed Bhutto 'selfish' and Kissinger thought him 'violently anti-Indian and pro-Chinese' but added 'in a way we gain a lot if he comes in.'[12] Perhaps he thought that in Bhutto the US would have a counterweight to India which was too independent for America's liking.

Continuing the discussion, Nixon asked if Bhutto would make a deal with Mujib to which Rogers replied in the negative. Digressing somewhat, Nixon asked the two if they had met Bhutto but more importantly 'have you ever met his wife? Boy, she is one of the most beautiful women in the world.'[13] Without disagreeing Kissinger joined in with a quip: 'It depends, Mr President.' Nixon was clearly suspicious of Bhutto and said that he 'is a total demagogue'; recalling the rundown given to him by Ayub who he thought was a pretty good judge of men, Nixon said that Ayub described Bhutto as 'just bad news.'[14]

On 11 December—five days before the surrender—a telephonic conversation took place between Kissinger and Haig, deputy assistant for national security, on the one side (in Washington) and Bhutto and N.A.M. Raza, Pakistan's ambassador to the US, on the other (in New York). Bhutto by then had been designated deputy prime minister (but not sworn in) and had been despatched to the UN to seek a ceasefire. It appears that Bhutto wanted to meet Nixon while Kissinger was not too keen to let that happen and deflected Bhutto's request by saying he (Kissinger) had to go for dinner and was being held up by the telephone conference. Bhutto was evasive in stating the purpose of his proposed meeting with Nixon; Kissinger was of the view that at that late stage of the crisis, a meeting would 'create a tremendous amount of excitement... before we find out what we will do jointly.'[15] Obviously the US policy was to allow the crisis to play itself out, the overriding consideration being not to upset Yahya by doing something pre-emptive.

Bhutto and Ambassador Raza pressed Kissinger for a firm public statement in support of Pakistan, and a warning to India to cease intervention. There was also a muted complaint that the US State Department and George Bush, head of the CIA, were hobnobbing with the Bangladeshis. To this Kissinger first said that Bush 'received somebody he did not know was Bangladeshi,' and then added that as far as the Bangladeshis were concerned 'the US doesn't do anything seriously and are marking time (whatever that means).' For fear of revealing something sensitive Kissinger attempted to end the discussion by saying, 'I didn't want to raise all these things on the phone.'[16]

Bhutto then talked about the resolution in the Security Council and wanted a joint position with China and the US. When pressed to state what Pakistan wanted in the resolution or how did it want China to vote on a 'ceasefire alone' resolution, Bhutto was not forthright.[17] With only five days to go before the Pakistan armed forces in East Pakistan were to formally lay down their arms, Yahya too was not sure what he wanted from the Security Council. Or at least that is what Bhutto seemed to suggest.

Reacting to the news that India had offered an assurance that it would not attack West Pakistan, Nixon and Kissinger discussed the position the Russians and the Chinese would adopt in the UN Security Council. Nixon was convinced that the Chinese and Russians were playing ball 'as a result of the President's ultimatum.'[18] The Chinese he thought would go along with the resolution tabled in the Security Council but would abstain from voting. Nixon wanted the Chinese to consult the Americans before making their position known. When Kissinger informed Nixon that the Chinese had told Bhutto (of what they would do in the Security Council), Nixon thought they shouldn't have and expressed his anger by lashing out at Bhutto.[19]

Gul Hassan reserves his utmost contempt for Bhutto although it was Bhutto who appointed him the chief of army staff; and after his abrupt

removal as the army chief, in which Ghulam Mustafa Jatoi and Ghulam
Mustafa Khar had a part to play in what would appear as his near
abduction, appointed him Pakistan's ambassador to Turkey. Gul Hassan
has difficulty in acknowledging that Bhutto was a popular leader and
prefers to ascribe the huge turnouts at Bhutto's public meetings prior to
the 1970 elections 'to the government agencies (who were) at his beck
and call'.[20] Since Bhutto held no office, the agencies must have been
directed by Yahya Khan. So where indeed were these agencies when
Bhutto continued to attract large crowds many years later, both before
and after the elections of 1977? And subsequently too, when Bhutto was
free for a brief period after being released by Ziaul Haq who had earlier
arrested him in the dragnet before overthrowing his government? Gul
Hassan has difficulty in understanding that popular leaders do command
a following, which military leaders have always craved but failed in
getting.

The pressure Bhutto put on Yahya to hand over power continued to
rankle with Gul Hassan. He threatened Bhutto's emissaries in his choicest
vocabulary—of which he had admittedly a vast store—against disturbing
peace in the West (having written off the East) and warned that 'Yahya
Khan or anyone else in his situation would not hesitate to employ all
means at his disposal to save Pakistan' but that 'he would use all means
at his disposal to save Pakistan.'[21] Having earlier launched the mission to
'save' East Pakistan, he now wanted to 'save' West Pakistan—from its own
people by keeping Bhutto out of power through military means.

Gul Hassan is furious at Bhutto for telecasting the surrender film
'several times'.[22] In reality it was screened only once and that too without
warning. Very few people actually saw it. One might be able to conceal
the truth from one's own people but one can't do so from the world at
large. Gul Hassan rues the fact that Bhutto was pleased at the humiliation
of the army and wanted to show people the film of the surrender at
Dhaka. To be honest, any right thinking person who saw great injustice
in the denial of the democratic rights to the Bengalis would have been
pleased to see the logical end of an unjust campaign of state terror.
Pakistanis might be the only people who did not see the shameful images
of the surrender that the military junta had brought upon the nation.

Aziz Ahmad, a very senior bureaucrat and minister of state for defence
in Bhutto's cabinet, is treated by Gul Hassan with similar contempt. To
the minister's daily meetings with the service chiefs, Gul Hassan started
off by sending his vice chief, then held him back and sent a brigadier and
finally an officer only of the rank of major. Instead of updating the war

book that Aziz Ahmad required, the generals chose to prepare contingency plans of taking over from Bhutto.[23] He even talks of his younger officers who would have sorted Bhutto out if he had created problems for the generals. What gross contempt for civilian authority! Bhutto is not alive to give his account because he was hanged (in 1979) much before Gul Hassan's book saw the light of day (in 1993).

Bhutto is accused by Gul Hassan of politicizing the army and thriving on mischief, hell bent on wrecking the army.[24] But this needed no effort on Bhutto's part because the army had already been politicized to the core. In 1954, General Ayub Khan as Commander-in-Chief of the Pakistan Army was given the additional charge of minister of defence. Accusing the masses of lapping up meaningless bombast, Gul Hassan berates leaders involved in politics. While referring to the refusal of the army to fire on the crowds in Lahore during the Pakistan National Alliance (PNA) movement, Gul Hassan says this was the first incident of disobedience of orders in the Pakistan Army. Unfortunately, that is not true. The Pakistan Army has refused to carry out legal orders of civilian authority by usurping power right from the time the first prime minister of Pakistan, Mr Liaquat Ali Khan, was murdered in a conspiracy. Why didn't the army refuse to fire on the Bengalis too? Was it because they were racially different or inferior? Or, was it to be in aid of military power?

The period 13 to 19 December 1971 is characterized by Gul Hassan as the most crucial. He terms 19 December 'the momentous and eventful day.' In his own words: '19 December was indeed a day that I will never forget—it was the worst I had ever experienced in all my long service. The discipline in the army was on the verge of snapping.'[25] No one in Pakistan knows to this day what momentous events took place on 13 or 19 December or in between—perhaps some rumbling of disgruntled junior officers in a few cantonments, which is all. It might have mercifully brought an end to the generals' rule, may be. Although it is the surrender at Dhaka on 16 December of that year which stands out as the day of national humiliation and ignominy which is etched on everybody's mind, Gul Hassan finds 19 December a more momentous event of his life.

NOTES

1. Gul Hassan Khan, op. cit., p. 419.
2. Ibid., p. 336.

3. US Department of State, op. cit. Telegram from US Consulate General (Dhaka) to the Department of State, 28 February 1971, Document 121. (http://www.state.gov/r/pa/ho/frus/nixon/e7txt/47238.htm).

4. Ibid., Memorandum Prepared in the Central Intelligence Agency, 9 December 1971, Document 170 (http://www.state.gov/r/pa/ho/frus/nixon/e7txt/50160.htm).

5. Gul Hassan Khan, op. cit., p. 283.

6. US Department of State, op. cit., Telegram from US Embassy (Islamabad) to the Department of State, 25 February 1971, Document 119. (http://www.state.gov/r/pa/ho/frus/nixon/e7txt/47236.htm).

7. Ibid., Telegram from US Consulate General (Dhaka) to the Department of State, 28 February 1971, Document 121. (http://www.state.gov/r/pa/ho/frus/nixon/e7txt/47238.htm).

8. Ibid., Conversation between Nixon and Kissinger, 9 December 1971, Document 171. (http://www.state.gov/r/pa/ho/frus/nixon/e7txt/48567.htm).

9. Ibid.

10. Ibid.

11. Ibid., Conversation among Nixon, Kissinger and William Rogers, 24 November 1971, Document 156. (http://www.state.gov/r/pa/ho/frus/nixon/e7txt/48559.htm).

12. Ibid., Conversation among Nixon, Kissinger and William Rogers, 24 November 1971, Document 156. (http://www.state.gov/r/pa/ho/frus/nixon/e7txt/48559.htm).

13. Ibid.

14. Ibid.

15. Ibid., Telephone Conversation between N.A.M. Raza and Bhutto with Kissinger and Haig, 11 December 1971, Document 175. (http://www.state.gov/r/pa/ho/frus/nixon/e7txt/49202.htm).

16. Ibid.

17. Ibid.

18. Ibid., Conversation between Nixon and Kissinger, 12 December 1971, Document 178, (http://www.state.gov/r/pa/ho/frus/nixon/e7txt/48571.htm).

19. Ibid.

20. Gul Hassan Khan, op. cit., p. 378.

21. Ibid.

22. Ibid.

23. Ibid., pp. 352-3.

24. Ibid., p. 364.

25. Ibid., p. 344.

21

Mujib's Role

Pakistanis are convinced that Mujib was responsible for the break-up of the country. They believe that Mujib was determined to create an independent Bangladesh and his six-point programme was nothing but a smokescreen for his real intention to break away from Pakistan. Kissinger, too, was aware of Mujib's political goals and although he believed Mujib was 'basically friendly towards the US' he felt that the Bengali leader 'may use independence as a negotiating ploy.'[1]

An unbiased assessment would suggest that Mujib was in fact keen on a political settlement and approached the US and other diplomats to play a peacemaking role to avoid an East–West Pakistan 'civil war'. On 10 March 1971 he sent a message to the US consul general in Dhaka to convey that he 'wanted very much to work out with Yahya some political settlement' and find a solution to the crisis 'along lines of confederation, with separate constitutions...and one army and foreign ministry.'[2]

Mujib had earlier stated this position when he met Ambassador Farland in Dhaka on 28 February 1971 saying 'he did not want separation but only a form of confederation.' He however alluded to an impression that the US 'had a reputation for deserting their friends when disagreeable problems' arose.[3] Mujib did not raise the matter of recognition of an independent Bangladesh, as he evidently did not intend separation.

The US report—'Contingency Study on Pakistan: East Pakistan Secession (NSSM-118)' dated 3 March 1971—said that Mujib and his party 'are believed to prefer to remain in a unified federal state of Pakistan with maximum provincial autonomy rather than secede.'[4] This nails the lie Yahya repeatedly told people that Mujib wanted East Pakistan to secede. It's another thing that Nixon disregarded the recommendations and assessments of his own administration and ran the foreign policy from the White House in order to reward Yahya for his role in opening up a channel to China and then facilitating the president's visit to Beijing.

The National Security Council's Interdepartmental Group for Near and South Asia prepared a paper (undated) for the Senior Review Group (SRG) in Washington to assess the crisis in East Pakistan and its impact on US relations with Pakistan. It also weighed US interests in South Asia and outlined policy options for dealing with the crisis. This was sent to Kissinger in his capacity as chairman of the NSC Review Group for use by the Senior Review Group at its 19 April meeting. The Paper clearly pointed out that 'The military's...action against the Awami League leadership has apparently converted what was once only autonomist sentiment into widespread demand for independence. Those killed on the days following March 25 are already viewed as martyrs to that demand.'[5] The Paper said the US historically assumed that their interest in regional stability was best served by a united Pakistan but that assumption 'now requires re-examination.'[6]

For the duration of this nine-month lurid drama Mujib was in the custody of Inter-Services Intelligence with no access to newspapers and radio and was hardly in a position to influence events. His incarceration ensured that whatever little hope there might have been for moderating his hot-headed supporters evaporated. So the responsibility for the break-up of Pakistan must lie elsewhere and with people who were free to do what they willed.

Mujib was arrested on 26 March 1971 and moved to West Pakistan where he was lodged in the Faisalabad jail and tried for 'treason'. He was taken to Rawalpindi in a jail van on 22 November 1971 after India had launched a full-scale attack on East Pakistan. Sultan M. Khan, who was Yahya's foreign secretary, says Mujib and Kamal Hussein 'had been kept in total isolation in prison and were unaware of developments in East Pakistan.'[7] According to Sultan Khan, who heard a secret tape-recording of the meeting between Mujib and Bhutto, the former was 'highly emotional and cried and laughed by turns.' Again and again he would ask Bhutto, 'Am I a free man? Can I go now?'[8]

Mujib was no traitor. It was his captors who ought to have been tried for this charge. He was a patriot and remained one until the end. Bangladesh became a reality only after he had been incarcerated. Following his release by what was then a truncated Pakistan he could not have disowned Bangladesh. According to Sultan Khan 'even if he had wished to modify this view he was no longer free to do so, extremists in the Awami League had taken control and they would have killed him rather than see him compromise on the issue of Bangladesh. A clash between the irresistible and the immovable thus became inevitable.'[9]

In fact Mujib should be credited for keeping his bitterness in control. He visited Pakistan for the Islamic Summit in 1974 and did not insist on the trial of the ninety-odd military personnel for war crimes although he had made a great public demand for that to take place.

Is this the profile of a secessionist that the military junta attempted to portray of Mujib in West Pakistan? The report of US Ambassador Joseph Farland on his meeting with Mujib in Dhaka on 28 February 1971 is significant as it provides insight into Mujib's position on various critical issues.

On his six-point programme Mujib told Farland he could not and would not compromise because he had made it 'a part of life of East Pakistan for a period of now some ten years'.[10] Mujib did expose a sordid aspect of his personality while telling Farland 'that the communists had killed three of his leaders and that he in turn had promised the communists that for every Awami League[r] killed, he would kill three of theirs and that "this we have done".'[11] Was Mujib perhaps admitting to murder?

Dilating on the subject of foreign aid, Mujib told Farland that Pakistan was then in a precarious financial situation with its foreign exchange reserves virtually exhausted but for Mujib 'this was a blessing in disguise' as this meant Pakistan 'did not have the financial power to subjugate his party.'[12] Mujib feared that if Pakistan succeeded in obtaining aid, say from Japan, whom it was begging, 'then they [the West Pakistanis] will bang us.' He also asked that friends of Bangladesh 'exert maximum influence on "those who would use the force of arms to keep my people in a colonial status",' adding 'that he had been a student of world affairs long enough to know the United States and other aid-contributing countries could exert this type of influence if they desired to do so.'[13]

The ambassador avoided a direct answer to a question from Mujib if the US and the consortium would support the 'rebuilding of Bangladesh.'[14] Understandably! The Americans were not interested in giving a fair deal to the Bengalis. They only had their strategic interests to safeguard. Those were not served by being squeamish about the democratic aspirations of the Bengalis.

Mujib was the creation of a political struggle and a democratic process although not unlike most of our other leaders he demonstrated an abysmal lack of respect for democratic principles. He ruled the new state of Bangladesh more or less like a dictator. He tried to establish a one-party rule and was planning to recruit his party office holders and others as District Governors which included MPs, civil servants, army officer, lawyers, politicians and tribal chiefs, another form of lateral entry far more blatant than the one introduced by Mr. Bhutto in Pakistan that allowed the latter to recruit all his cronies who could not pass any competitive examination. DCs as party office holders; I was told this by Irshadul Haq, my batch mate from Bangladesh. His plans were abruptly brought to an end when he and all members of his family who were present at home at the time were brutally murdered by officers of his own army. There is no dearth of people here who ascribe Mujib's tragic fate to divine justice. If divine punishment was as certain as its advocates believe then there are a large number of candidates deserving such punishment, Yahya being no exception—yet he drew full pension and benefits so long as he lived, and was buried with military honours when he died.

NOTES

1. Department of State, op. cit., Memorandum from Kissinger to Nixon, 22 February 1971, Document 118. (http://www.state.gov/r/pa/ho/frus/nixon/e7txt/47235.htm).
2. Ibid., Telegram from US Consulate General in Dhaka to Department of State, 10 March 1971, Document 124. (http://www.state.gov/r/pa/ho/frus/nixon/e7txt/47240. htm).
3. Ibid., Telegram from US Consulate General in Dhaka to Department of State, 28 February 1971, Document 121, (http://www.state.gov/r/pa/ho/frus/nixon/ e7txt/47238.htm).
4. Ibid., Contingency Study on Pakistan: East Pakistan Secession (NSSM 118), 3 March 1971, Document 123. (http://www.state.gov/r/pa/ho/frus/nixon/e7txt/47239.htm).
5. Ibid., Paper Prepared by the (US) National Security Council's Interdepartmental Group for Near East and South Asia, undated, Document 132. (http://www.state.gov/r/pa/ ho/frus/nixon/e7txt/50130.htm).
6. Ibid.
7. Sultan M. Khan, *Memoirs and Recollections of a Pakistani Diplomat,* The London Centre for Pakistan Studies, 1997, p. 406.
8. Ibid.
9. Ibid., p. 403.
10. Department of State, op. cit., Telegram from US Consulate General in Dhaka to Department of State, 28 February 1971, Document 121, (http://www.state.gov/r/pa/ ho/frus/nixon/e7txt/47238.htm).
11. Ibid.
12. Ibid.
13. Ibid.
14. Ibid.

22

Can Ayub be Blamed?

Yahya's defenders oftentimes blame Ayub's decade-long dictatorial rule for the eventual break-up of Pakistan. Ayub may have contributed to the Bengalis' sense of betrayal and estrangement yet he cannot be blamed for the final act of an eternally inebriated, ambitious Yahya in pushing East Pakistan out of the federation. Nevertheless, the *Diaries of Field Marshal Mohammad Ayub Khan 1966–1972*[1] do provide confirmation that Ayub was a bigoted man who had utter contempt for the Bengalis.

Ayub was Pakistan's first military ruler and must be held responsible for derailing the constitutional evolution of the country and thwarting development of its democratic institutions. *Diaries* expose Ayub's hollow intellect and character, and reveal his lack of understanding, narrow-mindedness, bigotry and egotistic self-esteem—all reflective of a personality that is both bizarre and frightening.

A few extracts from his 'pearls of wisdom' appear in the following paragraphs. Ayub could have been spared the embarrassment if his progeny had not undertaken the intellectual burden of publishing his private thoughts which appropriately should have remained confined to his diaries lying in the family heirloom.

It appears that Ayub read very few books but he claims to have read *The Anatomy of Greatness* by Mrs P.T. Lanine, an American writer. When Mrs P.T. Lanine asked him who had the greatest influence on his thought and action, Ayub named two individuals: his father and the late His Highness the Aga Khan. Although he claims to have met many leading personalities from different walks of life[2] he was not impressed by any of them.

Ayub was tormented by Pakistan's problems and believed these could be solved by introducing socialism but this needed leadership of a very high calibre. 'I don't see it emerging in this country. He (Gohar Ayub, his son and former captain of the Pakistan Army) said it will emerge, and from the Army, but it will take one or two more martial laws.'[3] Three more martial laws later Pakistan is in a bigger hole with little signs of things improving anytime soon and is still digging.

Referring to the politicians' contrivances Ayub says that civil authority can become supreme only if the politicians run the country well. That means never. 'If not, the Army has perforce to step in. This is an inescapable law and is the experience of all emerging countries.'[4] According to him the army is the only disciplined institution in the country with a nationalistic and patriotic outlook, and that it is responsible for both internal and external defence of the country. With that kind of an assumption of the military's role how could one expect constitutional evolution in this unfortunate country?

In an entry on 12 November 1969, eight months after Yahya overthrew him, he refers to himself as a great man whose services have been lost to Pakistan.[5] Was he indeed a great leader or simply a megalomaniac completely out of breath?

Once out of power, Ayub realized that the army had feet of clay. In a contradiction of his own conviction, Ayub finally acknowledged the growing resentment of the people against the army. 'The Army was being regarded as an occupation force and [an] instrument of oppression.'[6] He made this remark to an un-named person who said that Yahya suffered from constant fear that as a result of a popular upsurge he (Ayub) might stage a comeback. In his retirement he seemed to have few visitors—either people did not have time for a retired 'saviour' or they were afraid lest Yahya take offence. Ayub seemed to have forgotten that he was the man responsible for leading the army into politics. His views underwent a change because he was then no longer the army chief and was looking in vain for a popular upsurge to restore him to power.

Ayub did not understand even the basics of democracy and could not visualize the natural emergence of the Bengalis as a majority in a democratic dispensation. Referring to this possibility he is horrified and says such an eventuality would be disastrous that 'the Bengali majority will be the arbiter of the future of the country.'[7]

In his diary entry of 29 January 1970 he talks of the visit of veteran politician Mahmoud Haroon who amongst other things told Ayub that 'Sindhis were politically most unreliable. They have been known to have gone back on their signed pledges on the Quran. Bhutto is not an exception.'[8] Ayub's implicit acceptance of such wild generalizations should be enough to frighten an ordinary citizen of this country.

While ruminating over economic and food issues Ayub gives vent to his frustration saying that East Pakistan was 'a millstone around our neck. Their (Bengalis) main and constant effort was to grab whatever they could.'[9] Ayub blames them for 'demanding two million tons of food' in spite of so much extra outlay on imports for East Pakistan. In making such remarks, Ayub failed to cognize that East Pakistan was earning more foreign exchange than West Pakistan and much of the industrialization in the western wing had been financed by earnings from East Pakistan. Ayub wonders how the two wings could stay together because he felt the real problem was that the Bengalis did not want to work but only wanted solutions to their political issues.

Ayub was still president when he wrote (on 15 December 1967) that the Bengalis were 'by nature treacherous and unreliable, but they have faith in me. Even the opposition seem to think that their personal safety is due to me. What would have happened in the last war (1965) if I were not at the helm of the affairs?'[10]

Ayub noted in his diary (1 October 1968) that he wrote to the governors of East and West Pakistan on the importance of high-quality education and good management of the student community. Commending his own model of education Ayub said the same

> is necessary throughout the country but more so in East Pakistan. There the immigrants (referring to Mohajirs generally called Biharis) feel for Muslim unity but the Shudhra converts (meaning Bengalis), who are indigenous, composing the bulk of the population, and especially those who have got the smattering of education, have a great urge to revert to Hinduism by the language and customs if not temple.[11]

Referring to racial and cultural differences between the Bengalis and the people of West Pakistan which resulted in tension and hostility, he came to the profound conclusion that Pakistan could not exist without a strong centre—a euphemism for control by the West Pakistani elites. For him 'it is obvious that Bengali thinking of autonomy and eventual separation is common to politicians of most shades.'[12]

On 8 December 1970, a day after the general elections, Ayub noted with horror the prospect of a coalition between Mujib and Bhutto describing it '…most dangerous and disastrous for the country as the former would seek almost separation while Bhutto would get busy in forming cells in the army etc.' Ayub was pained at the outcome of the elections and wrote that 'Mujeeb and Bhutto's victory would have been of no great concern if they were normal people,' wondering how could the public put the fate of the country in the hands of such persons. He probably held Bhutto in slightly better esteem, as may be inferred from this: 'One (Bhutto) is educated and sophisticated; the other (Mujib) is an uneducated and uncouth political goonda.'[13]

Ayub felt he was eminently qualified to analyse the Bengali social and cultural milieu and as a result his profound observations on Mujib were that he:

...may be exploiting parochialism but its causes are probably much deeper. The Bengalis have a long history of exploitation by outsiders. Their hot and humid climate puts them at a physical disadvantage and the marshy nature of terrain with poor communication make[s] them exclusive, mother attached and inward looking. No wonder they are secretive, unsocial and unpredictable.[14]

This and a few other remarks on the Bengalis by Ayub are revealing: 'Talking of Governor Monem Khan, though a very good man, [he] knows nothing about economics, development or higher administration.' One wonders why had Ayub appointed him in the first place and then suffered him for so long? Then he talks of Dr Huda, a Bengali civil servant and describes people like him 'limited, bigoted, provincialist.' Ayub Khan goes on to say, 'it does not require a prophet to predict the future of East Pakistan.'[15] But what could be worse for the people of East Pakistan than to be in perpetual bondage to the West Pakistani military elites? If Ayub could predict the future of East Pakistan, why didn't he take steps to avert it and address the grievances of the Bengalis by allowing them some autonomy?

Ayub was deeply troubled by the problems confronting Pakistan and wrote on 7 September 1967:

There are two things that concern my mind continuously: (1) Hindu India's intentions against Pakistan and (2) Frustrating tendencies of behaviour of East Pakistanis. God has been very unkind to us in giving the sort of neighbours [India] and compatriots [Bengalis] we have. We could not think of a worst combination. Hindus and Bengalis. I told Khawaja Shahabuddin [minister of information 1965–9 in Ayub's cabinet] not to lose heart. If worst comes to the worst, we shall not hesitate to fight a relentless battle against the disruptionists in East Pakistan. Rivers of blood will flow if need be, unhappily. We will arise to save our crores of Muslims from Hindu slavery.[16]

His successor Yahya received training in the same military academies as his benefactor and followed his script both in concept and compliance.

Yahya implemented Ayub's political philosophy and caused 'rivers of blood' to flow to 'save crores of Muslims from Hindu slavery.' Yahya may or may not have succeeded in achieving the goal of saving the Muslims from Hindu slavery but he certainly helped in liberating the Bengalis from the occupation of the Pakistan military.

Ayub was of the view that the Bengalis were not thankful for the blessing of freedom 'unknown in their history...Any normal people should have recognized and rejoiced at this blessing.'[17] He noted that they had been exploited by caste Hindus, Muslim rulers and even the British and it was only after the creation of Pakistan that they received the blessing of freedom and attained equal status in society. If Ayub's dictatorship and a quarter of a century of dominance by West Pakistani elites was 'freedom' then he was perhaps right. It didn't occur to Ayub that he was the antithesis of the whole concept of freedom because of the tightly controlled dictatorship he ran.

Ayub hated everything about Bengalis, even their love for their own language which had given them the only poet laureate of the subcontinent. According to him they had to have love for the Urdu language to deserve his affection and pass muster. 'I am surprised at the Bengali outlook. They have cut themselves off from Muslim culture through abhorrence of the Urdu language...making themselves vulnerable to Hindu culture.'[18]

Ayub comes across as a rabid racist. He describes the Bengalis as 'shudhra converts' with a great urge to revert to Hinduism by adopting its language and customs: 'Saving them from serfdom is a supreme task in East Pakistan.' This concern of Ayub to protect their religion as well as freedom placed the Bengalis in a peculiar position of personal obligation to him. He quotes the Nawab of Kalabagh narrating what his cousin, the Sardar of Kot Fateh Khan, said in 1946 at Delhi: '...what this man Jinnah (mark the disrespect shown towards the Father of the Nation) is doing, he is wanting us to go under the shudhras of Bengal.' Ayub says he was annoyed when he was first told this story but after seeing Bhashani and Mujib, he was convinced that they (the Bengalis) indeed were shudhras and felt the danger was real.[19]

Ayub intensely hated India. His aversion for the Indians was no less than that for the Bengalis. He thought the Indians were waiting for an opportunity to take police action against East Pakistan in order to annex it. But his forecast based on limited understanding proved wildly wrong. India took full military action (and not just police action) and did not annex East Pakistan—instead it liberated the country from the clutches of a ruthless military dictatorship. The people of East Pakistan finally

became masters of their own destiny but only after much loss of life and
destruction of property.

Ayub detested all his opponents and characterized them interchangably
as communists or anti-Pakistani or both. He thought Mujib, G.M. Syed,
the Baloch Sirdars, the Red Shirts and the communists were all anti-
Pakistan elements. You were either with him or against him. A ruler with
these views and harbouring such distorted notions about 56 per cent of
Pakistan's population cannot be expected to unite the nation. In an entry
dated 12 August 1970, Ayub writes that his son-in-law, Mian Gul
Aurangzeb (for whom Ayub doesn't seem to have much affection),
reported on return from Dhaka that:

> ...when Yayha landed in Dhaka, he was dead drunk; he had ostensibly gone
> there to supervise flood relief work, but in reality was busy relaxing with
> women and drinking. He was surrounded by women even when going down
> on river trips; Mujib had a vast following. He would come with big majority;
> there was no sign of anti West Pakistan feelings. People were talking in terms
> of one country.[20]

This assessment clearly did not sit well with Ayub's bizarre notions of the
Bengalis and their commitment to Pakistan, and so he wryly comments:
'...this, of course, depends on what sort of people he met.'[21] I have known
Mian Gul Aurangzeb for several years and have seen him speak his mind
without fear or favour. Even though Ayub did not think much of his
son-in-law and dismissed his report on the Bengali sentiment, in my
assessment Aurangzeb's impressions were substantially correct.

In an entry dated 14 August 1970, Ayub quotes one Asghar Ali Shah
from Rawalpindi (not a public figure) telling him that the Yahya
administration was terrified of Mujib's popularity and was anxious to
postpone elections in the hope that he might lose ground.[22] On 26 August
1970, he notes that 'Yahya goes around saying that the politicians had no
business claiming credit for my removal. It was he who had given me the
push.'[23] This rings true and people who underestimate Yahya's ambitions
should take note. There is a widespread belief carefully cultivated in
Pakistan that Yahya was not in control of his faculties and whatever
happened during his watch could either be blamed on his advisers, both
military and civil, or the failure of his inebriated faculties.

When after the surrender people blamed Ayub for handing over to
Yahya, he notes in his entry of 17 December 1971 '...what else could I
do? He (Yahya) was the C-in-C of the army. I am told alcoholism changes
a man's personality.'[24] This is an admission of complete helplessness in the

dying days of his presidency and reflective of a failure to correctly read Yahya, attributing the man's despicable conduct to alcoholism.

In the diary entry of 26 March 1971, Ayub reflects on Yahya's character saying he 'is a wily and cunning man and is an expert at concealing his intentions.' Then without naming the person whom he quotes Ayub writes that 'Mujibur Rehman has shown willingness to sign any constitutional arrangement the government wants.'[25] If what was reported to Ayub was indeed true, it brings into focus Yahya's intentions of creating a crisis by taking precipitate military action.

On 1 December 1970, Ayub noted that Yahya and his associates were hoping that the elections would return mushroom political parties to the National Assembly who would not be able to frame a constitution within the 120 days allowed under the Legal Framework Order and would thus turn to Yahya to give one to them.[26]

The diary entry of 28 September 1970 records the remarks of Khawaja Shahabuddin, a respected and seasoned Muslim League politician from Dhaka, who said that the army would attempt to obstruct the process of constitution-making to strengthen Yahya's hands.[27] Conspiracies by Yahya and his cohorts to deny power to the people were afoot. Coming just ahead of the general elections originally scheduled for October and rescheduled for December on account of the cyclone that hit East Pakistan, Shahabuddin's warnings was prescient.

On 27 November 1970, Ayub noted that Mujib attacked the regime for its lack of sympathy for the cyclone affected province and an inadequate relief effort for the victims and worried that failure to hold elections in time would be taken as a sure indication of the regime's reluctance to give autonomy to the Bengalis.[28]

In his view '7th December 1970 (the day general elections were held) may well prove to be the darkest day in the history of Pakistan and an unmitigated tragedy.'[29] He abhorred elections and the political leadership that emerged in consequence. Only a dictator who ruled Pakistan for over a decade could characterize elections—the only means of ascertaining people's wishes—an 'unmitigated tragedy'. No wonder he avoided them like the plague—he thwarted the first general elections which were to be held under the 1956 constitution by imposing martial law a few months before they were due, and then held fake elections including a referendum to have himself and a rubber-stamp assembly 'elected' by 80,000 nominated Basic Democrats.

On 23 December 1970, Ayub records that he has started to read the *Pakistan Observer*, a newspaper published from Dhaka, in order to understand the views of the Bengalis.[30] It took him a good twelve years since seizing power to recognize the need to be aware of Bengali aspirations. It's a sad commentary on Pakistan's political culture that a man ruled the country for a decade without in all this time considering it necessary to understand the views, needs and hopes of over half the nation.

In his diary entry of 12 January 1971, Ayub notes 'Yahya has decided to visit Larkana for a shoot and accept the hospitality of Bhutto.'[31] This was a very crucial visit because it sounded the death knell of a united Pakistan; it was here that Yahya decided to subvert the verdict of the people given on 7 December 1970. In his diary entry of 22 January, Ayub notes that Yahya's meeting with Bhutto 'was designed to explore the possibility of using him against Mujibur Rehman.'[32] On 29 January Ayub writes that the discussion between Yahya and Bhutto at Larkana was on the planned separation of East Pakistan, with West Pakistan then adopting a draft constitution to form a government with Yahya as president and Bhutto as prime minister. Ayub empathized with Yahya for the situation he had dug himself into because he was a comrade in arms but described Bhutto as a mischief monger because he was a politician. Comparing the two he wondered '...fancy Yahya Khan identifying himself with him [Bhutto].'[33]

Writing about Bhutto and Mujib, Ayub ruefully remarks that those who created Pakistan must be turning in their graves, lamenting at the renegades who succeeded them.[34] But the creators of Pakistan would have viewed Ayub with even greater horror because he was the biggest calamity visited upon Pakistan. This obvious truth clearly eluded him.

Yahya—a renegade according to Ayub—was heard saying that if Francisco Franco could rule Spain for thirty-five years why could he (Yahya) not do the same in Pakistan.[35] The generals nurse such grandiose notions about their capabilities and God-given right to rule that they turn blind to their own shortcomings. Franco is a widely reviled dictator and should not be a role model except to those on the lunatic fringe.

In his diary entry of 3 April 1971, Ayub talks of Mujib's six points and says 'in reality they are not six points but only one point. They [the Bengalis] had no intention of making a Muslim nation and living with West Pakistan.' Ayub avers that Bengali nationalism took birth from the day Pakistan came into being, and that Muslim nationalism was regarded a deadly poison for it. He views the agitation on the question of language as only a camouflage for such feelings and a means to show Bengal's hostility for West Pakistan and non-Bengali Muslims.[36] I would be surprised if Ayub ever read the six points. How could he? He started reading East Pakistani newspapers after he was overthrown.

On 6 April 1971, when East Pakistan was in the throes of a military crackdown, Ayub takes notice of the long letter of protest written by Soviet President Nikolai Podgorny to Yahya about the situation in East Pakistan; the letter was polite but according to Ayub it towed the Indian line.[37] Ayub too failed to appreciate that Podgorny's advice was well intended and timely and could have saved both Yahya and Pakistan. Under similar circumstances Ayub would have acted no different from Yahya except that he possibly might not have ordered such mass-scale murders.

On 30 November 1971, Ayub makes a one-line entry: 'Indira Gandhi, in a show of Brahamanic arrogance, has invited Pakistan to withdraw its troops from Bengal.'[38] Ayub was out of touch with reality and unable to recognize that it would become increasingly difficult for Pakistan to extricate itself from an already difficult and dangerous situation. Inevitability, just sixteen days later Pakistani troops in East Pakistan surrendered to the Bangladesh–India joint command having lost the opportunity of withdrawing. This national humiliation could have been averted if the opportunity offered by Indira Gandhi had been accepted.

Ayub notes on 11November 1971 that a young army officer brought to the CMH Rawalpindi for psychiatric treatment had supposedly killed nearly 14,000 people (in East Pakistan).[39] This gives lie to claims by the military that it committed no crimes in East Pakistan

A day before the army finally surrendered, Ayub noted that if the Bengalis wanted separation, 'it could have easily been obtained in a peaceful manner'[40] little realizing that Yahya and his military were not looking for a peaceful resolution and under no circumstances were prepared to offer this option to the Bengalis.

In the entry of 21 December 1971 Ayub noted that 'in spite of Yahya's betrayal and disloyalty with me I feel sorry for him and the manner and circumstances under which he had to go'[41] although in an earlier entry (16 January 1971) he had been forthright in saying that 'he (Yahya) is utterly shameless, lacking in dignity and self respect.'[42] Oddly enough Ayub shows no comparable regret for the loss of East Pakistan, the surrender of the armed forces or the national humiliation!

Ayub had some very unkind words for almost everyone. Based on information from an unnamed but reliable person Ayub charges Bhutto of making money (10 April 1972). He doesn't spare the Quaid-i-Azam either—referring to Bhutto's ambitions to grab every job, he wrote, 'I suppose he wants to follow the footsteps of the Quaid-i-Azam who was a governor general, head of cabinet (not true), the Muslim League President and the leader in the Assembly.'[43]

NOTES

1. Ayub Khan, op. cit.
2. Ibid., p. 256.
3. Ibid., p. 339.
4. Ibid., p. 349.
5. Ibid., p. 339.
6. Ibid., p. 393.
7. Ibid., p. 341.
8. Ibid., p. 360.
9. Ibid., p. 390.
10. Ibid., p. 188.
11. Ibid., p. 267.
12. Ibid., p. 415.
13. Ibid., p. 419.
14. Ibid., p. 364.
15. Ibid., p. 187.
16. Ibid., p. 145.
17. Ibid., p. 210.
18. Ibid.
19. Ibid., p. 312.
20. Ibid., pp. 402-3.
21. Ibid., p. 403.
22. Ibid.
23. Ibid., p. 406.
24. Ibid., p. 507.
25. Ibid., p. 470.
26. Ibid., p. 417.
27. Ibid., p. 407.
28. Ibid., p. 414.
29. Ibid., p. 420.
30. Ibid., p. 429.
31. Ibid., p. 440.
32. Ibid., p. 443.
33. Ibid., p. 444.
34. Ibid., p. 445.
35. Ibid., p. 449.
36. Ibid., p. 473.
37. Ibid., p. 475.
38. Ibid., p. 501.
39. Ibid., pp. 498-9.
40. Ibid., p. 506.
41. Ibid.
42. Ibid.
43. Ibid.

PART III

23

Last Days before the Break-up

When the situation in East Pakistan showed little signs of improving and India's interference was getting increasingly overt and intrusive Yahya sought help from the United States. On 15 November, a month before the actual break-up, Pakistan's Foreign Secretary Sultan Khan met Nixon and Kissinger. He wanted US help to get India off Pakistan's back. After briefing Sultan Khan on the conversation he had had with Indian Prime Minister Gandhi, Nixon said that the president (Yahya) was a good friend of his and Kissinger's, but 'some of the nuts in our own party (the Republicans)—soft heads...have completely bought the Indian line.'[1] This was his way of saying that unlike Yahya he was not the absolute ruler but had to contend with domestic public opinion. The 'Indian line' so derisively dismissed by Nixon was in fact a demand that bloodshed in East Pakistan must stop and that power should be transferred to the majority party. 'Soft heads' was a contemptuous reference to the intellectuals and pro-democracy elements who saw merit in the Indian stance.

Nixon suggested the only sensible and correct course of action for Pakistan:

> This is one of those terrible problems that, frankly, must be solved by a political solution; it must not be solved by force...We will try to restrain to the extent that we have influence (on) the Indians...We don't control the Indians. That is accurate...I would like to be totally honest.'[2]

This was a clear message from Nixon that much as he would have liked to help there was little he could do to deflect India and that Pakistan better seek a political solution. But the country's foreign secretary was equally helpless as he had no control over either the domestic or foreign policy. Sultan Khan could do little to change the course of history even if he disagreed with Yahya and his policies or privately agreed with the US understanding of the crisis.

On 22 November 1971, India attacked East Pakistan. Early the next morning, Secretary of State William Rogers and Kissinger spoke on the telephone and talked about the US response to the attack. Although there were differences between the two, Kissinger characterized them as less of substance and more of nuance. He thought 'there is a shade of difference between the State's and President's view. He [Nixon] would like to tilt towards Pakistan and not India and your people go the other way.' Rogers rejected the notion that there were differences and proposed that the two meet the president together 'so he knows my position.' Kissinger's own position throughout the crisis remained close to that of President Nixon.[3]

On 24 November 1971, Nixon met with Rogers and Kissinger to review the crisis and examine US options. It was Roger's view that militarily Yahya's position was extremely weak, to which Nixon added, 'He will be demolished there (East Pakistan).' In the end, Nixon did not want to take the heat 'for a miserable war that we (the US) had nothing to do with.'[4] But surprisingly the US administration did little to encourage Yahya to find a political solution to the crisis although at that point it was perhaps already too late.

Rogers did suggest that 'we should engage in the maximum diplomatic efforts to do everything we can to caution restraint on both sides (Pakistan and India) at the highest level' and should continue to be very close to Yahya, with whom 'our relations are very good.' But Rogers cautioned against trying to 'mastermind a political solution.'[5]

Acknowledging that the US did not have leverage over India, the three discussed the option of taking the issue to the United Nations General Assembly or the Security Council and the votes that the Americans could garner. Nixon was however categorical that the US 'shouldn't push the UN game if there is any feeling that it might be to the detriment of Pakistan.' Rogers was of the opinion that the USSR was trying to restrain India but Nixon, always suspicious of the Russians, had doubts and felt they were 'not (trying) hard enough.' Kissinger was quick to agree with the president and said India was trying to reduce West Pakistan to the status of 'something like Afghanistan' so that it then becomes 'the only significant country' in the subcontinent.[6]

Rogers said that Yahya needed to survive through December 'because he has got plans made for this new Constitution to go into effect. If we can keep peace there for a couple of months then he may feel that he is on the road to a political solution.'[7] The Americans were naïve to expect that Yahya who had failed up till then to reach a political settlement would in two months time succeed in giving a new Constitution that would be acceptable to all political parties and diminish the Bengali resolve to break free from the shackles of West Pakistani colonial rule.

On 26 November, just twenty days before the surrender, Nixon and Kissinger spoke on the telephone to discuss the situation in the subcontinent. Both were pleased with an editorial in *The New York Times* which Kissinger described as 'a scorcher against India.' By then US aid to Pakistan had been cut off but Nixon wanted to make a distinction between India's aggression and Pakistan's military crackdown in East Pakistan. He asked that Pakistan be informed that the punitive action against them was taken 'because of their internal conduct not for their external conduct.'[8]

The crisis, in the meanwhile, progressed to an inevitable denouement. Suppressing people and forcing millions to flee to neighbouring India was described by Nixon as Pakistan's 'internal conduct' even though it evoked worldwide condemnation. Nixon was obviously angered over India's act of 'busting into Pakistan.' But how could Pakistan's military crackdown on its own people be deserving of any less condemnation than India's act of busting into Pakistan? Public opinion in the US ran counter to presidential preferences but in defiance of domestic pressures Nixon resorted to every trick to stand by his friend, Yahya.

On 6 December, three days after hostilities with India broke out on Pakistan's western front, Nixon and Rogers discussed the situation in the subcontinent and the bleak prospects facing Pakistan. 'This conflict,' the president said, 'was apparently inevitable.' Terming it unfortunate for having come at the wrong time (as if there is a right time for hostilities to break out between two sovereign countries), the president said, 'I certainly wouldn't want to be in the position of the Indians trying to take West Pakistan.' Rogers expressed the hope that Pakistan would do some good in Kashmir 'and make some offsetting gains' to which the president said 'that would be a good trade.' Rogers thought 'geographically it would make a lot more sense if they could have Kashmir and...' (lose East Pakistan!)[9] But in the event we lost both. They had a poor understanding of the material and moral strength of the Pakistan Army. Pakistan's military, long used to meddling in politics, had neither the professional capability nor the appetite to fight India. The Americans seemed interested in both countries ending up hurting each other without either gaining an overwhelming advantage over the other. The US policy was reduced to pathetically observing events from the outside hoping that Pakistan would be able to take Kashmir by force.

NOTES

1. Department of State, op. cit., Conversation among Nixon, Kissinger and Sultan Khan, 15 November 1971, Document 154 (http://www.state.gov/r/pa/ho/frus/nixon/e7txt/48558.htm).
2. Ibid.
3. Ibid., Telephone Conversation between William Rogers and Kissinger, 23 November 1971, Document 155 (http://www.state.gov/r/pa/ho/frus/nixon/e7txt/49193.htm).
4. Ibid., Conversation among Nixon, Kissinger and William Rogers, 24 November 1971, Document 156 (http://www.state.gov/r/pa/ho/frus/nixon/e7txt/48559.htm).
5. Ibid.
6. Ibid.
7. Ibid.
8. Ibid., Telephone Conversation between Nixon and Kissinger, 26 November 1971, Document 157 (http://www.state.gov/r/pa/ho/frus/nixon/e7txt/50145.htm).
9. Ibid., Conversation between Nixon and William Rogers, 6 December 1971, Document 161 (http://www.state.gov/r/pa/ho/frus/nixon/e7/48650.htm).

24

Role of the US

The infamous 'tilt' towards Pakistan was the substance of the US administration's policy to resolve the crisis in the subcontinent brewing for at least a year, since elections in December 1970, although public opinion in the United States as well as the Congress was strongly opposed to it.

The United States did not play any significant role before, during or even after the crisis. It essentially mouthed some inanities and lent firm diplomatic support to Yahya by characterizing the situation as Pakistan's internal matter. In his memorandum to President Nixon (22 February 1971) on the 'Situation in Pakistan', Kissinger reiterates that the 'US position has been that we support the unity of Pakistan.' This was an euphemism for permitting a military dictator to crush the democratic aspirations of the Bengalis.[1]

As early as March 1971 the Americans started to feel that there was a possibility of imminent separation of the two wings of Pakistan. In order to assess US interests and policy options in the eventuality of this occurring, a report ('Contingency Study on Pakistan—East Pakistan Secession: NSSM-118' dated 3 March 1971) was prepared for consideration by the Administration's Senior Review Group. This study offered three alternatives to the US government: continue to support the independence, unity and integrity of Pakistan, recognize the rising sense of nationalism in East Pakistan and adjust policies accordingly, and finally, to privately urge Yahya Khan to make every effort to reach an accommodation with Mujib.[2]

The second and third options offered the best hope for averting a bigger crisis but Nixon and Kissinger were determined to avoid them because they were both more concerned about supporting Yahya than resolving the situation; the ultimate result of this short-sighted policy was a disgraceful end to Yahya's career. Even though the study highlighted the rising sense of nationalism in East Pakistan, Nixon failed to recognize that a political settlement with the Awami League was necessary to preserve the integrity and unity of Pakistan. A share in governance to the Bengalis and some titular role for Yahya would have saved both a united Pakistan as well as Yahya.

The study acknowledged that American influence over events in Pakistan was limited. But so was the understanding of the American administration of the dynamics of political currents. The study's assumption that 'Yahya is doing his utmost to effect an accommodation between the two contending forces' was untrue and showed the disconnect between perception and reality. Yahya was doing precisely the opposite. Following on the false assumption that Yahya was doing everything to bring about a compromise between the two political leaders—Mujib and Bhutto—the study said that any US effort 'to urge compromise could be resented as unwarranted interference in Pakistan's internal affairs.'[3] Aware of the US influence over Pakistan, Mujib tried to seek its help in breaking the stalemate. But because the American president was not prepared to compromise Yahya's position the US ignored Mujib's plea for help and virtually followed a policy of drift and paralysis.

It was early March 1971 and Yahya had already created deep resentment in East Pakistan by postponing the National Assembly session yet the study believed it was very unlikely that 'West Pakistan would intervene militarily in East Pakistan to attempt to preserve the unity of Pakistan by force.'[4] But the study did make an allowance and said that 'Despite the unlikelihood of military intervention, we nonetheless should plan for it on a contingency basis on the theory that an irrational action is always possible.' In the event that an 'irrational action' was taken, the Contingency Paper listed some possible responses, i.e., (1) take no action; (2) urge West Pakistan to cease military action; (3) consult with India regarding mutual interests and urge it not to intervene militarily; (4) and finally (if West Pakistan and possibly India were to intervene militarily) use the threat of sanctions.[5]

It is clear that the US government chose to accept the first option and allowed itself to be overtaken by events. In all fairness to the Contingency Paper it did recommend the second and third options but Nixon's overriding consideration of not doing anything that could compromise Yahya paralysed the American government into inaction which remained a silent spectator in the whole sordid affair. As it turned out both countries took 'irrational' action—Yahya by arresting Mujib and ordering a military crackdown in East Pakistan and India by its military intervention.

Fortunately for the rest of the world this irrationality remained confined to the subcontinent.

That the US did not see the 25 March operation coming must be attributed to a massive failure of its intelligence. People in Pakistan had seen all the telltale signs. Flights full of military personnel had started arriving at Dhaka via Sri Lanka during the period between 1 and 25 March while Yahya kept up the charade of holding talks with political leaders, particularly Mujib. Although Yahya 'spoke in a tone of despair of "Blood and Chaos" which might ensue' if the impasse between Mujib and Bhutto was not broken,[6] it should be pointed out that the impasse was between the military and the politicians, and by extension the people they represented, and not between Mujib and Bhutto. Yahya and his military establishment were apprehensive of Bhutto's party, not the least because of his socialist leanings, but they were more averse to the right-leaning Mujib.

The Contingency Study also failed to anticipate India's military intervention, saying it was 'doubtful that India would send troops into East Pakistan since West Pakistan forces there are so weak as to make it unnecessary to take that rather great risk of escalation.'[7] This proved completely wrong on two counts. For one, it became necessary for India to intervene and end the crisis in East Pakistan because it was being burdened with a large number of refugees entailing a huge cost to its economy. Second, Pakistan's military had enough lethal power to be able to crush the Bengalis and sustain the cost of insurgency for a little longer than the study's estimate. The assessment was however right to the extent that military intervention by China was 'even more unlikely'. But in what may be considered the essence of US policy, the study recommended that 'we should avoid direct military involvement, recognizing that the area is not a vital security interest to the US.'[8]

In April 1971, a Paper was prepared by the National Security Council's Interdepartmental Group for Near and South Asia to assess the crisis in East Pakistan and its impact on US relations with Pakistan. This Paper, which was sent for use by the Senior Review Group (SRG) in its meeting on 19 April, presented three basic strategies which it said the US might adopt: one, a relative hands-off policy; second, the use of selective influence; and third, an all-out effort to bring an early end to hostilities. Assessing China's major interest in South Asia, the Paper estimated that China wanted to ensure 'there be no major military threat on its borders' and in this context it (China) regarded 'Pakistan as the most effective counterforce to India.'[9] It seems more than China, the West in general and the US in particular are better served by the geopolitics of a divided subcontinent, as so convincingly brought out in Narendra Singh Sarila's *In the Shadow of the Great Game: The Untold Story of India's Partition* (HarperCollins Publishers India, 2005).

In the same month (April 1971), the CIA also prepared a study to assess 'the present and prospective state of the Pakistani civil war, the role of India and other powers, and the outlook for Pakistan's two components—if the Bengali uprising should be put down, and if it should succeed.'[10] The CIA study said that the refusal of military leaders to honour the election results 'and their attempt to terrorize the Bengalis into submission...have almost certainly ended any general desire in East Bengal to see the Pakistani union continue.'[11] In assessing India's incentives in aid of the Bengalis, the study said that

> whatever the extent of Indian support to the Bengalis, the West Pakistanis will face increasingly serious difficulties in East Bengal. The area is principally riverine. With the advent of the monsoon in late May or early June, there will be extensive flooding which will further isolate the Pakistani Army in a few urban strong-points.[12]

In consequence it was estimated that the army would be reduced to maintaining a tenuous hold on a half dozen or so places that could be reached by helicopters and 'conduct occasional forays into nearby areas.'[13] While this uneasy control could last for months and conceivably years, the political and economic pressures could force the military leadership to change strategy. The economic costs of a 'civil war' are high.

The CIA also estimated that China could increase deliveries of military equipment to Pakistan but would not risk a major conflagration as it would be inhibited by Moscow.[14] China in the event did not interfere consistent with its policy of assiduously avoiding entanglement in an external adventure in which it has no strategic interests.

US intelligence estimates were not validated because the crisis ended sooner than the predicted months and years, besides these had not taken into account the deluge of refugees that provided India the much needed excuse to interfere militarily on the side of the Bengalis while the Nixon administration helplessly looked on. After all, Nixon believed this was an 'internal' matter for Pakistan to handle.

The West has all along used Pakistan to foil India's ambition to emerge as a significant regional power. Contrary to general belief that the US did not want China to interfere in the subcontinent, Nixon and his advisers felt that China should be encouraged to intervene on the side of Yahya to sustain his 'democratic' set up. Any notion of the Americans supporting democratic aspirations of people around the world is a lie that is given currency by the propagandists of the US government.

The role of the Soviet Union during the crisis was more honourable. The Chairman of the Presidium of the Supreme Soviet of the USSR Nikolai Podgorny took a principled stand and sent a message to Yahya asking him to accommodate the political demands of the Bengalis by entering into a dialogue with their leadership. The CIA characterized this as serving to support the Indian position but in reality the Soviet advice offered the only possibility for Yahya who had already painted himself into a corner to make a democratic exit. This would have averted the eventual break-up of Pakistan and would have spared the Bengalis and the Pakistan military unnecessary agony extending over nine months. Yahya spurned the message of the Soviet leadership because it interfered with his designs to continue in power until death. Yahya Khan's bravado was cheered in West Pakistan.

On 25 May 1971, the US department of state sent a 'Contingency Study on Indo–Pakistan Hostilities' to Henry Kissinger for discussion by members of the Washington Special Action Group. The study warned that:

> ...over the longer term there is the danger that the Pakistanis will provoke a conflict in order to distract international attention from the internal situation in East Pakistan and in order to convince the East Pakistani people that there is a threat from India sufficiently great to justify the continued unity of Pakistan and the West Pakistani military presence in the East.[15]

It was also assessed that Pakistan would come under increasing pressure to take action against India 'if an effective insurgency gains momentum as a result of Indian involvement' or on account of the refugees fleeing East Pakistan and their impact on India. In both cases 'as long as there is no fundamental solution to the underlying political problem, the danger of war will remain.'[16] But Yahya did not intend to address the underlying political problem because that would have meant an end to his career.

The study recommended steps to prevent escalation of the crisis, some of which were to 'continue to stress to the GOP the urgent need for political accommodation and indicate that our ability to assist Pakistan depends on progress toward such an accommodation,' and also to 'consider a more active use of the leverage of our military and economic assistance programmes to induce Pakistan to begin political negotiations with the Bengalis.'[17] In the event of escalation, the study recommended amongst other actions that the US 'withdraw the four C 130s which may be in the area of conflict carrying out a refugee airlift.'[18]

These recommendations were ignored. Unnecessary bloodshed of Bengali civilians could have been avoided had the US pursued a little forcefully the principled policy of supporting the democratic aspirations of the people of East Pakistan.

A study was also prepared by the National Security Council in July 1971 to assess US policy options in South Asia in light of the crisis in East Pakistan. It stressed that the US should avoid taking steps that could mortgage excessively its 'as yet undefined future relationship with East Pakistan'[19] more so because prospects for the continued viability of Pakistan as a united country were doubtful. The study may be quoted at length as it encapsulates US interests in the region.

> ...the problems facing South Asia have increased in complexity and intractability. Although the Pakistan Army has re-established general control over East Pakistan, military actions have not completely ceased against separatist elements and minority communities. Guerrilla activity, supported from sanctuaries in India, has developed. A massive flow of refugees engendered by the Pakistan Army's activities has taken place. According to Indian sources over six million East Pakistanis, mostly Hindu, have sought refuge in India. To date only a few have returned to East Pakistan and those that remain in India pose a massive threat to the political and economic stability of the sensitive eastern regions of India and to peace in the Indian subcontinent. The situation in the last three months has moved from a level in which our interests were only secondarily involved to one that, because of the danger of war, could pose a direct threat to the bases of US policy in South Asia.[20]

While dilating on 'US interests and Objectives' the study said that:

> ...the United States has no vital security interests in the South Asian subcontinent. However, as a global power we are inevitably concerned for the stability and well being of an area in which one-fifth of mankind resides and which holds a geopolitically significant position between China and the Soviet Union. Our interest is that India and Pakistan succeed in their development efforts, and withstand political pressures, which could lead to the dominance of an external power in the region.
>
> Peace is the essential precondition for the maintenance of our interests in South Asia. Hostilities could easily disrupt the economic, social, and political life of the subcontinent, and open the way for outside players to extend their

influence. If, despite our efforts (no efforts were made by the US government), hostilities did break out it would be our objective to ensure that neither we nor any of the other principal external powers became directly involved. Within South Asia itself both India and Pakistan are important to US interests. Our interests in India, however, are of greater significance. India, the world's second-most populous country, with strong and stable political institutions, the fourth largest armed forces and ninth highest GNP, is a force in South Asian regional affairs and in the broader context of the Indian Ocean and Southeast Asia. India aspires to be one of Asia's major powers in the next decade.

Pakistan, although the world's fifth most populous country, has neither the resources nor the ambition for such a role in world affairs. Its political and economic viability have been seriously weakened by recent developments. Overall, it has a much smaller capability for influencing US global interests. On the other hand, India's internal problems could in time bring about a situation in which it also could exercise little external influence. In formulating US policy in the region the relative pre-eminence of our interests in India should be an underlying factor in decisions which we take.

Given our interests in South Asia and recognizing that over the long-term the prospects for the continued viability of Pakistan as a united country are doubtful, US objectives have been to maintain a constructively close relationship with India and reasonable relations with Pakistan avoiding any steps which would mortgage excessively our as yet undefined future relationship with East Pakistan.[21]

This sums up US policy in South Asia, a policy that prevails to this day. Continued viability of Pakistan has always been in doubt and its break-up has been consistently forecast by sceptics. On the other hand, despite its irritatingly independent foreign policy India has continued to be treated with respect because it is perceived to be more crucial to US interests. Given this context, US policy makers were mindful not to mortgage future relations with what was then East Pakistan to decisions taken in support of a military dictator.

The study said that US policy in the face of the crisis in South Asia had three elements: counselling restraint on both sides, support of international efforts to provide humanitarian aid for the refugees and the people of East Pakistan, and emphasizing the need for political accommodation. It said the most crucial element was political accommodation because that would allow the refugees to return and diminish the danger of war with India. The study noted that half-hearted measures during the previous few months at persuading Yahya failed to yield much barring a few public statements by him that were 'designed for international consumption' while his junta continued 'victimizing the Hindus.'[22] But the Hindus were not the only victims of the junta's policy—every Bengali was an enemy and every Bengali young man a potential target for indiscriminate killing.

Unfortunately the White House acted at variance with the policy outlined in the study because it wanted to appease Yahya. In the end, US policy was held hostage to the whim of a president beholden to a dictator because of which India and Pakistan went to war and innocent Bengali civilians were slaughtered. The administration continued its policy of military and economic assistance to Pakistan because it was surmised that the US 'should not exaggerate the effect of our aid, which leaves untouched the social and political problems.'[23] It remained unclear what practical actions were taken by the US to address the social and political problems that were the root cause of the crisis.

The study rightly recommended suspending all arms shipments to Pakistan 'including any residual shipments, which remain from the pre-March 25 period.' This, the study observed, would restore a degree of credibility in US calls [to India] for restraint and help support the 'relative pre-eminence of our [US] interests in India.'[24] Referring to the shipment of military hardware licensed prior to 25 March or under one-time exception allowed in 1970, the study noted that the 'program has been strongly criticized by India which sees any arms to Pakistan as a direct support for the Army's suppressive actions in East Pakistan.' This in turn, the study concluded, 'damaged our [US] ability to maintain a constructive relationship with India.'[25]

In a preamble to its recommendations on US military and economic assistance to India and Pakistan, the study said these programmes had taken on considerable importance in view of the US desire to develop cooperative relations with both countries but noted that 'The dilemma inherent in those programs in Pakistan is that while they support our interests in Pakistan they simultaneously damage our interests in India.'[26] In a specific reference to Pakistan the study cognized that 'The stability of the Martial Law Administration is heavily dependent on the continued strength and morale of the military. Military sales therefore are of paramount psychological and practical significance to the martial law regime.'[27] In ignoring this clear reminder, the US implicitly supported a martial law regime by continuing to provide military assistance to Pakistan, much like what it has continued to do since then.

Discussing the pros and cons of pursuing a more coherent policy, the study pointed out that the proposed measures would certainly have the effect of irritating Pakistan but on the other hand serve a larger purpose of helping Americans influence India to exercise restraint.[28] Yet the administration risked its long-term interests for the sake of supporting just one individual—Yahya Khan.

On the other hand, by recommending that the US 'adhere to (its) policy of deemphasizing political criteria for aid,'[29] the study clearly encouraged Yahya to disregard the need to make a political accommodation with the East Pakistani leadership. This amounted to giving a blank cheque to the Pakistani regime to do as it pleased. The pitfalls of this policy were acknowledged but the recommendation appears to be in accord with presidential preferences of not putting any pressure on Yahya.

The study noted that 'Because the refugee burden represents the most likely proximate cause for escalation, our efforts have concentrated on mitigating the burden which the refugees represent for India.'[30] It reviewed various options for international assistance including discussions with the Soviets and UN involvement. But in view of the White House policy of not giving any offence to Yahya, none of these avenues were seriously explored. This policy of inaction was justified on the basis of a notion that 'there is no way in which we can directly address the political problem which the refugees pose for India.'[31] The root cause of the problem, however, was not the refugees or their influx into India but the military action taken by the dictatorial regime in West Pakistan to deny democratic rights to the Bengalis.

In reviewing various options to resolve the problem of refugees, the study reported that 'From all evidence available to us a substantial portion of the Hindu refugees may never wish to return to East Pakistan. At present the Government of India is not prepared to consider permanent resettlement…as that would imply that political accommodation was impossible.'[32] But the study said that 'any public acknowledgement by the US that it regarded the return of refugees as impractical would be of concern to the Government of India.'[33]

The study said that an integral element of the current US strategy vis-à-vis the crisis in South Asia was 'to urge the Government of Pakistan to proceed as expeditiously as possible with political accommodation' but at the same time cautioned that Yahya would consider any suggestions to show accommodation as political interference in view of 'his domestic requirements for a more delayed transfer of power.'[34] Delayed transfer of power was not Yahya's domestic requirement but his own personal need to perpetuate himself. A consuming desire to hang on to power has characterized all our military saviours.

Yahya had devised his own political timetable and had no intention to part with power, believing that the consequences of his actions would somehow be averted through efforts of his friends, particularly the US and China. Any half-hearted effort to persuade Yahya to directly negotiate with Mujib, who Yahya believed was a traitor, would have been fruitless. In any case, the US administration did not pursue the thought.

In assessing the prospects of hostilities in South Asia, the study noted that 'with the experience of 1965 in mind Indian decision-makers are aware that a decisive victory over Pakistan cannot easily be won' besides which they were conscious that 'the costs of war are high.' It was nevertheless estimated that despite this India could go to war with Pakistan because of 'domestic political pressures, and an assessment that the influx of refugees is likely to lead to radicalization in Bengal.'[35] In the event of war, the study emphasized that it was in the US interest to ensure that hostilities are short-lived and not permitted to 'expand to include third parties, particularly China.'[36] Prolonged hostilities, the study warned, 'would do profound damage to the political, economic and social fabric of India and Pakistan.'[37] Mercifully, remained confined hostilities were brief and between the two countries only. Short duration wars, so long as they were limited to the two subcontinental neighbours, presented no problem whatsoever to the Americans as the strategic balance remained unaffected.

The study considered the possibility of Chinese involvement in the South Asian conflict with much concern but this was counter to President Nixon's own view who had rather hoped that China would get involved and put India under pressure. The study estimated that India would 'wait to see whether international pressures and domestic compulsions in Pakistan will bring about a political accommodation, the restoration of peace and security in East Pakistan and a start to the process of repatriation of the refugees' but warned that 'if no progress is made in these areas by September or October, the chances for hostilities will increase.'[38] Unsurprisingly, this turned out to be true. The warnings went unheeded, and the purpose of the exercise lost.

In the event that hostilities between India and Pakistan did break out, the study outlined three broad strategies for the US: (a) adopt a passive hands-off role, (b) provide military support to the victim of the attack, and (c) intervene politically to localize the conflict. The study said that by adopting a passive role the US would retain the flexibility to act as events unfolded and preserve the relationship with both nations. As for providing military support, the study said that the US had limited commitments to both sides, with Pakistan under SEATO and CENTO and with India through the 1964 Air Defence Agreement. It was emphasized that neither agreement 'provides for automatic US involvement.' Determining the possibility of military support to India as less likely, it was assessed that 'if we judged it to be in our interest to assert the paramountcy of our interests in Pakistan and in its national unity and integrity we might offer to assist Pakistan's defence effort...although not with US combat personnel.'[39] So it was not the agreements or obligations that the US government had signed in the past that determined its policy but the interpretation of national interests at that point in time. Except for positioning an aircraft carrier in the Bay of Bengal when it was too late anyway, the US administration lent no material help in thwarting Indian military operations in East Pakistan and safeguarding the national unity and integrity of Pakistan. It would have made far more sense for the US to compel the West Pakistani regime to reach accommodation with the East Pakistani leadership and thereby deny India any excuse for military intervention.

On the political process the study correctly concluded that: 'Given our interest in maintaining relations with both India and Pakistan and our desire to prevent Chinese involvement and to limit external influence in the subcontinent, a policy of political intervention would give us considerable flexibility. The principal purpose of our political efforts would be to localize hostilities and end them.'[40] The study also listed pre-hostilities contingency actions which amongst others things required intensification of intelligence coverage of Chinese intentions and capabilities to intervene in South Asia. It appears that the US was not overly concerned to resolve the crisis until such time when actual hostilities broke out but also when hostilities did break out, so long as they remained confined to the subcontinent and did not hurt their global interests, the US had no cause to worry.

But by early December it was becoming increasingly clear to the Americans that Pakistan would lose the war in East Pakistan while the outcome in the west was still to be determined. In a memorandum prepared for the Washington Special Actions Group ('Implications of an Indian Victory over Pakistan') the CIA listed what they believed to be India's war objectives: 'liberation of Bangladesh, incorporation into India of southern parts of held Kashmir and the destruction of the Pakistani armoured and air force strength so that Pakistan could never again threaten India.'[41] On the assumption that India would achieve these objectives the CIA discussed the implications this would have in the post-war situation. In the CIA's assessment it was possible that 'West Pakistan might fall apart politically...based on the assumption that the Pakistani army is not simply defeated but virtually ceases to exist in the West as well as in the East.'[42]

In the eventuality that the Pakistan army was annihilated and the country started to fall apart, the CIA's assessment was that the Afghans would move to detach the NWFP from Pakistan and bring it under their protection. The Pashtuns on either side of the international border have close ties and consider that the existing Pak–Afghan border is no more than 'a line arbitrarily and unfairly drawn by the British Raj.'[43] As for Balochistan, described as 'primitive, frequently lawless, and isolated,' the assessment was that 'it is not likely to be able to assume the status of an independent state. It could thus remain attached to the Punjab, though it is conceivable that it would be absorbed by either Afghanistan or by Iran.'[44] The CIA was wide off the mark on this; Balochistan is least likely to remain with the Punjab more so because the Baloch accuse the Punjabis of having exploited their province ever since independence. Besides, with its rich mineral resources, a vast coastline and a favourable man-land ratio, Balochistan has greater prospects of survivability in comparison with some member-states of the United Nations.

For the Punjab it assessed that 'it would probably recover economically, fairly rapidly.' It was estimated that if India's war objectives were met, the Punjab would no longer pose a threat to India, and 'would probably be viewed by most powers as a state on the order of Afghanistan: remote and of no great consequence.'[45]

The assessment of the CIA with regard to the viability of the four provinces of West Pakistan proved to be wrong in all material respects, at least during the next several decades. India, on the other hand, failed to achieve its war objective of incorporating Azad Kashmir into India and only managed to grab small chunks of territory, which it was allowed to retain as a result of the Simla Agreement. Neither did India succeed in destroying the Pakistani military.

The CIA assessed that an Indian victory with Soviet help would have the effect of lending greater weight to Soviet influence in the world. Also, a victory would encourage the Soviets to believe 'that its power and influence were growing and that it could entertain the idea of playing a stronger hand in some other contests.'[46]

The CIA report is extensively interspersed with 'ifs' and 'buts' and does little credit to its understanding of the region. Even at the international level things did not happen as per its estimates. The Soviet Union did not gain any more influence in the region while its internal dynamics proved fatal to its continued status as a superpower. China did not turn against India, but on the contrary improved relations with her. The dust in the region settled down as soon as the aberration of the military junta was removed, but unfortunately not for long. The subcontinent is yet again a flashpoint that causes much concern to the international community.

NOTES

1. Ibid., Memorandum from Kissinger to Nixon, 22 February 1971, Document 118 (http://www.state.gov/r/pa/ho/frus/nixon/e7txt/47235.htm).
2. Ibid., Contingency Study on Pakistan: East Pakistan Secession (NSSM 118), 3 March 1971, Document 123. (http://www.state.gov/r/pa/ho/frus/nixon/e7txt/47239.htm).
3. Ibid.
4. Ibid.
5. Ibid.
6. Ibid., Telegram from US Embassy (Islamabad) to the Department of Sate, 25 February 1971, Document 119. (http://www.state.gov/r/pa/ho/frus/nixon/e7txt/47236.htm).
7. Ibid., Contingency Study on Pakistan: East Pakistan Secession (NSSM 118), 3 March 1971, Document 123. (http://www.state.gov/r/pa/ho/frus/nixon/e7txt/47239.htm).
8. Ibid.
9. Ibid., Paper prepared by the (US) National Security Council's Interdepartmental Group for Near East and South Asia, undated, Document 132. (http://www.state.gov/r/pa/ho/frus/nixon/e7txt/50130.htm).
10. Ibid., SNIE 32-71: Prospects for Pakistan, 12 April 1971, Document 131. (http://www.state.gov/r/pa/ho/frus/nixon/e7txt/50127.htm).
11. Ibid.
12. Ibid.
13. Ibid.
14. Ibid.
15. Ibid., Memorandum from the Executive Secretary of the Department of State (Eliot) to Kissinger, 25 May 1971, Document 133, (http://www.state.gov/r/pa/ho/frus/nixon/e7txt/47247.htm).
16. Ibid.
17. Ibid.
18. Ibid.
19. Ibid., Study Prepared in Response to National Security Study Memorandum 133, 10 July 1971, Document 140, (http://www.state.gov/r/pa/ho/frus/nixon/e7txt/49185.htm).
20. Ibid.
21. Ibid.
22. Ibid.
23. Ibid.

24. Ibid.
25. Ibid.
26. Ibid.
27. Ibid.
28. Ibid.
29. Ibid.
30. Ibid.
31. Ibid.
32. Ibid.
33. Ibid.
34. Ibid.
35. Ibid.
36. Ibid.
37. Ibid.
38. Ibid.
39. Ibid.
40. Ibid.
41. Ibid., Memorandum Prepared in the Central Intelligence Agency, 9 December 1971, Document 170, (http://www.state.gov/r/pa/ho/frus/nixon/e7txt/50160.htm).
42. Ibid.
43. Ibid.
44. Ibid.
45. Ibid.
46. Ibid.

25

How did the US Consul General in Dhaka View the Crisis?

Archer Blood was the US Consul General (CG) posted in Dhaka and Joseph S. Farland, the American ambassador stationed in Islamabad. The two had diametrically opposite views on the traumatic events in East Pakistan following the military operation. According to Arshad-uz-Zaman, 'The story of Archer Blood, the US Consul General, is a dramatic one. He openly threw his support on our (Zaman being a Bengali) side whereas his ambassador in Islamabad was a staunch supporter of united Pakistan.'[1] Accounts of the CG were closer to the truth and that of the ambassador's were in harmony with what the US administration wanted. The CG was frank, forthright and objective in reporting the situation as he saw it but in the process jeopardized his career. He appears to be an honourable man who was sensitive to human, legal, and constitutional aspects of the crisis.

One finds much anecdotal evidence to validate the contents of the CG's reports. In a telegram to the State Department on the subject of 'Selective Genocide' sent on 28 March—three days after the military crackdown was launched—the CG highlighted the atrocities committed by the Pakistani troops. 'We are mute and horrified witnesses to a reign of terror by the Pakistan military,' he wrote.[2] He said there was mounting evidence that the military authorities were systematically eliminating the Awami League (AL) supporters by seeking them out and shooting them down. Among those marked for extinction in addition to the Awami League leaders were student leaders and the university faculty and that the full horror of the atrocities would come to light sooner or later. He wrote:

> I, therefore, question continued advisability of present US Government posture of pretending to believe Government of Pakistan's (GOP) false assertions in denying for understood reasons, the detailed accounts of events in East

Pakistan this office is communicating. We should be expressing our shock, at least privately to GOP. I, of course, would have to be identified as source of information and presumably GOP would ask me to leave.[3]

But Blood was a man of conviction who stood up for principles and was unconcerned that the host government might demand his removal or that he might jeopardize his career. According to Arshad-uz-Zaman, 'Kissinger vowed that as long as he was Secretary of State, Blood would be in the dog house in the State Department. Kissinger made good his vow.'[4]

The next day, on 29 March, he sent another telegram and quoted American priests, whose names were protected. They reported that:

...army acted with no provocation...[and was] exclusively responsible for all fires. Technique was to set houses afire and then gun down people as they left their homes. [The priests were] unwilling to estimate number of casualties but advised that [they] must be very high. Hindus [were the] particular focus, although areas including non-Hindus [were] also burned out. [The priests] Stated [the] army [was] looking [for] Awami Leaguers, but [were] really more indiscriminate...in approach. Most [of the] army [actions for] destruction [took place on] nights of 25 and 26 March.[5]

The CG reported that according to a reliable account a family of eleven was killed on the night of the 25th, and said that on the night of 25 and 26 March the army attacked the police headquarters at Muhammadpur and killed 1800 policemen. They razed Razarbagh Police Lines to the ground and 'practically demolished [the] Special Branch building.' They also attacked the East Pakistan Rifles (EPR) headquarters and killed about 700 people.[6] The same message also said there were 'recurrent reports [of] many university professors [being] killed' adding that 'although circumstances [are] vague many [people] say attempt [is] underway [to] wipe out all source [of] potential intellectual ferment.'[7] This savagery was intended to break the will and motivation of the Bengalis to offer resistance to the occupation forces.

Civil servants living in official houses were not spared either. Some sources were quoted by the CG as telling him that there had been cases of random violence and forced entry into the homes of three or four senior civil servants whose inhabitants were killed. Readers will recall that on my last day in Dhaka (31 March 1971) I met Dr Fakhruddin Ahmad, the deputy secretary of the services department, whose house had been similarly raided and its inmates subjected to violence.

Troops were reported to be involved in widespread looting of homes and beating up those who objected. When they tired of looting, they allowed the non-Bengalis to indulge in the activity. Children were not spared either. The report quoted a USAID provincial director as having witnessed 'unprovoked firing by military on children and fishermen' on the afternoon of 29 March.[8] The CG concluded:

> As details of horror stories of varying reliability filter in, it appears [that] army [is] seeking: [to] terrorize population in general and thereby crush [the] will to resist, although resistance in Dhaka ended several days ago, and [to] eliminate all elements of society that pose [a] potential threat to consolidation and maintenance of martial law authority.[9]

In yet another message the CG wrote that an American working with the Food and Agricultural Organization in East Pakistan toured Dhaka University on 27 March and reported that in Iqbal Hall 'students were either shot down in rooms or mowed down when they came out of the building in groups.'[10] University halls had become the Dhaka base for students in the Awami League movement. All this happened on the night between 25 and 26 March. He saw a pile of twenty-five corpses tightly packed for removal by the army. This was the last pile as others had been removed earlier.

The CG reported that the army did not even spare the girls. Troops set their hostel known as Rukayya Hall ablaze and machine-gunned the girls in their rooms including those that tried to flee.[11] I found confirmation of this crime in a verbal account given to me by Major Saeed Jung of the Pakistan Army some years later who claimed to have participated in the carnage. He described the horror of the massacre and said there was blood all over the rooms of Rukayya Hall. No one was allowed to escape. The boys had weapons but the girls had nothing. The army burnt all university files. But the burning of papers, books or libraries is not a new phenomenon as barbarians have employed this as an act of war against civilizations throughout recorded history. This is the surest way to decimate collective memory.

In all it was estimated about 1000 students and faculty members were killed. According to this account mass graves were found on the campus and because of rain on the night of 29 March some bodies were exposed, and were giving out a strong stench. The CG concluded his account by saying that the 'figure of thousand dead at University nonetheless strikes us as exaggerated, although nothing these days is inconceivable.'[12]

Occupation armies are proverbially brutal and show extreme savagery in suppressing dissent. The systematic slaughter of intellectuals in Iraq by the Americans when they occupied that country in 2003 is a case in point. Asma Rashid documented American barbarities in an article in *Dawn* of 18 March 2006 and reported that Iraqi intellectuals were systematically hunted down and killed. Rashid wrote:

> US backed special units conducted strikes against leaders of the so-called insurgency. A force of paramilitary death commandos was formed and trained by veterans of the US's dirty wars in South America, including the former US Ambassador to Iraq, John Negroponte.[13]

Horrendous torture, extra-judicial executions and arbitrary arrests became the order of the day in Iraq. Mutilated corpses littered the garbage dumps, and morgues overflowed while hundreds of people simply disappeared. But the events of 1971 took place before the advent of modern tools of mass communication like the satellite television and the Internet. The Pakistani army had little reason to worry that the media might expose their gruesome activities; hence one may assume that it acted with equal brutality in suppressing the Bengali uprising.

On 6 April 1971, the US Consul General in Dhaka sent a hard-hitting telegram to the State Department to register the strong dissent of numerous officers of the American Consulate, USAID, and USIS in Dhaka to the US policy towards East Pakistan. In a stunning and admirable show of moral courage, these officers accused their government of 'moral bankruptcy':

> Our government has failed to denounce the suppression of democracy. Our government has failed to denounce atrocities. Our government has failed to take forceful measures to protect its citizens while at the same time bending over backwards to placate the West Pak (istan) dominated government and to lessen likely and deservedly negative international public relations impact against them. Our government has evidenced what many will consider moral bankruptcy, ironically at a time when the USSR sent President Yahya a message defending democracy, condemning arrest of leader of democratically elected majority party (incidentally pro-West) and calling for end to repressive measures and bloodshed.[14]

The State Department must have been taken aback at this show of strong dissent by its own officers, but moved with caution and hollow hypocrisy to placate them saying that it 'welcomed the expression of strongly held views.' Yet it defended US actions (or inaction) on the grounds that there had been 'conflicting reports' and that media in the US had 'been carrying stories of atrocities on both sides.'[15] Responding to the charge that the US government had failed to denounce atrocities, the State Department said that 'we are naturally concerned at the reported loss of life, damage and hardship suffered by the people of Pakistan. What is impossible for us to establish at this time is any reliable set of facts regarding the recent events in the area....'[16]

With so much intelligence and information coming from various sources, the mass exodus of millions of refugees, and with suspicions heightened due to the expulsion of all journalists from East Pakistan, it should not have been difficult for the American government to rely on reports sent by its official representatives in the region. In the end, the CG was punished and sidelined for a number of years for showing dissent to the US policy in East Pakistan.

The American ambassador in Islamabad had different notions as a responsible civil servant and he was more in tune with the views of the State Department and even more so with those of Kissinger who, of course, mirrored Nixon's thinking. Responding to Archer Blood's observations on the atrocities committed in East Pakistan on 25 March and beyond, the ambassador commented that:

> Incidents involving wanton military force which Consul General Dhaka and others have reported arouse our indignation and we can appreciate the sense of horror felt by witnesses at the scene. Since we are not only human beings but also government servants, however, righteous indignation is not of itself an adequate basis for our reaction to the events now occurring in East Pakistan. The constituted government is using force against citizens accused of flouting its authority.[17]

By describing Yahya's government as 'constituted' the ambassador justified use of force on the grounds that it was employed against 'citizens accused of flouting its (government's) authority.' One marvels at the lack of training in law and constitutionalism of this career diplomat who could describe a military government that seized power by force as 'constituted'— implying its legality—and characterize resistance by citizens as 'flouting authority'.

The US ambassador analysed the crisis in East Pakistan from a historical perspective and concluded: 'deplorable as current events in East Pakistan may be, it is undesirable that they be raised to [the] level of contentious international political issue.'[18] Although the ambassador called for a review of the US political relationship with the government of Pakistan, the US stance towards East Pakistan and the various US operational programmes in the country, he was categorical in his assessment that 'Yahya was sincere in his effort to bring about a political solution under a system recognizing the majority of East Pakistan population.'[19] The basis on which he formed this view is difficult to understand. He was perhaps too gullible and believed the self-serving claims made by senior members of the regime. He characterized the Awami League's actions of civil disobedience as acts of insurrection in as much as they were running a parallel government, raising Bangladesh flags and creating impediments in the way of the government of Pakistan's civil and military activities. This was an echo of the regime's propaganda and the ambassador's appetite for mendacious justification offered by it to swallow hook, line and sinker. And yet the ambassador maintained that the US should keep its options open so as to promote its own interests. And this he intended to do by not interfering in Pakistan's harsh military crackdown deemed essentially to be an internal matter requiring no outside interference or comment.

In the event his view and *realpolitik* prevailed while Archer Blood, the US CG in Dhaka, suffered for his audacity and was hounded by the State Department.

In a telegram sent to the State Department on 10 April 1971, the Consulate in Dhaka expanded on its objections to the US response to the crisis in East Pakistan first outlined on 6 April vide telegram 1138. It explained the 'specific areas of dissent with current US policy toward East Pakistan' and underscored the staff's concern that the US posture in the event of a West Pakistani military intervention proposed in an official document dated 2 March had been 'ignored':

> ...we note NSCIG/NEA. 71-9 dated 2 March suggests in section ii, part c, a proposed US posture in [a] contingency [if] West Pakistan military intervention appeared imminent or actually occurred to squash the independence movement on part of Bengalis. 'If West Pakistan intervention becomes imminent or actually occurs, we would have an interest in doing what we could [to] avoid bloodshed and restore peace, and to prevent the conflict from escalating beyond a purely East-West Pakistan clash we should be willing to risk irritating the West Pakistanis in the face of such a rash act on their part, and the threat of stopping aid should give us considerable leverage.' We concur with this proposal but are concerned that it seemingly has been ignored.[20]

The staff at the CG also questioned 'Yahya's bonafides in seeking a political solution' and endorsed Mujib's characterization of Pakistani politics as 'politics of conspiracy.'[21]

The CG's staff took exception to the State Department's line that 'we are not only human beings but [also] government servants and righteous indignation is not of itself an adequate basis for our reaction to events occurring in East Pakistan' and responded by saying that 'in a country wherein our primary interests [are] defined as humanitarian rather than strategic, moral principles indeed are relevant to [the] issue.' The army in East Pakistan was defending interests at variance with those of the general populace and in consequence killing people indiscriminately. They took issue with the state department's characterization of Yahya's government as 'constituted' and described it as an 'extra-constitutional martial law regime of dubious legitimacy.'[22]

The CG's staff challenged the regime's attempt to characterize the elected representatives of East Pakistan as 'miscreants', although they had mustered about 73 per cent of the vote in that province. They did not see the 'issue as distinctly internal' and pointed to the genocide of the Hindus and Awami League followers; for them the situation represented colonial rule. They averred that 'the people of East Pakistan want to live as free people of a free country, preferably within Pakistan, but if given no other choice, outside it.' They described Ambassador Farland's view that 'deplorable as current events in East Pakistan may be, it is undesirable that they be raised to level of contentious international issue' as a 'woefully inadequate reaction to events' which contrasted sharply with the 'more decisive reaction' of the Russians. They concluded that for them an independent Bangladesh was inevitable.[23] In just eight months time, this actually came to pass.

Elaborating their concern over the evacuation of US nationals and their earlier charge that 'our government has failed to take forceful measures to protect its citizens', the CG's staff took serious issue with their government's decision 'to accept "with appreciation" GoP's counter-proposal to use PIA as a method of evacuation action rather than US aircraft.'[24] They recalled their previous experience with the Pakistan Air Force, which had taken over Pakistan International Airlines (PIA) operations in East Pakistan, and said that they had predicted 'the confusion, delays and indignities which were in fact experienced.'[25] But this was bound to happen because the air force is a military organization which has neither the expertise nor the experience to manage the operations of a commercial airline.

The staff reported that US citizens in East Pakistan were 'virtually unanimous' in their repugnance of the indiscriminate killing by the military. Americans waiting at the airport to be evacuated saw the planes that were to fly them out unloading troops from West Pakistan and being marched onto trucks. According to them this amounted to Pakistan 'underwriting half of the costs of bringing more troops to East Pakistan to continue the military action.' The staff accused the State Department of placating the West Pakistan government by disguising evacuation as 'thinning' and of jeopardizing the lives of American citizens by failing to consult the CG on timely evacuation. They said that the government of Pakistan 'lied to us' regarding its plans to launch an operation against the people of East Pakistan and as a result the evacuation of American citizens was delayed.[26]

Endorsing his own personal comments in conclusion, Archer Blood emphasized that 'these recommendations do not stem from any dissenting group but rather are the fully staffed out recommendations of USG agencies in East Pakistan' adding that 'accordingly I propose to dispense with the NODIS (not for distribution) channel and to forward these recommendations in the normal way, restricting them as appropriate according to their sensitivity.'[27]

But Archer Blood was not the only person with whom the US administration was at odds over the crisis in East Pakistan. Nixon and Kissinger were equally irritated with Kenneth Keating, the US ambassador in India, whom they agreed was a 'traitor.'[28] In fact, Nixon was unhappy with Keating on account of his dissenting views and on an earlier occasion had told Kissinger, 'I am not too damned impressed with Keating.'[29]

During an informal meeting at a party in early June, Nixon told Keating that he would see him formally when he (Keating) came back (to Washington) later that month. Discussing this with Kissinger the next day (4 June), Nixon asked what it was that Keating wanted the US to do with respect to the situation in South Asia. Kissinger said that Keating 'thinks we should cut off all military aid, all economic aid [to Pakistan], and in effect help the Indians to push the Pakistanis out.'[30] Obviously irked, Nixon shot back: 'I don't want him to come in with that kind of jackass thing with me' and added that Keating had been 'sucked in' [by the Indians] just 'like every ambassador who goes over there [India].'[31] In fact this is a malaise known as 'localitis' to which most diplomats are generally susceptible.

Kissinger reiterated his well considered negative opinion about the Indians and Nixon chimed in with his own comment saying that 'they are no good.' Both agreed that 'if East Pakistan becomes independent, it is going to become a cesspool' and that it 'would bring pressure on India because of West Bengal.'[32] Kissinger complained that the 'Indians have never lifted a finger for us, why should we get involved in the morass of East Pakistan?'[33] This conversation concluded with Nixon accusing the Indians of having the destruction of Pakistan at the back of their minds. He was only echoing the views of the Pakistani military and had not arrived at this conclusion by means of his own intellectual endeavour.

The conversation clearly shows that these two leaders were devoid of any morality and ethics and failed to realize the magnitude of the crisis. They refused to see that the crisis was man-made and that their dictator-friend Yahya was fully responsible for it. The world would be a more manageable mess if people had the good fortune of having intelligent leaders. Decision-making is only as good as the leaders a country has.

The president finally met Ambassador Keating on 15 June with Kissinger in attendance. The ambassador gave his appreciation of the developing crisis in South Asia and briefed the president and his assistant for national security on their impending meeting with the Indian Foreign Minister Swaran Singh. Keating started by making two points: one, the significant commercial interests of the US in India and second, his own relationship with Indira Gandhi. The ambassador informed the president that Indira Gandhi and her Congress Party had been returned with a large majority, winning 350 out of 520 seats in the Lok Sabha (the lower house of the parliament) but this apparently failed to impress Nixon. Keating then described his relationship with Indira Gandhi saying that she 'has always been pleasant' and 'never turned me down when I wanted an appointment', adding that 'she couldn't be nicer in her dealings with me.'[34] He informed the meeting that he had sent two cables to the State Department—one shortly after the Pakistan Army 'started the killing in East Pakistan'—which represented his assessment of the situation in the subcontinent.[35] But these cables in all probability were simply ignored because the reality was that the State Department was not in the policy-making loop; policy was conceived, conceptualized and finalized in the White House by Nixon and Kissinger.

A palpable sense of hostility marked the meeting because both Nixon and Kissinger disliked the Indians as well as their own ambassador. The president asked Keating what the Indians would want the US to do, and without waiting for an answer asked, 'Break up Pakistan?' The ambassador emphatically denied this assumption and said 'when the [Pakistan] army walked in and knocked out the elections of course they [Indians] were upset.'[36]

Briefing Nixon on what the Indian foreign minister would likely say to the president in the meeting scheduled for next day, the ambassador said Swaran Singh would point to the basic issue of getting the refugees to return to Pakistan because they were placing a great strain on India and would cost around $400 million if the crisis were to last a year. Keating said that refugees from East Pakistan were pouring into India at the rate of 100,000 to 150,000 a day. He alleged that the Pakistan army had started indiscriminate killing and 'it is almost entirely a matter of genocide killing the Hindus.'[37] The president asked if the total number of refugees was 300,000 and when told by Keating that the figure was five million, Nixon remarked: 'Why don't they [Indians] shoot them?'[38] This from the president of the world's second largest democracy! He seemed to have no respect for life particularly of the ordinary people of the subcontinent or of East Pakistan. He thought nothing of the Indians shooting dead the incoming refugees if that would save Yahya from losing power and the US administration the bother of having to find an equally subservient replacement.

Ambassador Keating recommended that 'new pressure' be applied on Pakistan to seek a political settlement but being mindful of the president's inclinations hastily added '...I am conscious of the special relationship that you have with Yahya. And I respect it...' The president was not pleased by this reference to his personal association with Yahya, which impliedly coloured US policy in South Asia, and shot back: 'Not only just that but there are some other major considerations.'[39] There indeed were none but Nixon did not consider it necessary to enunciate them. In effect, Nixon succeeded in shutting off his ambassador from influencing policy.

Nixon perhaps realized he had been overtly hostile in his attitude towards the Indians and did not want Keating to 'get the wrong impression.' Emphasizing the importance and size of India, Nixon said 'There are 400 million Indians.' When Keating corrected him and said the number was 550 million, Nixon callously remarked: 'I don't know why the hell anybody would reproduce in that damn country?'[40]

Returning to the issue at hand and without going into the reasons, Nixon remarked that Pakistan's collapse 'may not be in our interest' and while conceding that 'we have to find a way to be just as generous as we can to the Indians' he emphasized that at the same time 'we do not want to do something that is an open breach with Yahya—an open breach, an embarrassing situation.'[41] The president also noted that India was not a popular country with Congress either. He refused to be dragged into the South Asian mess and directed his embassies to not 'allow the refugee problem to get us involved in the internal political problems. You see that is our policy.'[42]

This was mid-June and events in the subcontinent were moving fast. Yet, Kissinger remained either unconcerned or unmindful of the rapidly deteriorating situation and asked for three to four months 'to have a direct communication with Mrs Gandhi.'[43] Now both Nixon and Kissinger appeared to be hedging the issue and were avoiding taking charge of the brewing crisis for the sake of small cynical gains. Three to four months would be an eon in the context of the developing crisis. Being one of two superpowers at the time it would have been easy for the US to make a phone call to Indira Gandhi asking her to cool things down. But the real policy induced by their shared hatred of India and whatever it represented was to avoid engaging India and allow maximum leeway to Yahya to do what he willed with his own people whom he had held hostage for two years. As for the Indians 'we will find some money, we will gradually move into position to be helpful, but we have got to do it our way. Just to shut them up.'[44] The crisis to them seemed to stem from an Indian desire to get 'some money'. And the money would not be taken out of Pakistan's allocation because that 'would bring down the Pakistan government'.[45]

Kissinger also suggested setting up a separate channel with the Chinese 'so that we are not so vulnerable.'[46] That implied China putting her diplomatic and military weight on the side of the Americans to deter India from any adventure. But throughout the discussion, the underlying cause of the brewing crisis was scrupulously avoided.

Ambassador Keating's position was principled and in tune with the sentiment in India. His recommendations were in accord with moral principles because the majority province of East Pakistan had won the general elections and yet was being denied power by a ruthless military junta. Sadly, his views carried no significance for Nixon and Kissinger because as ambassador to India he was perceived as having a 'weakness' (for the US)—the former described him as 'soft' and Kissinger only reiterated his dislike for the man.[47]

NOTES

1. Arshad-uz-Zaman, op. cit., p. 109.
2. Department of State, op. cit., Telegram 959 From the Consulate General in Dacca to the Department of State, 28 March 1971, Document 125, (http://www.state.gov/r/pa/ho/frus/nixon/e7txt/47241.htm)
3. Ibid.
4. Arshad-uz-Zaman, op. cit., p. 110.
5. Department of State, op. cit., Telegram 978 From the Consulate General in Dacca to the Department of State, 29 March 1971, Document 126, (http://www.state.gov/r/pa/ho/frus/nixon/e7txt/47242.htm).
6. Ibid.
7. Ibid.
8. Ibid.
9. Ibid.
10. Ibid., Telegram 986 From the Consulate General in Dacca to the Department of State, 30 March 1971, Document 127, (http://www.state.gov/r/pa/ho/frus/nixon/e7txt/47243.htm).
11. Ibid.
12. Ibid.
13. *Dawn*, 18 March 2006.
14. National Archives, RG 59, Central Files 1970-73, POL 23-9 PAK., Telegram (No.1138) From the Consulate General in Dacca to the Department of State, Dacca, 6 April 1971 (http://www.state.gov/documents/organization/45582.pdf).
15. Department of State, op. cit., Telegram 58039 From the Department of State to the Consulate General in Dacca, 7 April 1971, Document 129 (http://www.state.gov/r/pa/ho/frus/nixon/e7txt/47245.htm).
16. Ibid.
17. Ibid., Telegram 2954 From the Embassy in Pakistan to the Department of State, 31 March 1971, Document 128 (http://www.state.gov/r/pa/ho/frus/nixon/e7txt/47244.htm).
18. Ibid.
19. Ibid.
20. Ibid., Telegram 1249 From the Consulate General in Dacca to the Department of State, 10 April 1971, Document 130 (http://www.state.gov/r/pa/ho/frus/nixon/e7txt/47246.htm).
21. Ibid.
22. Ibid.
23. Ibid.
24. Ibid.
25. Ibid.
26. Ibid.
27. Ibid.
28. Ibid., Conversation among Nixon, Kissinger, and William Rogers, 24 November 1971, Document 156 (http://www.state.gov/r/pa/ho/frus/nixon/e7/48533.htm).
29. Ibid., Conversation among Nixon, Kissinger, the Indian Foreign Minister (Singh), and the Assistant Secretary of State for Near Eastern and South Asian Affairs (Sisco), 16 June 1971, Document 138 (http://www.state.gov/r/pa/ho/frus/nixon/e7txt/48554.htm).

30. Ibid., Conversation between Nixon and Kissinger, 4 June 1971, Document 136 (http://www.state.gov/r/pa/ho/frus/nixon/e7txt/48552.htm).
31. Ibid.
32. Ibid.
33. Ibid.
34. Ibid., Conversation among Nixon, Kissinger, and Keating, 15 June 1971, Document 137 (http://www.state.gov/r/pa/ho/frus/nixon/e7txt/48553.htm).
35. Ibid.
36. Ibid.
37. Ibid.
38. Ibid.
39. Ibid.
40. Ibid.
41. Ibid.
42. Ibid.
43. Ibid.
44. Ibid.
45. Ibid.
46. Ibid.
47. Ibid., Conversation between Nixon and Kissinger, 6 December 1971, Document 162 (http://www.state.gov/r/pa/ho/frus/nixon/e7txt/48560.htm).

26

Nixon's Malevolence towards India

When India gained independence in 1947, the Cold War between the United States and the Soviet Union had divided the world into two major blocs. From the very outset, India adopted a foreign policy that was independent and free from superpower influence. In fact, India's Jawaharlal Nehru together with Gamal Abdel Nasser of Egypt and Josip Tito of Yugoslavia founded the non-aligned movement (NAM) in 1955 in order to ensure 'the national independence, sovereignty, territorial integrity and security of non-aligned countries.' Ever since India has followed a foreign policy that is designed to serve its own national interests and not those of the superpowers. The US, which has long been used to dealing with lackeys and subservient dictators in Third World countries, found India's independence irksome and annoying. It is only natural then that successive US administrations have always borne a degree of hostility towards India.

But Nixon had an additional reason to hate India and the Indians. He was denied the pomp and ceremony when he visited India as a private citizen before being elected president. To quote Nixon as part of his conversation with his national security adviser on 6 December 1971: 'First of all, I visited India in 1953, and I visited there on two other occasions, but for a considerable time in 1967 and of course briefly as President.'

But Nixon had other reasons to dislike India. On 7 December 1971, following a report to Nixon by Secretary of Commerce Maurice H. Stans on his trip to the Soviet Union, Nixon, Kissinger, Haig, and Press Secretary Ron Ziegler met to discuss a background briefing Kissinger intended to give the press concerning the crisis in South Asia. In order to placate the Indians who were by now clearly winning the war, Kissinger suggested that in his press briefing he would 'first say a lot of nice things about the Indians.' Nixon agreed and added:

> ...why don't you put it a little bit stronger? First of all, I [Nixon] visited India in 1953, and I visited there on two other occasions, but for a considerable time

186

in 1967 and, of course, briefly as President. I have great interest, as I've said [in India], and I said when she [Indira Gandhi] was here, expressed our views that it is the policy of the United States to help the largest nation of the world, free nation, [to] succeed because [unclear] very important that they succeed. That's why we're one of the strongest supporters [of India] in terms of [unclear].[1]

But apparently Nixon's experience in India had not been pleasant; he sounded unenthused when he remarked: 'Oh my God, when I was in India in 1967, I was there 3 days, and I saw Mrs Gandhi, the President, the Vice President, every…Indian.'[2]

Nixon made no secret of his antipathy towards India. Earlier in May when war clouds were gathering ominously over the subcontinent, Nixon and Kissinger met to discuss a letter that had been received from the Indian Prime Minister Gandhi and another that was to be sent to Yahya. In fact India had seen a great opportunity of cutting Pakistan to size, both literally and figuratively. It launched a vigorous campaign asking for international support to compel Pakistan to stem the flow of refugees and seek a political settlement with the Awami League. At the same time India brought its armed forces to a high state of preparedness. Indira Gandhi's letter to the US president was part of this diplomatic offensive.

At one point during this discussion, Nixon burst out and said that what the Indians really needed was 'a mass famine.' He then rued the fact that 'they aren't going to get it,' adding that 'if they are not going to have a famine the last thing they need is another war in East Pakistan—let the goddamn Indians fight a war.'[3] As always, Kissinger agreed with his president and commented that 'They [the Indians] are the most aggressive goddamn people around there.'[4] But in making this comment he obviously overlooked the many aggressions Americans committed in their relatively brief history as a nation; and one cannot forget that the US is the only country that has used nuclear weapons and destroyed two Japanese cities inhabited by hundreds of thousands of innocent men, women, and children.

With regard to Indira Gandhi's letter, Kissinger advised the president that 'we should answer it' and suggested that Nixon write to Yahya too who 'might appreciate a letter, which would give him an excuse to answer all the things by saying, listing all the things he's doing…'[5] Nixon of course was concerned for Yahya and sought confirmation from Kissinger that his letter to the Pakistani president would not contain anything that could compromise the latter's position. So he asked, 'But we don't say anything against Yahya?' Kissinger reassured Nixon and said, 'No, no. You just say you hope the refugees will soon be able to go back to East Pakistan. He [Yahya] will then reply to you...that's exactly what he wants.'[6]

Indira Gandhi visited Washington in early November 1971 as part of her diplomatic drive to garner support for India's position vis-à-vis the crisis in the subcontinent. On 5 November, Nixon, Kissinger and H.R. Haldeman (the president's chief of staff) met to discuss Nixon's conversation the previous day with Indian Prime Minister Gandhi, and agree on the approach to take in the meeting he was scheduled to have with her later the same day. Nixon's intense dislike for Indira Gandhi had clearly been heightened; he gloated over the fact that he had 'really slobbered over the old witch' in the previous day's meeting. Kissinger had some choice words of his own and said 'the Indians are...starting a war there.'[7]

On 24 November, two days after India attacked East Pakistan, Nixon, Kissinger and Rogers met to discuss the implications of the crisis and the approach to be taken in dealing with India and Pakistan. It was debated whether the US should take action against India but the consensus was that even if action was taken it would be 'symbolic rather than substantive', more so because the leverage the US had on India was very minimal.[8]

Condemning India was not an appealing option because it was believed this would not help and on the contrary might result in a general war in the subcontinent. Even as late as November the US administration failed to appreciate the seriousness of the crisis. It suffered from a complete paralysis of policy for fear of compromising Yahya. But there appeared near consensus to take the case to the Security Council in order to stop the war in East Pakistan and end hostilities. Apparently, the fact that a dictator was riding roughshod over the democratic aspirations of the majority population of a country the size of Pakistan escaped the president's notice. That an elected leader of an abiding democracy could overlook such a serious violation of democratic principles was appalling. Yahya on the other hand had not made up his mind to approach the United Nations as he continued to rely on his powerful friends in the White House to prevent the Indians from interfering with his designs. Yahya thought until the end he would somehow, with the help of his American and Chinese friends, tide over the crisis. The role of the Americans was reduced to that of a helpless Goliath who could do little except watch the crisis unfold. Besides, since no vital American interests in the region were at stake, the US was likely to suffer no harm if it opted to remain a silent spectator and restricted itself to making some appropriately friendly noises.

Yet, there were lighter moments in this otherwise sombre conversation among Nixon, Rogers, and Kissinger. The relationship between India and Pakistan was characterized in matrimonial terms when Nixon remarked that both countries 'hate each other so much that they are totally irrational' Rogers elaborated, 'Just like a man and wife...too jealous to care about the welfare of their children.'[9]

In a telephone conversation on 26 November between Nixon and Kissinger to discuss the fighting in East Pakistan, Nixon said he 'would like the Indians to be embarrassed,' and on this occasion again expressed his aversion for the Indian leadership. When Kissinger criticized Indira Gandhi and said she 'has betrayed her father,' Nixon promptly countered the implied admiration for Nehru and said, 'Of course her father was just as bad as she is.'[10]

On 6 December—three days after the war started in the west—Nixon and Kissinger discussed the crisis in South Asia, focusing on the approach to take with the Soviet Union and China, and the best way to deal with Indira Gandhi. Nixon was clearly frustrated with the progress of the war because it was clear by then that Yahya was going to be demolished. He probably felt Indira Gandhi had outmanoeuvred him and said 'this woman suckered us.' Wanting to exact revenge, Nixon said, 'But let me tell you, she's going to pay...on this aid side.'[11] The ever-prescient Kissinger felt that the Democratic Party could make the suspension of aid to India an issue in the next elections and advised the president that 'let's fight it in the campaign.' Nixon countered: 'They'll probably say we are losing India forever...All right, who is going to care about losing India forever?'[12] The White House was obviously frustrated because it had failed to coerce India into subservience over the crisis in the subcontinent.

Earlier in the discussion, in a reference to Indira Gandhi's visit to Washington the previous month, Nixon regretted that he had been 'too easy on the...[Indira Gandhi] when she was here.' Kissinger agreed, as was his wont, and said 'looking back now could we have recommended to you to brutalize her privately?' and to say that 'you do this [attack Pakistan] and you will wreck your relations with us for 5 years and we will look for every opportunity to damage you.'[13] But Indira Gandhi was a tough lady and would perhaps not have countenanced being bullied by the American president.

Nixon complained that Indira Gandhi 'attacks us', but Kissinger pointed out that 'she's been pretty cautious about attacking us...She's never mentioned us by name.' Nixon then said he would not conduct a press conference because he did 'not want to be in a position of attacking [Indira Gandhi].' Kissinger endorsed this, and advised Nixon not to get into an argument with her fearing that 'it will look as if she's winning.'[14]

Henry Kissinger shared with Nixon in equal measure his contempt for India and the Indians. The two met on 9 December and concluded that, while East Pakistan could not be saved, they would have 'accomplished a lot' if they managed to 'save a strong West Pakistan.'[15] Discussing ways to stop an Indian onslaught on West Pakistan, Kissinger said: 'What I would do with the Indians, Mr President, is keep them in the deep freeze until after your (re-)election. After you're elected they'll come to you hat in hand.' Assuming that all Americans shared his personal feelings towards India, Kissinger wondered if any American would like India. President Nixon agreed and said, 'Nobody.'[16]

The Indians had been trying to convince the US that there was a need for American role in trying to defuse the crisis created in East Pakistan by Yahya and his crew. Some six months later, President Nixon had met Indian Foreign Minister Swaran Singh in the White House on 16 June. The stratagem Nixon and Kissinger had privately devised to deal with the unwelcome visitor and his demand for applying 'overt pressure on Pakistan', which they thought would have a 'counterproductive effect', was to tell him in vague terms that 'we are working with Yahya in our own way.' Kissinger went on to add: 'It is a little duplicitous but these… understand that.' They had decided to 'give him a combination of sympathy' and 'great firmness' so that he could go home satisfied.[17] Both wanted him off their hands as fast as possible.

Kissinger told Nixon that 'I am just trying to keep them from attacking for three months.'[18] He was perhaps hoping that Pakistan would collapse during this period and thus save him the painful task of offending Nixon's friend in Islamabad. In the event the Indians waited longer and did not attack for six months but the US continued to follow a policy of drift and did nothing to address the basic causes of the conflict and prevent a war.

Pleasantries were exchanged as Swaran Singh along with L.K. Jha, the Indian ambassador to the US, Keating, and US Assistant Secretary of State Joseph Sisco entered the Oval Office. In the discussion that followed Singh emphasized the 'tremendous problem' created for India by the influx of refugees. To determine what India's views were on the possibility of East Pakistan becoming an independent country, Nixon asked Singh how he saw the 'historical process working down'.[19] Singh said that there was a very good chance of saving Pakistan but added that continuation of the current policy in which the military was pitted against the united will of almost all the people of East Pakistan was not going to help. Nixon continued to probe Singh about India's view on the creation of an independent country and asked 'you don't have a feeling that the situation would be to your interest to have...an independent country? What would be in India's best interest? The Indian foreign minister was non-committal and very diplomatically said: 'We have no fixed position on that.'[20] India did not to wish to close its options or even disclose them.

Nixon counselled patience while the US would provide additional funds to India to deal with the refugees and used quiet diplomacy, a euphemism for doing nothing, to try and mediate a settlement in Pakistan. He pressed hypocrisy into service and praised his ambassador by saying, 'And on our part we couldn't have a person who is more vigorous in presenting this point of view which you have described.' This was in sharp contrast to what Nixon and Kissinger thought or said of Keating in private. The excuse Nixon could muster for not exerting any pressure on Yahya was that he did not want 'to do anything that...has the opposite results from what we want...' and elaborated by adding: 'The question is how we can discuss the matter with them in a way that may...lead to amelioration of the situation.'[21] Between applying public pressure and private persuasion, Nixon went on to say 'I have always believed in the latter as the most effective way, particularly when I know the individuals fairly well.'[22] But the problem is that 'private persuasion' can neither be seen nor verified. And one finds no evidence in the Nixon Presidential Materials of the promised private persuasion. Nixon then offered some financial crumbs to India and complained that 'The French and Germans have just as great an interest...and are doing very little' although they were 'making all sorts of big statements.'[23]

Nothing much happened in the US until 2 July when Kissinger left Washington for what was publicly described as a fact-finding trip to South Vietnam, Thailand, India, and Pakistan. In actual fact the trip also included a secret visit to China that Kissinger undertook while in Pakistan. He returned to Washington on 11 July.

During Kissinger's meeting in New Delhi with the Indian Defence Minister Jagjivan Ram and the Indian Defence Secretary K.B. Lall, Ram asserted that 'Mujibur Rahman never wanted secession. He was a moderating influence.'[24] This was quite true and did not controvert the US estimates. Ram expressed the hope that the US would use its influence on Pakistani leaders more aggressively than it had in the past. Referring

to the balance of power in the subcontinent, Kissinger succinctly stated
the fundamentals of the US policy saying 'that the only balance of power
the US is concerned with is the global balance—and the problem of
preventing an outside power from dominating South Asia. The local
balance within South Asia is not an American concern. The difficult
problem we now have between us as nations is to maintain that long term
perspective.'[25]

They discussed the overall situation in the region—East Pakistan must
have been uppermost in their minds—during which Ram complained
about the tension with Pakistan on the western front and gave Kissinger
his perception of the threat posed by China; he was of the view that a
surprise attack by the Chinese 'would be difficult.' Ambassador Keating
who was also present quoted the Chinese as having declared that 'they
would support Pakistan in a war.' Kissinger said that the US would take
a 'grave view' of any Chinese move against India.[26] The US policy must
have changed dramatically in the intervening five months because
according to declassified papers, in a conversation on 10 December, Nixon
asked Kissinger to urge China to act and move, 'some trucks, some
planes...You know some symbolic act' or move a division. He asked
rhetorically, 'The Indians are cowards, right?' and Kissinger agreed but
added that India had Russian backing.[27]

When Lall accused the US of using its influence with Pakistan in
questionable ways, Kissinger responded by saying 'that the amounts of
military equipment that Pakistan had received of late were relatively
insignificant, though we [the US] recognize that the Indian reaction
resulted as much from strong emotion as from actual assessment of the
impact on the military balance.'[28] Lall conceded that 'nothing capable of
offensive use was going to Pakistan' yet added 'but it must not be ignored
that the "bits and pieces" that were being shipped were sufficient to restore
weapons to their full use.'[29]

However, declassified papers now reveal that the administration had
been advised that arms supplied by the US 'have been used extensively by
the army in East Pakistan.'[30] These included Chafee M-24 tanks and F-86
fighter aircraft. Suspension of aid and military supplies, it was argued 'may
not provide us with the leverage to achieve a major reorientation of
Pakistan policy'; although it was emphasized that 'Pakistan needs us more
than we need it.'[31] It was also said that 'because of the Indo–Soviet
relationship, Pakistan is unlikely to turn to the USSR to meet gaps and
will therefore continue to look to us for help even in the event we adopt
a more positive attitude towards Bengali aspirations.'[32] The US

administration defied all moral and legal norms that demanded a firm stand against the West Pakistani military clique and abdicated its responsibility for ensuring regional peace.

Discussing the possibilities of a Chinese attack on India, Lall asked Kissinger 'whether he thought the Chinese would do anything without some provocation.' Kissinger thought this was unlikely yet cautioned that the Chinese could intervene 'if there were a war with Pakistan.' Lall said that there would be no justification for a Chinese attack as according to him 'India is not going to war with Pakistan.'[33]

Complaining of constant tension on its western borders with Pakistan, Ram told Kissinger that the US would have to judge if Pakistan could retain Bangladesh and asked, 'Will it be in US interest for Pakistan to stay together?' Kissinger replied that the US was considering that question but followed up with a query of his own: 'What can the US do?' The Indian minister promptly pointed out 'that the US could do a lot. All of Pakistan has been sustained by the US,' adding that there were now seven million refugees in India which could become 'a problem of great social concern.' The minister emphasized the need to find a solution to the 'Bangladesh problem' and said, 'Pakistan ought to have another election. "I would not mind that."'[34] But this seemed far-fetched and not a very well considered proposal. One would have expected India to come up with something more cerebral. What was the guarantee that the fresh elections would be fair? Anything other than absolute transparency would have only deepened the crisis. And even if the elections were fair and free and yielded a different outcome from the previous elections, the results would have been equally unacceptable to the military junta. The time for fresh elections had gone. The point had long since passed. The only option left for Yahya now was to reach some settlement with Mujib. But that would have involved transfer of power that Yahya was not prepared to approve, whatever the cost to the country or its people.

The Indians also wanted the US to 'tell Yahya that he will have to find a solution that responds to the will of the people in East Pakistan.' Lall pointed out that, 'The Pakistanis do not seem to understand that they cannot go on maintaining a country with an army drawn from six or eight different districts' and Ram added: 'The Punjabi rulers have not put faith in the Bengalis. Now, there is not even a constabulary in East Pakistan.'[35] Had the advice given by the 'enemy' been heeded the Pakistan Army would not have suffered the humiliation of surrender and the people of Pakistan would not have been subjected to the shock of losing half the country and more than half the population.

Kissinger was conscious of the drift in the crisis and asked the Indians for their assessment on how long could the Pakistanis fight in the event of war. Lall responded with, 'Not very long' and the Indian minister elaborated by saying that the 'logistics problem for the Pakistani military forces is a real one. It would be difficult for them to continue fighting over a prolonged period.'[36] With far weightier problems on his mind including the secret trip to China, which would prove to be the legacy of Nixon and Kissinger, the short war scenario was perhaps enough to put any worries of the visitor to rest. So his government continued to pursue its hands-off policy.

Earlier in this discussion Lall had underplayed the current misunderstanding between the US and India as 'lovers quarrels.' The Indian defence minister wanted to end the discussion on a conciliatory note and concluded the meeting by reiterating 'the common objective which the US and India have in peace and stability and in a solution to the present problem that would contribute to those objectives.'[37]

After India attacked East Pakistan, Nixon realized that the end was near and conceded that Pakistan would 'eventually disintegrate.' He was convinced Indira Gandhi was the person responsible for this and said, 'Despite what she says that's what she wants, there's no question about that.' In the given circumstances Nixon counselled that, 'it is very much in our interest to get the damn thing cooled' but qualified this by adding, 'that our policy wherever we can should definitely be tilted toward Pakistan and not towards India.'[38] In many ways this tilt towards Pakistan can be attributed to Nixon's personal affection for Yahya and his animosity towards for Indira Gandhi.[39] A dictator's 'decency' thus became the guiding principle and the cornerstone of American foreign policy. The American love for democracy had once again been amply demonstrated in 1953 when they engineered a *coup* against the hugely popular Iranian Prime Minister Mohammad Mossadeq and replaced him with their local gendarme, Reza Shah Pahlavi.

Kissinger was unconcerned with the political realities of the subcontinent and thought 'Yahya is a better man for reconciliation (with Mujib).'[40] He didn't ask the Bengalis what they thought of him because it was they who had been at the receiving end of his ruthless rule nor did he wonder what the people of West Pakistan felt about living under a military dictatorship. US administrations spawn dictators and are enamoured of them! Yahya vehemently detested Mujib and had planned to execute him before he was forced to hand over power to Bhutto. Nixon's Secretary of State, William Rogers, was not to be left behind and joined the chorus: 'My problem is I dislike the Indians so…much. I had trouble even being reasonable with them.'[41] All three were letting sentiment interfere with rational discourse on foreign policy!

At the fag end of the crisis the Americans assessed there was danger that West Pakistan too might collapse. Nixon desperately looked for ways to prevent this from happening. With not many options available to him, Nixon arbitrarily decided to penalize India by ordering $25 million taken out from its aid money and re-allocated to Indonesia. That, he said, was an order.[42] Continuing to vent his anger against India, Nixon said that they were right in deciding to move the aircraft carrier into the Bay of Bengal, to which Kissinger added, 'In fact, even if there is a settlement (between India and Pakistan), we should move the force in there just to show we can do it…'[43] But this was all sabre rattling—Nixon neither had the intention nor the political will to commit his forces in this regional conflict.

Throughout the crisis, Nixon remained convinced that China could restrain India, and reiterated this on a number of occasions. Nixon had earlier asked Kissinger to talk to the Chinese and urge them to make military moves towards the Indian border. On this occasion Nixon asked Kissinger if he had acted 'on my (Nixon's) proposition with regard to the Chinese' and when Kissinger said he had done nothing till then, Nixon said, 'I think we've got to tell them that some movement on their part we think toward the Indian border could be very significant.'[44] Nixon explained why this could be significant: '…the only thing the Indians fear is the possibility of [unclear–sanctions?]…But damn it, I am convinced that if the Chinese start moving, the Indians will be petrified.'[45] But Kissinger had a better understanding of world politics and cautioned the president that 'we shouldn't urge them to do it because they will get too suspicious' and suggested an alternative approach which was to say to the Chinese that '…if you consider it necessary to take certain actions we want you to know that you should not be deterred by the fear of standing alone against the powers that may intervene.'[46]

This conversation shows a remarkable lopsidedness in priorities and a pathetic lack of options for a superpower that would much rather rely on encouraging China to petrify India than command respect itself. But respect could only come if the US had played by the rules, and ceased to support an illegal and immoral assault on civilians by a country's military junta. That the US is a bastion of democracy proved no more than a myth.

Nixon's ire against India was no less than his thirst for revenge. When Kissinger suggested that 'the Indian Ambassador must not be seen under any level higher than the country desk officer (at the State Department)' Nixon was quick to see the possibility of snubbing the Indians and ordered: 'I want it as an instruction on my part…Also, I want you to send a message to Keating. He is to be totally cold in his relations.'[47] In his quest to settle scores with India, Nixon reversed the role of his ambassador from being a builder of bridges between the county of his accreditation and the mother country to one of being a spoiler.

Nixon was constantly looking to get even with Indira Gandhi for having 'suckered' him, and vowed that she would have to pay for this. He intended to make her suffer by cutting off aid. Kissinger reinforced Nixon's view and offered the rationale in support of this: '…they (the Indians) have to know they paid a price. Hell, if we could reestablish relations with Communist China, we can always get the Indians back whenever we want to later a year or two from now.'[48]

In pursuit of his compulsion to seek retribution, Nixon then resorted to his 'dirty tricks' and asked Kissinger if there was a way he could get the confidential Helms Report into the hands of columnist Joe Alsop. Nixon wanted this to be 'put into the hands of a columnist who will print the whole thing' because 'it will make her [Indira Gandhi] look bad.' Telling Kissinger to give the report to anyone who would print the story, Nixon cautioned him 'don't get caught…Just be sure to get it yards away from the White House.'[49]

In fact, on this occasion Nixon was particularly irked with India because Kissinger said that the operation (against Pakistan) had 'been great for the Indians' and predicted that it would certainly 'lead to the overthrow of Yahya.' This saddened Nixon who mused: 'It's such a shame. So sad.'[50]

The administration was at pains to appear interested in peace. On 7 December, during a discussion on the background briefing Kissinger intended to give the press concerning the crisis in South Asia, Nixon encapsulated the theme he wanted Kissinger to put out: 'We only have an interest in peace. We are not anti-India, we are not anti-Pakistan. We are anti-aggression as a means of solving an internal, a very difficult internal problem.'[51] But in reality, he had done nothing substantive to demonstrate this commitment. Passivity was the policy.

It's a commentary on Kissinger's lack of awareness that he had little idea about the fact that there was no mutual security treaty between the United States and Pakistan. His repeated reference during the crisis that the United States would come to Pakistan's assistance in the event of Indian aggression against Pakistan stemmed from the fact that both he and Nixon were 'ill-informed.' In a telephone conversation with Pakistani Ambassador Raza on 8 December, Kissinger suggested that Pakistan invoke its mutual security treaty with the United States even when no such treaty existed. The explanation posted by the US State Department in reference to this conversation makes interesting reading:

> No mutual security treaty has ever been concluded between the United States and Pakistan. The references to such a treaty and unqualified references to an assurance offered to Pakistan by the Kennedy administration indicate that Nixon and Kissinger were ill-informed about the nature and extent of a US commitment to take military action to assist Pakistan in the event of an attack by India. Kissinger's reference to a mutual security treaty during this conversation is an apparent reference to the Agreement of Cooperation signed by the United States and Pakistan on 5 March 1959, in the context of Pakistan's membership in the Baghdad Pact. The agreement (10 UST 317) obligates the United States to take appropriate action 'as may be mutually agreed upon' to defend Pakistan against aggression. The agreement cites the Joint Resolution to Promote Peace and Stability in the Middle East of 9 March 1957. (PL-7, 85th Congress) The Joint Resolution contemplated, among other things, the use of armed forces to assist nations against aggression by 'any country controlled by international communism' so long as such use of force was consonant with the treaty obligations and the Constitution of the United States.

The assurance offered to Pakistan in 1962, which was cited by Kissinger repeatedly during the crisis, was that the United States would come to Pakistan's assistance in the event of Indian aggression against Pakistan. The assurance was delivered in an *aide-mémoire* presented to Pakistani President Ayub Khan on 5 November 1962. (For text, see *Foreign Relations,* 1961-1963, volume XIX, page 372, footnote 6) The *aide-mémoire* did not subject the assurance to any qualification relating to constitutional constraints. A Department of State press release issued on 17 November 1962, however, stated that the United States had assured Pakistan that, if India misused United States military assistance in aggression against Pakistan, the United States would take 'immediately, in accordance with constitutional authority, appropriate action to thwart such aggression.'[52]

Under the circumstances Kissinger's advice to Raza was meaningless. Nothing of the sort happened and Yahya's hopes of direct US assistance were dashed to the ground.

References to a non-existent mutual security treaty or subsequent assurances were hollow noises intended to deter India from pursuing its military option in East Pakistan but there was little American interest in a region of marginal strategic significance. The reality is that the Nixon administration was unable or unwilling to directly intervene on behalf of Pakistan. This only proved the point that US commitments for security assistance couldn't be invoked by lesser powers like Pakistan unless the US itself chose to interpret the understanding differently. Third World client-states and their rulers should take no comfort from such commitments.

By the second week of December the creation of Bangladesh had become a near certainty. On 10 December, Kissinger gave Nixon an update of the situation in the subcontinent and started by telling him that the commander of the Pakistani forces in East Pakistan was asking for a ceasefire—a fact that was widely reported in the media but was denied by Yahya. Both understood that East Pakistan was gone but they now needed to take immediate steps to save West Pakistan. Nixon, of course, was furious and wanted a public relations campaign to fix the blame for the crisis on India. He was explicit: 'I want the Indians blamed...We can't let these...Indians get away with this.'[53] And neither was Nixon prepared to forgive India for its independent stance on the Vietnam War: 'They've pissed on us on Vietnam for 5 years' and then, as if to expose Indian duplicity, added: 'Here they are raping and murdering, and they talk about West Pakistan, these Indians are pretty vicious...'[54]

Despite Nixon's malevolence towards India, it was Indira Gandhi who had the last laugh. With the war objective of liberating Bangladesh successfully achieved, it was now time for her to pay Nixon back. In an interview she gave to a journalist on 22 December 1971, the substance of which was reported by the US embassy in New Delhi to the State Department, Indira Gandhi spoke of her willingness to normalize relations with the US but only if the Americans recognized that India was the predominant power in the subcontinent. Euphemistically referring to the American 'tilt' towards Pakistan as a 'misunderstanding by President Nixon of India's case' she declared that 'it's a question of recognizing what India is, what India stands for and what India wants to do. We have never accepted (the) theory of balance of power, and we have no intention (of) doing it now.'[55] Indira Gandhi then trashed reports of Indo–Soviet collusion saying that 'there is fantastic nonsense being talked about in the US about our [India] having received promises from the Soviet Union (i.e., concerning Soviet intervention against the 7th [US] fleet and against China)'.[56]

NOTES

1. Ibid., Conversation among Nixon, Stans, Kissinger, Haig, and Ziegler, 7 December 1971, Document 163 (http://www.state.gov/r/pa/ho/frus/nixon/e7txt/48561.htm).
2. Ibid.
3. Ibid., Conversation between Nixon and Kissinger, 26 May 1971, Document 135 (http://www.state.gov/r/pa/ho/frus/nixon/e7txt/48551.htm).
4. Ibid.
5. Ibid.
6. Ibid.
7. Ibid., Conversation among Nixon, Kissinger and the President's Chief of Staff (Haldeman), 5 November 1971, Document 150 (http://www.state.gov/r/pa/ho/frus/nixon/e7txt/48557.htm).
8. Ibid., Conversation among Nixon, Kissinger and William Rogers, 24 November 1971, Document 156 (http://www.state.gov/r/pa/ho/frus/nixon/e7txt/48559.htm).
9. Ibid.
10. Ibid., Transcript of Telephone Conversation between Nixon and Kissinger, 26 November 1971, Document 157 (http://www.state.gov/r/pa/ho/frus/nixon/e7txt/50145.htm)
11. Ibid., Conversation between Nixon and Kissinger, 6 December 1971, Document 162 (http://www.state.gov/r/pa/ho/frus/nixon/e7txt/48560.htm).
12. Ibid.
13. Ibid.
14. Ibid.
15. Ibid., Conversation between Nixon and Kissinger, 9 December 1971, Document 171 (http://www.state.gov/r/pa/ho/frus/nixon/e7txt/48567.htm).
16. Ibid.
17. Ibid., Conversation among Nixon, Kissinger, the Indian Foreign Minister (Singh), and the Assistant Secretary of State for Near Eastern and South Asian Affairs (Sisco), 16 June 1971, Document 138 (http://www.state.gov/r/pa/ho/frus/nixon/e7txt/48554.htm).
18. Ibid.
19. Ibid.
20. Ibid.
21. Ibid.
22. Ibid.
23. Ibid.
24. Ibid., Memorandum of Conversation, New Delhi, 7 July 1971, Document 139 (http://www.state.gov/r/pa/ho/frus/nixon/e7txt/47248.htm).
25. Ibid.
26. Ibid.
27. Ibid., Conversation between Nixon and Kissinger, 10 December 1971, Document 172 (http://www.state.gov/r/pa/ho/frus/nixon/e7txt/48568.htm).
28. Ibid., Memorandum of Conversation, New Delhi, 7 July 1971, Document 139 (http://www.state.gov/r/pa/ho/frus/nixon/e7txt/47248.htm).
29. Ibid.
30. Ibid., Paper prepared by the National Security Council's Interdepartmental Group for Near East and South Asia for the Senior Review Group, undated, Document 132 (http://www.state.gov/r/pa/ho/frus/nixon/e7txt/50130.htm).
31. Ibid.
32. Ibid.

33. Ibid., Memorandum of Conversation, New Delhi, 7 July 1971, Document 139 (http://www.state.gov/r/pa/ho/frus/nixon/e7txt/47248.htm).
34. Ibid.
35. Ibid.
36. Ibid.
37. Ibid.
38. Ibid., Conversation among Nixon, Kissinger and William Rogers, 24 November 1971, Document 156. (http://www.state.gov/r/pa/ho/frus/nixon/e7txt/48559.htm).
39. Ibid.
40. Ibid.
41. Ibid.
42. Ibid., Conversation between Nixon and Kissinger, 9 December 1971, Document 171. (http://www.state.gov/r/pa/ho/frus/nixon/e7txt/48567.htm).
43. Ibid.
44. Ibid., Conversation between Nixon and Kissinger, 6 December 1971, Document 162 (http://www.state.gov/r/pa/ho/frus/nixon/e7txt/48560.htm).
45. Ibid.
46. Ibid.
47. Ibid.
48. Ibid.
49. Ibid.
50. Ibid.
51. Ibid., Conversation among Nixon, Kissinger, Haig, and Ziegler, 7 December 1971, Document 163. (http://www.state.gov/r/pa/ho/frus/nixon/e7txt/48561.htm).
52. Ibid., Transcript of Conversation between Kissinger and Raza, 8 December 1971, Document 164 (http://www.state.gov/r/pa/ho/frus/nixon/e7/48213.htm).
53. Ibid., Conversation between Nixon and Kissinger, 10 December 1971, Document 172 (http://www.state.gov/r/pa/ho/frus/nixon/e7txt/48568.htm).
54. Ibid.
55. Ibid., Telegram 19600 From the Embassy in India to the Department of State, 23 December 1971, Document 194 (http://www.state.gov/r/pa/ho/frus/nixon/e7txt/49219.htm).
56. Ibid.

27

Was West Pakistan Threatened?

Kissinger conceded that the loss of East Pakistan was inevitable and that there was 'nothing to be done about that.'[1] This was on 9 December at which point it was clear that Kissinger's main concern then was to 'save' West Pakistan. He told Nixon that the 'Pakistanis are going to collapse in two weeks...If we can save West Pakistan it will be...an extraordinary achievement.'[2] Both Nixon and Kissinger believed they would have 'accomplished a lot' if they managed to 'save a strong West Pakistan.'[3] As if shedding off more than half the country would have added to a country's strength. It did not occur to them to ask Yahya to respect the election results and cease his own illegitimate hold over power. That Yahya was the problem and not a solution escaped their attention.

Attempting to absolve Nixon from any feeling of regret or a sense of failure in not being able to preserve the integrity of Pakistan, Kissinger once again assured the president that in his opinion East Pakistan could never have been saved. Nixon saw the opportunity to explain away his failed policies and shifted the responsibility on to the West Pakistanis saying they were 'too clumsy to have saved the damn thing.'[4] But the discussion was not without the usual compliments given by Kissinger to the president. Talking of the summit Nixon was to have with Brezhnev and how important it was for the Soviet leader to succeed, Kissinger reassured his president that despite little support from his own Congress and poor approval ratings '...outside this country you are the world leader right now.'[5]

In fact this discussion took place in the backdrop of a meeting Nixon had a few hours earlier with Soviet Minister for Agriculture Matskevich and Soviet Chargé d'Affaires Vorontsov; Kissinger was also present at that meeting. For Nixon, this was the moment of truth. He started by reviewing progress toward détente but then turned to the crisis in the subcontinent and asked Matskevich to inform Chairman Leonid Brezhnev that progress towards détente would be seriously jeopardized if the Soviet

Union did not act to restrain India from attacking West Pakistan. And then in an unexpected display of brinkmanship that must have caught Matskevich off guard, Nixon warned that if India were to attack West Pakistan there would be a confrontation between the United States and the Soviet Union.[6]

Nixon adopted a hard line throughout the conversation and was unequivocal about his own position: 'A better way is for the Soviet Union and the United States to find a method where we can work together for peace in that area. Now the first requirement is that there be a ceasefire. The second requirement is that, and this is imperative, that the Indians, who already have pretty much overcome the resistance in East Pakistan, the Indians desist in their attacks on West Pakistan.' He threatened India saying that the United States would not just 'stand by' if India did not stop and moved its forces against West Pakistan.[7]

Citing treaties that the Soviets had with India and the Americans with Pakistan, Nixon warned the Soviets in very clear terms that if 'the Indians...move against West Pakistan...we then inevitably look to a confrontation.'[8] Nixon had thrown the gauntlet!

Nixon also cautioned Matskevich that if the Soviets did not restrain the Indians, the United States would 'not be able to exert any influence with Yahya to negotiate a political settlement with the Awami League.'[9] As if he had all along urged Yahya to take that course of action! He also forgot that the time for such negotiations had long since passed. At this late stage, when India had commenced overt hostilities in East Pakistan, an insincere offer for political settlement in East Pakistan by Yahya's military regime would have been too late and too little.

Matskevich was stunned at this unexpected onslaught and stuttered that he 'was not prepared' for this discussion; he left with an assurance to Nixon that when he saw Brezhnev he would 'convey the spirit and letter' of what had been said.[10]

Kissinger and Nixon met within hours of Nixon's ultimatum to the Soviets and discussed the possible outcome of the impending summit. Both agreed that there was too much at stake for the Soviets to ignore the American proposals for resolving the crisis in South Asia. They also discussed the outline of a settlement that would form part of an appeal to be made by Nixon and Brezhnev after their summit; but before details of this appeal could be finalized they needed to get Yahya on board. Any settlement would have required Yahya to relinquish power completely or partially, something he was not prepared to do. Yahya was averse to the idea of having to reach a settlement with the Bengali leadership and favoured a military solution to the crisis just as the US administration was determined to reward a friend who had arranged a secret meeting between the Americans and the Chinese. Nixon decided to go to the UN Security Council in case the joint appeal by the US and the USSR failed to make any impact on India.

Nixon disregarded the assessment of his government agencies and instead ran the foreign policy from the White House. Kissinger characterized the liberal establishment 'intellectually and morally corrupt', and added for good effect that 'what they are telling you, Mr President, is to preside over the rape of an ally.'[11] Both Nixon and Kissinger were unhappy with the State Department for not being in tune with their views. Nixon went on to say that the State Department 'needs to get pounded into its goddamned head that we do not determine our policy solely on the basis of how many people are on one side...and whether a country is a democracy or not.'[12] This was a reference to India being a democracy of a more populous country and Pakistan a military dictatorship of a much smaller country. Nixon thought that an evil deed (by India) was not made good just by the form of (its) government. This summed up the political creed of the US government. Principles did not matter. Morality did not count for much. And democracy was a concept selectively applied to serve imperial interests.

With the crisis fast approaching denouement Nixon and Kissinger met regularly to review the latest situation. When the two met on 10 December, just six days before the surrender, it had become known that the Pakistani commander in East Pakistan had asked the UN to arrange a ceasefire and 'the immediate, honourable repatriation of his forces.'[13] Kissinger informed Nixon that he had 'told them (State Department) that they should link any discussion of ceasefire in the east with ceasefire in the west' adding that 'the major problem now is to protect the West.'[14] For Kissinger a ceasefire just in East Pakistan would not 'solve the overwhelming problem of the war in the West' to which Nixon added: '...the point is—our desire is—to save West Pakistan.'[15] Nixon ordered Kissinger 'to keep those carriers moving' towards the Bay of Bengal and wanted to give more money to Pakistan for its rehabilitation: 'I want to help Pakistan on the war damage in Karachi and other areas.'[16]

The two then considered measures that could serve to preserve the territorial integrity of West Pakistan. They talked about four options: to convert the economic assistance to Pakistan into military hardware; to enlist Russian help; threaten India of consequences; and go to the United Nations. They discussed the situation on war material which Pakistan had lost during the war and Kissinger informed the president that Pakistan 'had no spare parts from us for months. The army is ground down. And two more weeks of war and they are finished in the West as much as in the East.'[17] Nixon knew that 'it was impossible we can get through the Congress arms sales to West Pakistan' and so ordered, 'a hell of a lot of economic assistance.'[18] Kissinger understood Nixon's motives and chimed in with, 'I will let them convert into (military hardware).'[19] They decided to encourage Jordan, Turkey and Saudi Arabia to divert some planes to Pakistan and to ask the French to sell some planes. 'The French are just…they would sell to anybody,' said the president.[20]

Yet again Kissinger fawned over his president and said: 'If you can save West Pakistan, it will be an unbelievable achievement because West Pakistan has had all its oil supplies destroyed.'[21] Nixon was convinced that West Pakistan was on the verge of going under and that the Indians were determined to make that happen. But one finds no proof or evidence that would validate the apprehensions of these statesmen.

The CIA's assessment of the outcome of the war was somewhat different. In a memorandum on the 'Implications of an Indian Victory over Pakistan' issued on 9 December, the CIA estimated that 'what is now termed West Pakistan will face an uncertain future' and said 'though the Indian military would have withdrawn after its victory' there were possibilities that 'West Pakistan might fall apart politically.'[22] But the CIA report noted that the breakup of Pakistan was contingent on the eventuality that the Pakistani army was not simply defeated but ceased to exist in both wings of the country. The CIA assessed that 'it is doubtful that India will (or that it can) impose such a total defeat upon Pakistan.'[23] It was however rightly assessed that Yahya and his associates would be so discredited by the defeat that someone else would head the government. In the event of India's total victory, the CIA assessed that India would feel 'less beholden to the Soviets' because they would no longer face a strong and hostile Pakistan military machine, wryly noting that in any case 'Indian gratitude is not a very enduring matter.'[24]

As for an 'impoverished and overcrowded' Bangladesh, the CIA saw it emerging 'under a kind of Indian tutelage' but projected that 'the two Bengals will create considerable trouble and consume much of New Delhi's efforts and resources.'[25] This was based on the analysis that:

> …the Bengali propensity for extremism, radicalism and violence already apparent in the Hindu Indian state of West Bengal is likely to manifest itself in Muslim Bangladesh in fairly short order. And the troubles in that new

country and in West Bengal are likely to reinforce and stimulate one another. We do not believe that new Bengali nationalism is likely to be an effective force for the foreseeable future in sustaining independence.[26]

On 12 December, Kissinger walked into Nixon's office with the news that the Russians had given in to Nixon's demand to restrain India from attacking West Pakistan. Kissinger announced: 'They are giving us a full reply later. The interim reply is that they have an assurance from Mrs Gandhi that she will not attack West Pakistan.'[27] This of course meant that India would not threaten the integrity of West Pakistan as war on the western front had already started on 3 December. That West Pakistan had been 'saved' was a matter of profound satisfaction for Nixon, more so because his ultimatum to the Soviets had produced the desired effect of restraining India.

Kissinger was euphoric and unabashedly heaped praise on the president for his role in this 'achievement'. Eulogizing Nixon for standing against his own 'bureaucracy…against the Congress, against public opinion… alone…without flinching', even though that meant he might have been 'shooting (his) whole goddamn political future,' Kissinger described Nixon's behaviour as nothing short of 'heroic.'[28]

This prompted Nixon to ponder and in a rare display of introspection he mused, 'I do not know whether the US has a viable foreign policy.' Kissinger's adulation of Nixon was not over so he promptly replied: 'The United States has not a viable foreign policy; it luckily has a viable President.'[29] Pleased with what he was hearing, Nixon now wanted to measure his leadership with other leading Republicans and sought further approbation from Kissinger. In an apparent reference to the ultimatum Nixon had given to the Soviets to restrain India or else be prepared to face a confrontation with the US, Nixon commented: '[Vice President Spiro] Agnew could have done it.'[30] Kissinger, always quick to take the cue, replied, 'Agnew, Mr President, would have done it so stupidly.'[31] When Nixon suggested that Secretary of the Treasury John Connally would have been equal to the task, Kissinger agreed but once again pleased his president by adding that Connally lacked Nixon's 'subtlety.' Apart from his president for whom he had nothing but high praise, Kissinger had difficulty acknowledging merit in any other politician of the United States. Discarding Connally as an equal to Nixon, Kissinger remarked that 'his [Connally's] first instinct is often wrong, like when he said to cut off aid to both Pakistan and India [instead of India only].'[32] If anything it was Kissinger whose own instincts were entirely wrong.

Even though Prime Minister Gandhi had 'assured [Soviet] Minister Kuznetsov' that she would accept a 'ceasefire with no military action against West Pakistan'[33] the two remained convinced that West Pakistan was direly threatened. Or were they perhaps looking to claim credit for averting a hypothetical disaster? India's assurance backed by the USSR should have put the matter at rest, but not for Nixon and Kissinger who continued to 'worry' till the end.

The threat to West Pakistan was a figment of Kissinger's imagination and yet he has repeatedly claimed credit in books and articles for saving West Pakistan. All evidence points to Indian plans being limited to liberating East Pakistan. On the contrary, it was clear that Yahya was desperate because he was about to lose half the country and started hostilities on the West Pakistani borders with India in a bid to internationalize the issue and compel world powers to bail him out. That this did not work out the way it was intended starkly manifested the laws of unintended consequences.

The Russian assurance that India would not attack West Pakistan was apparently not enough to convince the two that this indeed was the case and both felt there was a need to do more. When Kissinger reassured Nixon that they had 'broken the back' of the crisis, Nixon remained sceptical and cautioned 'don't be too sure' and then shot at Kissinger, 'Why [do you believe] have we broken the back of it?'[34] Referring to the assurance offered to Pakistan in 1962 that the United States would come to Pakistan's assistance in the event of Indian aggression against Pakistan, Kissinger replied: 'Because, Mr President, when we showed, when I showed Vorontsov the Kennedy treaty, they knew they were looking down the gun barrel.'[35] But Kissinger wanted to continue ratcheting up the pressure and advised Nixon that there was a need 'to turn the screw another half turn' and not to 'let off the pressure too much and show any relief.'[36] Kissinger's 'strong recommendation' was to 'trigger this UN thing as quickly as we possibly can because it's the only way we can go on record now of condemning India;'[37] a statement coming directly from the White House was to be the 'trigger'.

Nixon asked to see the statement prepared by Kissinger and was pleased by what he read: 'Now you got it. It's better than what I had.'[38] But as always, he remained unsure if the White House statement would pass the State Department's muster and had to use his presidential authority to browbeat them into accepting it without question. He asked Kissinger to tell them that, 'The President dictated this thing. This is it gentlemen...and that there is frankly no appeal to this.'[39] The two were convinced that they had done a superb job by putting together a statement that was perfect in all respects.

The institutional strength of bureaucracy is to keep a check over the power of the executive, in this case the White House, and serve as a necessary safeguard. The two were running a conspiratorial, parallel administration away from the scrutiny of the formal government, the state department, Congress and the Press. An adversarial relationship between the Nixon White House and the State Department symbolized the Nixon presidency. Nixon had a poor opinion of the State Department and his distrust was monumental.

Since it was Nixon's view that 'Communists generally use negotiations, for the purpose of screwing, not for the purpose of settling—just like they screwed us on Vietnam'[40] it was considered prudent to take the case to the UN rather than just relying on the summit. But to approach the Security Council despite the Russian assurance would have shown that the US did not trust the Soviets and hence the move needed to be given a cover. Kissinger said that even though the hotline message to be sent to Brezhnev would not be made more conciliatory, it would explain the US action by offering the excuse that 'since your message (conveying Indira Gandhi's assurance that she would not attack West Pakistan) arrived too late we were already in the machinery.'[41] Nixon wanted to reinforce this line and suggested that the message could say: 'The President had already directed the Secretary General, I mean Ambassador Bush, to take this to the Security Council.'[42] This was a Freudian slip—the president was directing the UN Secretary General when in effect he meant the US ambassador.

On 9 December, when things had progressed beyond the point of no return, the BBC announced that Pakistani troops had deserted Jessore Cantonment in a great hurry leaving their lunch uneaten after the Indians appeared on the horizon. The West Pakistani junta continued to deny that it had suffered such a reverse and characterized the report as a malicious concoction. A large number of gullible people in West Pakistan did not want to face the bitter truth and genuinely believed that the BBC was an anti-Pakistan weapon and an Indian mouthpiece. They relied totally on Pakistan Television (PTV) and Radio Pakistan while their patriotism gave them faith in their armed forces, both in deed and their claims.

NOTES

1. Ibid., Conversation between Nixon and Kissinger, 9 December 1971, Document 171 (http://www.state.gov/r/pa/ho/frus/nixon/e7txt/48567.htm).
2. Ibid.
3. Ibid.
4. Ibid.
5. Ibid.
6. Ibid., Conversation among Nixon, Kissinger, Matskevich and Vorontsov, 9 December 1971, Document 169. (http://www.state.gov/r/pa/ho/frus/nixon/e7/48540.htm).
7. Ibid.
8. Ibid.
9. Ibid.
10. Ibid.
11. Ibid., Conversation between Nixon and Kissinger, 9 December 1971, Document 171 (http://www.state.gov/r/pa/ho/frus/nixon/e7txt/48567.htm).
12. Ibid.
13. Ibid., Conversation between Nixon and Kissinger, 10 December 1971, Document 172 (http://www.state.gov/r/pa/ho/frus/nixon/e7txt/48568.htm).
14. Ibid.
15. Ibid.
16. Ibid.
17. Ibid.
18. Ibid.
19. Ibid.
20. Ibid.
21. Ibid.
22. Ibid., Memorandum prepared in the Central Intelligence Agency, 9 December 1971, Document 170, (http://www.state.gov/r/pa/ho/frus/nixon/e7txt/50160.htm).
23. Ibid.
24. Ibid.
25. Ibid.
26. Ibid.
27. Ibid., Conversation between Nixon and Kissinger, 12 December 1971, Document 178 (http://www.state.gov/r/pa/ho/frus/nixon/e7txt/48571.htm).
28. Ibid.
29. Ibid.
30. Ibid.
31. Ibid.
32. Ibid.
33. Ibid.
34. Ibid.
35. Ibid.
36. Ibid.
37. Ibid.
38. Ibid.
39. Ibid.
40. Ibid.
41. Ibid.
42. Ibid.

Epilogue

An independent Bangladesh has failed to realize its true potential. In UNDP's Human Development Report for 2007/2008, Bangladesh was ranked at 140 in its human development index (HDI), four places below Pakistan which was placed 136 out of the 177 countries. Life expectancy at birth in Pakistan was calculated as 64.6 years as against 63.1 years in Bangladesh. Adult literacy rate for the two countries was estimated to be 49.9 and 47.5, combined primary, secondary and tertiary gross enrolment ratio as 40 and 56 (in percentage) and GDP per capita on Purchase Power Parity (PPP) in USD as 2370 and 2053, respectively.[1] Bangladesh continues to lay behind 38 years after independence.

While Bangladesh failed to make any notable improvement in the life of its people, it did succeed in controlling population growth. According to data from the Population Reference Bureau (PRB)—a US based non-profit organization—the population of Bangladesh in mid-2008 was 147.28 million as against 172.8 million in Pakistan. In 1971, the population of East Pakistan, now Bangladesh, was 56 per cent as against 46 per cent in West Pakistan. However, because Bangladesh has a much smaller area in comparison to Pakistan, its population density is 1023 people/sq km as against just 217/sq km for Pakistan. But Bangladesh has had greater comparative success in checking population growth, evident from the fact that by mid-2050 its population is projected to rise by 46 per cent to 215.08 million whereas Pakistan's population by then is estimated to rise by 71 per cent to reach 295.22 million.[2]

While most HDI indicators for Bangladesh are lower than Pakistan, it would be safe to suggest that these would have been worse had it remained part of a united Pakistan. Bangladesh has had a tumultuous political past and currently suffers from a severe scarcity of power and water; in combination with myriad other problems that it faces, Bangladesh is expected to remain a troubled nation for the foreseeable future. The unfortunate reality is that independence did little good for the common man. The failure of the government to alleviate poverty and improve the quality of life of its people resulted in the space being occupied by mammoth NGOs like BRAC (Bangladesh Rural Advancement

Committee) and Grameen. But Bangladesh can take pride in the fact that one of its distinguished citizens—Professor Mohammad Yunus—won the Nobel Peace Prize in 2006, an honour that was less likely to have come his way in a united Pakistan. When he tried to launch a political party of his own he did not receive the anticipated welcome from the people who remain committed to the Awami League or the Bangladesh National Party.

There is no reasonable explanation for the dismal failure of the leadership in both countries. Both the leaders exhibit little understanding of the rudiments of good governance and with each successive stint in power show no sign of having learnt any lessons. It may perhaps be a subcontinental syndrome. Even 'Shining India' may not attain the progress it strives for because many of its people remain illiterate. No nation can progress without first achieving a very high percentage of literacy. Sri Lanka has a comparatively higher rate of literacy and a reasonably good HDI but this country too has been a disappointment mainly because it failed to peacefully resolve the question of its Tamil minority. The war against Tamil militants compelled Sri Lanka to spend a large percentage of her limited resources on defence, a sure recipe for eventual decline.

Bangladesh's economy has performed better than it would have if it were still part of Pakistan. Self-rule has been a major factor in this partial success because in united Pakistan authority would reside in Islamabad. Secondly, the foreign exchange it earns from exports is now invested entirely in its own development instead of serving the industrialists of the erstwhile West Pakistan. It was for this reason that one of Awami League's six points required both wings to maintain independent foreign exchange accounts.

In terms of religious tolerance Bangladesh can be rated a little better than Pakistan, but unfortunately in recent times it seems to be heading in the wrong direction. But unlike Pakistan, they haven't yet written bigotry into their constitution and have desisted from branding an entire community a 'religious minority'. The people of East Pakistan are mostly Sunni Muslims with no notion of Shiism. But of late they have shown signs of religious intolerance and attacks on the mosques of Qadianis have become a favourite rallying point for bigoted clerics. Religious cadres have become more militant and have acquired greater political strength; they were part of Khalida Zia's coalition before it was replaced by the interim set up in 2007–08 and are suspected of being behind a number of terrorist attacks in the country.

Bangladeshis are more nationalistic and had no desire to opt out of the federation. In spite of being the majority they waited patiently for twenty-five years to get a fair share in governance. They adopted all possible means to persuade the West Pakistani rulers to share power with them but that was not to be. Once the 1970 elections were held, the pervasive gloom dissipated yielding place to new-found optimism that stemmed from the belief that finally the peoples' representatives would have an opportunity to rule the country. But the army high command was in no mood to part with power and used every ruse to frustrate its transfer. I was witness to the tragedy as it unfolded before my eyes. The calamity was not inevitable, it was mostly man-made.

Yahya reckoned that the US patronage of his regime would ensure that in spite of the military crackdown the situation in East Pakistan would remain a domestic issue and no foreign power would intervene. The US must serve her own national interests and this required that it maintain good relations with all countries of South Asia, in particular India, in part because of its size and democratic institutions. But the White House was solidly behind Yahya as he had been the conduit through which China had been opened up to the United States. Yet there are limits to American power. Ultimately Yahya's hopes were dashed. India first secured its flanks by signing a defence treaty with the erstwhile Soviet Union and then launched a military operation to carve out an independent Bangladesh. The military junta looked on helplessly, now more concerned with hanging on to power in a truncated Pakistan.

I visited Bangladesh in the late 1990s and then again in 2003. Dhaka has expanded in every conceivable direction because of the vast increase in population. People by and large are hopeful for the future and go about their business at a hectic pace with optimism. I noticed that Dhaka had become more crowded but appears more orderly. It is not as polluted as it once was because buses and rickshaws are required to operate on CNG. Islamabad is far more polluted than Dhaka.

Cycle rickshaws are very much part of the landscape. There was a call for a strike on the day I was leaving Dhaka because of which there was no vehicular traffic. This was in protest against a bomb explosion in a public meeting that the opposition Awami League leader Sheikh Hasina Wazed had addressed in Dhaka. Cycle rickshaws were going about through lanes and small streets. It was in one such rickshaw that I managed to reach the outskirts of the airport. A South Asia Free Media Association meeting was being held in Dhaka and a number of delegates including Mr Iqbal Haider of the Human Rights Commission had to catch the same flight. They rode to the airport from their hotel in an ambulance. People have learnt to overcome ordinary hurdles in life.

Bangladesh has not rid itself of the military monster which continues to exercise a disproportionate influence over national life. In spite of being provided alternative accommodation to relocate barracks situated in the heart of the city, the military continues to occupy that space, denying public access to a direct and shorter route which leads directly to Dhaka's new airport. Such methods are not different from the ones adopted here. After all Bengali senior officers have received training in the same staff colleges as our officers and were infected with the same ambition. Bangla Bundho Sheikh Mujibur Rahman was assassinated by his own military which then assumed power and ruled the country for decades. Generals Ziaur Rehman and Mohammad Ershad remained in power long enough to remind the people of Bangladesh that separation from Pakistan provided no guarantee against military rule.

Bangladesh has not been able to ensure complete civilian control of its military. But more than the military it is the politicians who are to blame. The founding father of the nation, Sheikh Mujib, was an undisputed and democratically elected leader but had a streak of the despot. He assumed the office of president rather than that of the prime minister. He tried to institute a one-party rule and was in the process of enlisting deputy commissioners into party cadres when he was murdered just three years into office along with all members of his family except those who were fortunate to be abroad. It has been assumed that the Bengalis have a great deal more democracy in them than the Pakistanis. And yet they could not pre-empt army intervention.

Until recently the country was under unconstitutional military rule although it had assumed a civilian façade. The military backed government attempted to discredit the country's two major political parties—headed by Khalida Zia and Hasina Wazed—by levelling corruption charges against them. These charges might have a basis in fact but not in public perception. The military in Bangladesh seems to have taken a leaf from the book of General Pervez Musharraf who made similar charges against Benazir Bhutto and Mian Mohammad Nawaz Sharif, jailing the latter and then sending him into exile and not permitting the former to land unless it was into his jail. Benazir was murdered during Musharraf's watch under very mysterious circumstances. Politics cannot be fixed through administrative means; popular support for the two Bangladeshi leaders, who were jailed and then released, forced the interim government to organize elections which swept the Awami League into power.

The interim government's Chief Adviser Fakhruddin Ahmed was at pains to dispel doubts about the promised polls. But in the period preceding the general elections, the country was placed under emergency rule and all political activities were banned. Indoor politics was reluctantly allowed. The interim government failed to improve the economy which remained wobbly during its tenure; businesses slowed down while soaring oil and food prices added to the country's woes.

The political strife in the country may be gauged from the fact that its leading politicians, Khalida Zia and Hasina Wazed, have refused to speak to each other although almost everyone of consequence tried to reconcile their differences including one of the world's most respected statesmen, Jimmy Carter.

Civil Service in Bangladesh has been politicized because of the war for independence. Such civil servants as could prove that they had taken part in the freedom struggle were given two years' seniority and promotion. Similarly, ordinary graduates who were able to show that they participated in the struggle were rewarded with selection into the civil service without having to qualify the competitive examination. Most deputy commissioners I met twenty five-years after the country had attained independence were such people. Every subdivision has been upgraded into a district.

Bangladesh shows a great deal more resentment towards India than Pakistan. Ordinary people in Bangladesh bear no animosity to the people of Pakistan. On the contrary they are affectionate and friendly. On my visit to Bangladesh such of my batch mates as could be found welcomed me very warmly. There was only an occasional show of bitterness or lack of civility. A young, successful businessman who was just a first-year college student in 1971 narrated with more sorrow than bitterness his personal experience of the military crackdown and how that compelled everyone to hide in their homes because they feared for their life. When the curfew was lifted after two or three days of incessant shelling, he went out and was horrified to see in and around the university opposite the British Council a large number of dead bodies being hurriedly removed in army trucks.

On another occasion I watched a Bengali feature film screened on board a BIMAN (Bangladesh National Airlines) flight. The theme of the film was based on the Bangladesh freedom struggle, depicting the Pakistan army at its worst. But the actors who played the role of the Pakistani military were diminutive and flabby and looked more like comic caricatures of a Pakistani soldier. The film could scarcely conceal its propagandist purpose.

The Awami League is now in power following a landslide electoral victory. Sheikh Hasina Wazed assumed the office of prime minister on 6 January 2009 after being in a political wilderness for about two years. One thought she may have learnt her lesson but I am told that this is not the case—business is being conducted much as before.

I recently asked a Bangladeshi friend if the leadership of his country had learnt any lessons from the bitter past. His reply was an emphatic no. Cronyism is the currency and merit takes second or third place. Because of its overwhelming majority, the Awami League shows little regard for the opposition. In the past when Wazed and Zia alternated in power they would not talk to each other and the party in opposition either boycotted the assembly or staged walkouts. One must wait to see if things get any better this time around. Prospects are not promising.

NOTES

1. UNDP Human Development Report 2007/2008, Table 1 (http://hdr.undp.org/en/media/HDR_20072008_Table_1.pdf).
2. Population Reference Bureau, (http://www.prb.org/DataFinder.aspx).

Index